中英双语珍藏本

吹小号的天鹅

E. B. White

THE TRUMPET OF THE SWAN

〔美〕E·B·怀特 著 任溶溶 译

上海译文出版社

译者的话

E·B·怀特（Elwyn Brooks White, 1899—1985），他本来就是美国著名的散文家，还有人说他是美国最优秀的散文家，后来他兴之所至，又写起了儿童文学作品。结果，在国际范围来说，他作为儿童文学作家的名声反而更大，因为他的儿童文学作品被介绍到了许多国家。

怀特1899年生在美国纽约州的芒特弗农市，1921年毕业于康纳尔大学，1926年起和《纽约人》杂志长期合作，担任特约编辑和作者。《纽约人》以其幽默风格驰名，幽默散文大家怀特对奠定这杂志的独特风格起了重大作用。

怀特在世界儿童文学上如此有名，其实他一共只写了三部童话，这就是《精灵鼠小弟》(1945)、《夏洛的网》(1952)和《吹小号的天鹅》(1970)。

《吹小号的天鹅》，原名《天鹅的小号》，是怀特最后一部儿童文学作品。书中写的是因叫声嘹亮被称为"吹号天鹅"的一种野天鹅的故事。怀特对这种天鹅感兴趣，是因为1965年《纽约时报》报道费城动物园一对稀有的吹号天鹅养了五只小天鹅，还刊登了照片。怀特于是写信给费城老朋友，说他真想到费城看看，并托他代拍那些天鹅的照片并加以观察。后来他又向他要费城一二十年来抒情流行音乐的资料。可见，他这部童话构思出来了。

他童话里写的一只小吹号天鹅，却是一只生下来就发不出声音的哑天鹅。名为吹号天鹅而发不出声音，麻烦就大了，等到有了心爱的天鹅小姐，也无法像所有天鹅那样用洪亮的声音求爱。这小天鹅却没灰心，找到它的老朋友，一个牧场孩子帮忙，让它进学校学会了读和写，脖子上挂着石板石笔回湖上来。可依然没有用，它看中的天鹅小姐不会读，看不懂它在石板上写的意思，飞走了。这回轮到天鹅爸爸想办法，它去城里冲破一家音乐商店的玻璃橱窗，给它叼来了一把小号。小号到底没有付钱，是偷来的，这又成了小天鹅的心事。它学会吹几个音符之后，脖子上除了挂石板石笔，又挂上了这个小号，随它那位孩子老朋友到夏令营去担任吹号手挣钱还债。它在夏令营听到了许多优美音乐，于是把右趾蹼割开，这样就能够按小号的按键，吹奏出好听的曲子来。夏令营结束后，它先后到波士顿和费城去演奏小号，越吹越好，名闻全国，成了美国小号演奏家路易斯·斯特朗第二——它也叫路易斯，这当然是作者给它起的，因为作者——这位安排书中人物命运的"上帝"——正是注定要它和那位小号大师并列在一起。这一来，它挣到了许多钱。也是无巧不成书，一场暴风雨把它心爱的那位天鹅小姐逼降在它寄居的费城动物园的湖上。吹号天鹅是种稀有动物，动物园准备剪掉天鹅小姐翅膀上的飞羽，让它永远留在动物园里。路易斯——就是那小天鹅——跟负责人谈判，让他放走天鹅小姐，答应在动物园需要时，它们把生下来要照料的小天鹅送给动物园。路易斯用它的小号声赢得了天鹅小姐的爱，带着它回到爸爸那里，把挣来的钱交给爸爸去还清小号欠款，然后带着新娘到它的出生地加拿大人迹罕至的沼泽地去生儿育女。吹号天鹅都是生在那里，然后飞到美国野生动物保护区生活的。当然，路易斯带着小儿女回美国的时候，一路上还会旧地重游，看看它那些老朋友。

这就是《吹小号的天鹅》的故事，可以看到，这是一只生下来就有不能发声这一致命缺陷的天鹅和命运抗争的故事，它克服种种困难到获得成功的故事。这只是个童话，我相信小读者会从中得到启发。作者又是一位知名的幽默散文大师，书中充满了机智幽默、带有善意讽刺的文字。

这本书出版以后得到不少好评。美国当代大作家厄普代克把怀特的三部童话归于儿童文学经典作品之列，并认为《吹小号的天鹅》写得"最无拘束，娓娓而谈"，"它的故事给了小朋友一个最有说服力的关于成长的寓言"。

任溶溶

2000年春节之年初五

总目录

〔美〕E·B·怀特/著

吹小号的天鹅

目 录

1. 萨姆

萨姆穿过沼泽地回营地去，一路上想，是不是要把他看到的事情告诉爸爸。

"我只知道一点，"他心里说。"明天我还要到那个小池塘去。我要一个人去。要是我把今天看到的事情告诉了爸爸，他就要跟我一起去了。我不敢说那是个非常好的主意。"

萨姆十一岁，姓比弗。按他那个岁数来说，他的身体挺棒，黑头发，黑眼睛，像个印第安人。萨姆走路也像印第安人，直着腿一步一步走，不发出什么响声。他穿过的沼泽地很荒凉——没有脚印，脚踩下去黏糊糊的，走起来很费劲。每走上四五分钟，萨姆就从口袋里掏出指南针看看方向，算准他是在朝西走。加拿大是个大地方。它的大部分是荒野。在加拿大西部的森林和沼泽地带一旦迷了路，那事情就严重了。

萨姆这么一路跋涉，心里一个劲儿琢磨着他看到的奇迹。世界上没有多少人看到过这种吹号天鹅①的窝。可在

1

这个春天日子里，偏让萨姆在荒凉的池塘上给找到了一个。他看见到了两只雪白的大天鹅，雪白的长脖子，黑色的嘴巴。他一辈子里以前见过的任何东西，还从来没有使他产生过一种感觉，跟他在这荒凉小池塘上看到这两只大天鹅时所产生的感觉完全一样。它们比他以前见过的鸟大得多。它们的窝也大——一个树枝和草堆起来的大墩。雌天鹅坐在几个天鹅蛋上，雄天鹅慢慢地走过来走过去在守护着它。

萨姆回到帐篷，又累又饿，看见他爸爸正在煎两条鱼做晚饭。

"你上哪儿去了？"比弗先生问他。

"探险，"萨姆回答说。"我去了离这里大约一英里半的一个池塘。就是我们来的时候从飞机上看见的那个。它不大——根本没有我们这里的这个湖大，连比也不能比。"

"你在那里看见什么了吗？"爸爸问他。

"这个嘛，"萨姆说，"它是个沼泽池塘，有许多芦苇和香蒲。我认为一点不适合钓鱼。很不好去——得穿过一片沼泽地。"

"到底看见什么啦？"比弗先生再问一遍。

"我看见了一只麝鼠，"萨姆说，"还有几只红翅膀的乌鸫。"

比弗先生从柴火炉子上抬起头来，鱼在煎锅里嘶嘶响。

2

“萨姆，”他说，“我知道你喜欢探险。可你别忘了——这里的森林和沼泽跟我们蒙大拿家乡周围不同。你再到那池塘去可小心别迷了路。我不喜欢你穿过沼泽地。它们危险。你不定会踩进一个泥沼，就陷下去了，那里不会有人把你拉出来。”

“我会小心的，”萨姆说。他很清楚，他要再回到那个有天鹅的池塘去。他可不打算在森林里迷路。他感到宽慰，到底没把他看见天鹅的事告诉爸爸。不过他也为此觉得奇怪。萨姆不是一个不老实的孩子，但有一点他是古怪的：他喜欢有事藏在心里不告诉别人。他喜欢孤独，特别是在森林中的时候。他喜欢蒙大拿甜草乡他爸爸的养牛牧场的生活。他爱他的妈妈。他爱他的小马“公爵”。他爱骑着它在牧场上走走。他爱看每年夏天到比弗牧场来住宿的客人。

但是在生活中，他最喜欢的莫过于和他爸爸这样到加拿大来旅行露营。比弗太太对森林兴趣不大，因此她难得同来——总是萨姆和比弗先生来。他们坐自己的汽车到美国和加拿大交界的边境，进入加拿大。到了加拿大这边，比弗先生就请当地一位专门飞行于人烟稀少地区的飞行员，开飞机把他们送到这里湖边，他们在这里搭上帐篷，待上几天，钓鱼、闲逛和探险。比弗先生主要是钓鱼和闲逛。萨姆探险。到了时间，那位飞行员又来把他们接回去。他的外号叫矮子。他们一听见他的飞机声，就跑出来向他招手，看着他把飞机降落到湖面上，靠到码头上来。这些日子，这些在森林中的日子，是萨姆生活中最快活的日子，它们远离一切——没有汽车，没有马路，没有人，没有喧闹声，没有学校，没有家庭作业，没有问题，除了一个问题，就是不要迷路。当然，还有一个问题，就是他长大了干什么。这个问题是每个孩子都有的。

那天晚上吃过晚饭，萨姆和他爸爸在帐篷门口坐了一会儿。萨姆在读一本关于鸟类的书。

"爸爸，"萨姆说，"你认为我们一个月以后还会再回来露营吗——我是说大约三十五天以后？"

"我想会的，"比弗先生回答说。"我的确希望再来。不过为什么是三十五天呢？为什么非三十五天不可呢？"

"噢，没什么，"萨姆说。"我只是想，三十五天以后这一带可能非常好看。"

"这是我听到的最傻的话，"比弗先生说。"这里所有的时候都是好看的。"

萨姆走进帐篷。鸟类的事他知道很多，他知道天鹅把小天鹅孵出来大概要三十五天。他希望他能在池塘上看到出壳的小天鹅。

萨姆有一个日记本——记下他一天天的生活。这是个廉价的记事本，一直放在他的床头。每天晚上上床睡觉以前，他总要在本子上写上点什么。他记下他做过的事，看到的东西，想到过的事情。有时候他画上一幅画。最后他总是给自己提出个问题，这样躺下来睡觉的时候，便有些什么可以想想了。在他发现天鹅窝的那一天，他在日记里是这么记的：

今天，我在我们营地东边一个小池塘上看见一对吹号天鹅。天鹅妈妈有一个窝，里面有天鹅蛋。我看见三个，不过我将在画上画四个——我想它正在下着一个。这是我一辈子里最大的发现。我没有告诉爸爸。我那本鸟类手册说，刚养出来的叫幼天鹅。我明天要回到那里去看那两只大天鹅。今天我听到了狐狸叫。狐狸为什么叫呢？是因为它发疯了，抑或是担心，抑或是肚子饿，还是因为它在给另一只狐狸传递信息呢？**狐狸为什么叫？**

萨姆合上他的小本子，脱去上衣，爬上他的床，闭上眼睛躺在那里，想着狐狸为什么叫。几分钟后，他就睡着了。

---

① 吹号天鹅是一种野天鹅，因叫出来的声音像吹号而得名。

5

2. 池塘

　　萨姆在那个春天早晨发现的池塘,是人迹罕至的。整个冬天,雪覆盖着冰,池塘在它这白毯子下面冰冷地躺着,静止不动。大多数时间一点声音也听不见。青蛙沉睡着。金花鼠沉睡着。偶尔有一只蓝木坚鸟叫两声。夜里有时候狐狸会号叫——叫声高亢刺耳。冬天好像就将这样一直下去,永远没有尽头似的。

　　可是到了一天,森林和这池塘起了变化。温暖的风,轻快柔和,在树木间吹拂。夜间变软了的冰开始融化。一道一道的水出现了。生活在池塘和森林的所有动物很高兴感觉到了暖意。它们听到并且感觉到了春天的呼吸,由于新的生活和希望,它们开始动起来。空气中有一种很好闻的新的气息,大地长睡后醒来的气息。一直埋在池底烂泥里的青蛙知道春天到了。山雀知道春天来了很快活(几乎每一件事情都会让山雀快活)。睡在洞里的雌狐狸知道它很快要有小狐狸。每一样动物知道,马上就要过上一种更好、更容易过的生活——更温暖的白天,更叫人高兴的夜晚。树木长出了绿芽，芽蕾逐渐长大。鸟儿们开始从南方飞来了，一对野鸭飞来了。红翅膀的乌鸫飞来了，并且在池塘上找地方筑窠。一只白喉咙的小麻雀飞来了，还唱着："噢，可爱的加拿大，加拿大，加拿大!"

在春天这样第一个温暖的日子，又是在临近傍晚的时候，如果你碰巧坐在池塘边上，你会听到从你头顶上的高空传来激动人心的声音——这声音很像是吹号。

"咯—嗬，咯—嗬!"

如果你这时候把头抬起来，你就会看到高高地在你的头顶上有两只白色的大鸟。它们轻快地飞着，腿笔直地伸向后面，白色的长脖子笔直地伸向前方，强健的翅膀拍打得有节奏、有力量。"咯—嗬，咯—嗬，咯—嗬!"空中一阵震耳的响声，天鹅吹出来的号声。

两只大鸟一发现了这个池塘，它们就开始打转，从空中把这地方好好看一下，然后滑翔下来，停到水面上，收拢它们的长翅膀，把头转过来转过去观察它们的新环境。它们正是两只吹号天鹅，黑嘴的雪白大鸟。它们喜欢上了这沼泽地池塘的景色，决定把它作为短期的家，在这里生儿育女。

两只天鹅长途飞来，累了。它们很高兴从天空中飞下来。它们慢慢地来回划水游了一阵，然后开始找吃的，把它们的脖子伸到浅水里,从水底拔出树根和植物。它们全身雪白,只除了嘴和脚,嘴和脚是黑的。它们高高昂起了头。它们来了,池塘好像也变样了。

接下来几天,两只天鹅都在休息。它们饿了就吃。它们渴了——这是经常的——就喝。到了第十天,雌天鹅开始到处看,找一个地方造它的窝。

在一年的春天,雌天鹅心中只想着造窝:这是最重要的事。如果它找了个好地方,它就能够下蛋和孵出它的小天鹅。如果它找了个不好的地方,它就无法生儿育女了。雌天鹅知道这一点,它知道它作出的决定是至关重要的。

两只天鹅先查看了池塘上游那一头,那里有一条小溪缓缓流进来。那里很可爱,有芦苇和灯心草。红翅膀乌鸫在池塘这一带忙着筑窠,一对绿头鸭在求偶。接着两只天鹅游到池塘的下游一头,这里一边是沼泽地和森林,另一边是一片有鹿出没的草原。这里很清净。在一处岸边,有一长条沙地伸进池塘,像个小小的半岛。在这条地带的尖端对面,隔水几英尺,是一个很小的岛,不比一张餐桌大多少。岛上长着一棵小树,还有岩石、蕨草和青草。

"看看这里!"雌天鹅打着转游来游去说。

"咯—嗬!"它的丈夫回答,它很高兴有谁征求它的意见。

雌天鹅小心翼翼地从水里出来,踏上小岛。这地点看来很合适——造窝正好。当雄天鹅漂浮在岛旁看着的时候,雌天鹅看来看去,直到最后在岛上找到了一个很好的地点。它蹲下来,看蹲在这个地方感觉如何。它决定它的大小正好适合它的身体。位置好,离水边只有两英尺。非常方便。它向丈夫转过身去。

"你看怎么样?"

"一个理想的地点,"丈夫回答说。"一个完美无缺的地点!我来告诉你它为什么是个完美无缺的地点,"它庄重地说下去。"万一敌人——狐狸,或者浣熊,或者狼,或者臭鼬——怀着杀心要到这地点来,它得下水,把身体也弄湿了。在它能够下水之前,它还得走完整条地带,在这段时间,我们就能看到它,或者听到它,我要让它吃一顿苦头。"

雄天鹅展开它的两只巨大翅膀,从这边翅膀尖到那边翅膀尖足有八英尺长,再在水上狠狠地拍了一下显显它的力气。这样让它马上觉得痛快多了。一只吹号天鹅用翅膀拍打敌人,敌人就像挨了一棒球棍。

它的太太装作没注意到丈夫在炫耀自己,不过它当然看到了,并且为它的力气和勇敢自豪。要说丈夫,它是个好样儿的。

雄天鹅观察着它蹲在那小岛上的美丽妻子。它感到万分高兴,看到它妻子开始慢慢地转来转去,但始终在同一个地点,践踏着烂泥和青草。雌天鹅正在做造窝的开头动作。首先,它在它选定的地方蹲下来。接着,它转过来转过去,用它宽阔的蹼足脚掌踏实泥土,把泥土踏出浅坑来,像个盘子。再下去,它伸长脖子把小树枝和青草拉到身边,撒在它四周和尾巴底下,造成它身体下面的一个窝。

雄天鹅靠近它漂浮着。它仔细看它妻子的每一个动作。

"现在来一根中等大小的树枝,亲爱的,"雄天鹅说。雌天鹅就把长长的美丽脖子尽量伸长,叼起一根树枝,把它放在自己身旁。

"现在再来一些粗的草,"雄天鹅十分威严地说。

于是雌天鹅伸出脖子去叼来青草,叼来苔藓,叼来小树枝——有什么叼来什么。慢慢地,小心地,它造起了一个窝,直到最后,它已经是蹲坐在一个大草墩上。它干了大约两个小时,然后这一天就做到这里,重新滑到池塘上去喝点吃点。

"这个头开得好!"雄天鹅回头看着新造的窝说。"一个完美无缺的开头!我真想不出你怎么会干得这样聪明。"

"这是天生的,"它的妻子回答说。"要做许多活儿,不过总的来说，这是一个开心活儿。"

"是的，"雄天鹅说。"等到造完，你就显示出你的劳动成果——有了一个天鹅窝，直径六英尺。有什么鸟能造得出？"

"这个嘛，"它的妻子说，"也许老鹰造得出。"

"对，不过那就不是天鹅窝，而是老鹰窝了，它会是在什么地方的某一棵老枯树高高的顶上，而不是在水边，有种种和水有关的方便。"

它们对这一点双双大笑。接着它们开始吹号，拍水，把水舀起来浇在它们的背上，冲过来冲过去，就像它们一下子乐疯了似的。

"咯—嗬！咯—嗬！咯—嗬！"它们叫道。

只要是在离池塘一英里半之内的每一头野兽，都能够听到这两只天鹅的号声。狐狸听见了，浣熊听见了，臭鼬听见了。还有一双耳朵听到了，但它们不是野兽的。可这两只天鹅并不知道这件事。

3. 不速之客

有一天，那是差不多一个星期以后了，雌天鹅轻轻地蹲到它的窝里，下了一个蛋。每天它想在窝里下一个蛋。它有时候做到了，有时候做不到。反正窝里如今有了三个蛋，它已经准备好下第四个。

它蹲坐在那里，丈夫优雅地漂浮在它旁边，这时候它有一种奇怪感觉，感到有人在偷看它。这弄得它很不舒服。鸟都不喜欢被人偷看。它们特别不喜欢当它们蹲在窝里的时候被人偷看。因此雌天鹅把头转来转去，到处张望。它目不转睛地盯住靠近它那个窝的那条伸进池塘来的地带尖端看。它用它锐利的眼睛在搜索附近岸上入侵者的迹象。可它终于看到的东西使它从未有过地惊讶。在地带尖端一根大木头上坐着一个小男孩。他非常安静，他没有枪。

"我看见的东西你看到了吗？"它悄悄地问它的丈夫。

"没有。你看见什么了？"

"瞧那边。那根木头上。是个男孩！现在我们怎么办？"

"一个男孩怎么会到这里来呢?"雄天鹅悄悄地说。"我们可是在加拿大荒野深处。周围多少英里连一个人也没有。"

"我也正是这么想,"雌天鹅回答说。"如果那边大木头上不是个男孩,那我就不是吹号天鹅。"

雄天鹅发火了。"我飞了那么远路到北边这加拿大来,可不是要跟一个男孩打交道的,"它说。"我们来到这里这个恬静的地点,这遥远的小小隐居处,是为了能够好好享受一点应该得到的清静生活。"

"是啊,"它的妻子说,"我也很抱歉会看到这个男孩,不过我还是得说,他很规矩。他看见了我们,可是不扔石头块。他不扔树枝。他不捣乱。他光是这样看着。"

"我不希望被人看,"雄天鹅抱怨说。"我飞了十万八千里来到加拿大的心脏,可不是来给人看的。再说我不要你被人看——只能被我看。你正在下蛋——我是说,我希望你是正在下一个蛋——你有权保持隐私。所有男孩都扔石头块扔树枝,这是我的经验——这也是他们的天性。我要过去用我强大有力的翅膀揍那男孩,他会以为他是挨了一警棍。我要把他揍昏!"

"不,等一等!"雌天鹅说。"没有必要去打他。这男孩眼前没有打搅我。他也没有打搅你。"

14

"可他是怎么到这里来的呢?"雄天鹅说,它已经不再说悄悄话,而是大叫大嚷了。"他是怎么到这里来的呢?男孩不会飞,加拿大的这一带又没有路。我们离开最近的公路也有五十英里远。"

"也许他是迷路了,"雌天鹅说。"也许他要饿死了。也许他想打劫我们的窝吃我们的蛋,不过我不这么想。他看上去不饿。不管怎样,我已经造好了这个窝,我已经下了三个漂亮的蛋,那男孩眼前也很规矩,我打算这就下出第四个蛋来。"

"祝你好运,我亲爱的!"雄天鹅说。"我守在你身边,万一有什么事,我保护你。把蛋下下来吧。"

接下来一个小时,雄天鹅绕着小岛,慢慢地划着脚团团转地游,守卫着。它的妻子继续安静地蹲在窝里。萨姆坐在大木头上,肌肉也难得一动。他看到这两只天鹅,像是中了魔法一样。它们是他有生以来看到的最大的鸟。他听到了它们吹号的声音,他在森林和沼泽地找了又找,终于找到了这个池塘,找到了这个窝。萨姆对鸟类大有研究,知道它们是吹号天鹅。只要在大自然里野生动物中间,萨姆一直会感到快活。他坐在他那根大木头上,观察着这两只天鹅,那种美好感觉就像人们坐在教堂里的时候那样。

看了一个小时以后,萨姆站起来。他慢慢地、安静地走开，一只脚一只脚直挺挺地移动，印第安人就是这么走路的，一点儿声音也没有。两只天鹅看着他离开。当雌天鹅离开它的窝时，转过身来回头看。在窝底柔软的羽毛堆上，安全地躺着第四个蛋。雄天鹅走到岛上来看这个窝。

"一个代表作！"它说。"一个比例匀称的最美丽的蛋。我得说，这个蛋几乎有五英寸长。"

它的妻子听了很高兴。

雌天鹅下了五个蛋，心里很满意。它得意地看着它们。接着它蹲在窝里使它那些蛋保持温暖。它小心地把嘴伸下去，把每个蛋拨弄得正好让它们能吸取到它身体的热量。雄天鹅在周围靠得近近地巡航，和它做伴，同时保卫它不受敌人侵犯。它知道有只狐狸在森林里什么地方潜行；它听到这狐狸夜里猎到东西时的号叫声。

一天天过去，雌天鹅始终安静地蹲坐在那五个蛋上。一夜夜过去。它始终蹲坐在那里给予这些蛋温暖。没有人来打搅它。那男孩走了——也许再也不会回来。在每个蛋里面有什么事情在发生，但是它看不见：一只小天鹅在成形了。等到一个星期一个星期过去，白天变长了，黑夜变短了。就算是下雨天，雌天鹅也是这样一动不动地蹲坐着，让雨去下。

"我亲爱的，"有一天下午，它的丈夫雄天鹅说，"你永远不觉得你的任务繁重或者厌烦吗?老在那么一个地方,用那么一种姿势坐着,覆盖着那些蛋,没有变化,没有乐趣,没有活动,没有逗乐,你永远不觉得厌烦吗?你从不觉得难受吗?"

"不,"它的妻子回答说。"不大觉得。"

"蹲坐在蛋上不舒服吧?"

"是的,不舒服,"它妻子回答说。"可为了把小天鹅带到世界上来,我能够忍受这一点儿不舒服。"

"你知道你还得再坐多少时候吗?"

"没有数,"雌天鹅说。"不过我注意到,池塘那头的鸭子已经孵出了它们的小鸭子;我注意到,红翅膀乌鸫也孵出了它们的小乌鸫;有一天傍晚,我看见一只条纹臭鼬沿着岸边猎食,它带着四只小鼬鼠。因此我想,我的日子一定也快到了。幸运的话,我们很快就能看到我们的孩子——我们美丽的小天鹅。"

"你从来不觉得饥饿难受,或者渴得要命吗?"雄天鹅问它。

"不,觉得,"它的伴儿说。"说真格的,我现在就得喝点水。"

这天下午很暖和,太阳很明亮。雌天鹅觉得它可以安全地离开那些蛋几分钟。它站起来,先把一些蓬松的羽毛推到蛋上面,遮住它们,让它不在的时候它们给暖和地盖着。接着它离开窝到水里去。它很快地喝了几口水。接着它游到一个水浅的地方,把头伸到水下,从水底拉上来一些柔嫩的植物。再下来它用水浇身体洗个澡。然后它走到青草岸边,站在那里用嘴整理它的羽毛。

雌天鹅觉得很舒服。它根本想不到敌人就在附近。它没有注意到,那头红狐狸正躲在一丛灌木后面盯住它看。狐狸是被泼剌水声引到池塘边来的。它本想找到一只鹅。现在它嗅着空气,闻到了一只天鹅。天鹅转过了身,于是狐狸开始慢慢地向它爬过来。天鹅对它来说太大了,叼不走,但是它决定无论如何把它咬死,尝尝血的味道。雄天鹅还在池塘上游着。是它首先发现了狐狸。

"小心!"它吹号似的叫起来。"小心狐狸,它正在向你爬过来,甚至在我说话的时候它还在爬。它的眼睛闪着凶光,它毛蓬蓬的尾巴伸直,它的心在渴望血,它的肚子几乎贴近地面!你极端危险,我们必须立刻采取行动。"

雄天鹅还在发表它这篇美丽的警告演讲词,一件事情发生了,这件事情使在场的每一个都大吃一惊。就在狐狸要跳起来把它的尖牙利齿咬进雌天鹅脖子的这一刹那,一根树枝飞过空中。它狠狠地打在狐狸的鼻子上,狐狸转身就逃。两只天鹅还没明白过来到底出了什么事。接着它们看到灌木丛里有动静。从那里面走出来的是萨姆·比弗，就是一个月以前来看过它们的那个男孩。萨姆露出了牙齿在笑。他的手里握着另一根树枝，以防狐狸再回来。但是狐狸丢了魂，不想再回来了。它的鼻子痛得要命，它已经没有胃口去吃新鲜的天鹅肉了。

"你们好，"萨姆用低沉的声音说。

"咯—嗬，咯—嗬!"雄天鹅回答。

"咯—嗬!"它的妻子说。

池塘充满了号声——打败了狐狸的欢呼声，胜利的欢呼声。

萨姆被两只天鹅的号声震聋了耳朵，有人说这种号声像吹法国号的声音。他慢慢地沿着岸边来到靠近小岛的那个小尖角，坐在他那根大木头上。两只天鹅现在明白了，毫无疑问，这男孩是它们的朋友。他救了雌天鹅的性命。他在合适的时候来到合适的地方拿起合适的武器。两只天鹅很感激他。雄天鹅向萨姆游过来，爬出池塘，靠近他站着，用友好的眼光看着他，很优雅地拱起它的长脖子。有一次，它把它的脖子小心地伸得很远，几乎碰到了这个男孩。萨姆一动也不动。他的心激动和高兴得怦怦直跳。

雌天鹅划水回到它的窝里，重新做它温暖那些蛋的工作，它觉得很幸运能活下来。

那天晚上，萨姆在帐篷里爬上他的床之前，拿出他的记事本，找来一支铅笔。这是他写的话：

在天底下，我不知道还有什么比一个有蛋的窝看起来更了不起了。一个蛋，因为里面有生命，它是最完美的东西。它又漂亮又神秘。一个蛋比一个网球或者一块肥皂要棒得多。一个网球始终就是一个网球。一块肥皂始终就是一块肥皂——直到它变得越来越小，小得没人要了，就把它扔掉。但是一个蛋有一天会成为一只活的动物。天鹅蛋会打开，从里面出来一只小天鹅。鸟窝几乎和蛋同样了不起而神秘。鸟怎么会知道怎样造窝呢？没有人教过它。**鸟怎么会知道怎样造窝呢？**

萨姆合上记事本，对爸爸说了声晚安，吹灭了灯，爬上他的床。他躺在那里想鸟怎么会知道怎样造窝。很快，他的眼睛闭上，他睡着了。

4. 小天鹅

　　夜里，雌天鹅觉得它听到身底下那些蛋发出叽叽的声音。就在天亮的那个小时，它断定它感到了它的胸口底下有轻微的动静，就像一个很小的身体在那里扭动。也许那些蛋终于孵化了。蛋当然是不会扭动的，因此雌天鹅断定，在它身体下面的已经不是蛋。它坐得完全纹丝不动，仔细倾听着，等待着。雄天鹅浮在附近，仔细守望着。

　　禁闭在蛋里的小天鹅要出来有一段艰苦的时间。如果大自然不提供它两样重要的东西，它就永远不能出来：一是有力的颈部肌肉，一是嘴尖上一只小尖牙。这牙很尖，天鹅娃娃就用它在蛋的硬壳上凿出一个洞。只要洞一凿出来，其余的事就好办。小天鹅现在能够呼吸了，它就是不断地扭，扭啊扭啊，直到从蛋壳里挣脱出来为止。

　　雄天鹅这时候正盼着随时成为父亲。做父亲的想法使它有一种诗意和自豪的感觉。它对它妻子说起话来了。

　　"我在这里照天鹅的样子游啊游的，"它说，"而大地沐浴在奇观和壮美之中。现在，一点一点地，白天的亮光来到我们的天空。迷雾低垂在池塘上。迷雾像水壶的蒸汽那样一点一点地升起，而我照天鹅的样子在游，蛋在孵化，小天鹅在来到世间。我游啊游啊。光越来越亮。空气越来越暖和。迷雾逐渐消散了。我照天鹅的样子游啊游。小鸟唱起它们的晨曲。叫了一夜的青蛙住了口，静下来了。我仍旧照天鹅的样子在不停地游。"

"你当然是照天鹅的样子游，"它的妻子说。"你还能照别的什么样子游呢?你不能照糜鹿的样子游，对吗?"

"对，不能。这话一点不假。谢谢你纠正我的话，我亲爱的。"雄天鹅听了它伴侣常识范围内的指点大吃一惊。它讲美丽的字句和漂亮的话讲得入了迷，喜欢想着自己照天鹅的样子游。它决定还是多游游，少讲话。

整个早晨，雌天鹅听着那些蛋壳叽叽响。它不时感觉到，有什么东西在窝里它的身体下面扭动。这是一种很奇怪的感觉。那么许多许多天以来———共三十五天———这些蛋都是安安静静的，可如今到了最后，它们却萌动了生命。它知道最正确的做法就是坐着不动。

到了下午晚半晌，雌天鹅的耐心得到了报答。它低下头来看，只见一个小脑袋顶开了它的羽毛伸出来——这是第一个小宝宝，第一只小天鹅。它毛茸茸，软绵绵。不像它的父母，它是灰色的。它的脚和腿是暗黄色。它的眼睛很亮。它两腿颤颤抖抖,拼命挣扎,直到最后在它母亲身旁站了起来,东张西望地看它第一次看到的世界。它的母亲温柔地对它说话,它很高兴听到母亲的声音。在蛋里关了那么久,它很高兴呼吸到空气。

雄天鹅紧张地观望了一整天,这时候看到了那小脑袋出现。它的心快活得蹦了起来。"一只小天鹅!"它叫道。"终于出来了一只小天鹅!我是爸爸了,有做爸爸的所有快活的任务和可怕的责任。噢,我亲爱的小儿子,这真是多么好啊:看到你的脸从你妈妈胸前保护着你的羽毛底下往外面看,在这美丽的天空下,这时池塘在下午长久的阳光里那么安静!"

"你怎么会想到它是一个儿子呢?"它的妻子问它。"你知道,它是个女儿。反正它是一只小天鹅,活着又健康。我还能感觉到我身体下面其他的小天鹅。我们也许会孵得顺利。我们甚至可能把全部五只都孵出来。到明天我们就知道了。"

"我完全相信我们会的,"雄天鹅说。

第二天一早,父亲还在睡觉,萨姆·比弗爬出了他的床。他穿好衣服,点上了炉子。他煎了几条熏肉,烤了两片面包,倒了一玻璃杯牛奶,就坐下来吃他的早饭。吃好了,

23

他找了支铅笔和一张纸，写了个字条。

我去散步了。回来吃中饭。

萨姆把字条留在爸爸找得到的地方，接着拿了望远镜和指南针，把猎刀拴在皮带上，就动身穿过森林，经过沼泽地，到天鹅它们待着的池塘去。

他小心地来到池塘，望远镜挂在肩上。才七点过一点儿，太阳苍白，空气凛冽。早晨闻上去香香的。萨姆来到那根大木头边，坐下来调正他的望远镜。从望远镜看出去，窝里的雌天鹅只有几步远。它坐得很近，一动不动。雄天鹅在附近。两只天鹅都在倾听着，等待着。两只天鹅都看到了萨姆，但对他在那里毫不介意——事实上，它们十分高兴他在那里。不过它们对望远镜确实惊奇。

"那男孩今天好像有一双大眼睛，"雄天鹅悄悄说。"他那双眼睛像铜铃似的。"

"我想那双大眼睛实际上是一副望远镜，"雌天鹅回答说。"我说不准，不过人用望远镜看东西，一切就显得靠近和变大了。"

"那男孩的望远镜会使我显得比我实际上还大吗？"雄天鹅满怀希望说。

"我想是的，"雌天鹅说。

"噢，我喜欢这样，"雄天鹅说。"我太喜欢了。也许那男孩的望远镜不仅让我显得比实际上更大，而且让我显得比实际上更漂亮。你也这样想吗?"

"有可能，"它的妻子说，"不过不大会。你最好别变得太漂亮——它会冲昏你头脑的。你是只很爱虚荣的鸟。"

"所有天鹅都是爱虚荣的，"雄天鹅说。"天鹅觉得自豪，漂亮，这对天鹅来说是对的——天鹅活着就为了这个。"

萨姆想不出两只天鹅在说什么，他只知道它们在对话，光是听着它们对话就使他热血沸腾。在荒野中和这两只大鸟做伴使他感到满足。他百分之百地高兴。

上午在太阳升得很高的时候，萨姆又举起望远镜看天鹅的窝。他终于看到了他特地来看的东西:一个小脑袋钻出它妈妈的羽毛，一个吹号天鹅娃娃的小脑袋。这小天鹅爬到窝的边上。萨姆能够看到它的灰脑袋灰脖子，它的盖满柔软茸毛的身体，它的黄色的腿和脚，脚上有趾蹼，适宜于游水。很快又出来了一只小天鹅。接着又是一只。然后那第一只又钻到它妈妈的羽毛底下去取暖。接着有一只要爬到它妈妈的背上，可是妈妈的羽毛很滑，它滑了下来，只好待在它妈妈身边。雌天鹅只管坐着不动，欣赏它这些小宝宝，看它们学会使用它们的腿。

一个钟头过去。有一只小天鹅比其他小天鹅胆子大，离开窝，在小岛的岸上啪嗒啪嗒走来走去。这一下，天鹅妈妈站了起来。它断定带它那些孩子下水的时间已经到了。

　　"来吧！"它说。"大家待在一起！仔细看着我怎么做。然后你们照着做。游水是很容易的。"

　　"一，二，三，四，五，"萨姆一只一只数。"一，二，三，四，五。一共五只小天鹅，跟我是活人一样错不了！"

　　雄天鹅一看见它的孩子们朝水边走，马上觉得它该做出爸爸的样子。它从发表演讲开始。

　　"欢迎到池塘和毗连的沼泽地来！"它说。"欢迎到这个世界来，它包括了这可爱的池塘，这呱呱叫的沼泽地，它们保持着大自然的风貌，没遭到过破坏！欢迎到阳光和阴影中来，风和雨中来！欢迎到水上来！水是天鹅的特别元素，你们很快就会发现的。对于一只天鹅来说，游泳丝毫不成问题。欢迎到危险中来，你必须时刻提防它——提防走路鬼鬼祟祟、尖牙利齿的恶棍狐狸，提防游到你们底下来要抓住你们腿的害人水獭，提防夜里出来觅食、混在阴影里的臭鼬，提防捕捉动物、大叫大嚷、比狐狸大的狼。小心猎人的枪留在所有池塘底下的铅弹。不要把它们吃下去——它们会毒死你们！要警惕，要强壮，要勇敢，要规规矩矩，要一直跟着我！

我走在最前面,你们排成单行跟着我游,热爱你们的妈妈会殿后的。入水要安静,有信心!"

天鹅妈妈很高兴它这番长篇大论终于结束,踏进水里,招呼它那些小天鹅。那些小天鹅朝水看了一秒钟,接着跌跌撞撞地走上前,往水里一跳,都浮在水面上了。水的感觉真好。游水很简单——根本没事。水可以喝。每个小宝宝都啜了一大口。它们快活的爸爸在它们上面弓起漂亮的长脖子保护它们。接着它慢慢地游开,小天鹅们排成单行跟在它后面。它们的妈妈游在最后。

"多么好看啊!"萨姆心里说。"真是好看得没命!七只吹号天鹅排成一行,其中五只才刚出壳。这真是我一个幸运的日子。"他简直没注意到,在大木头上坐了那么久,他人都坐僵了。

像所有爸爸一样,这位雄天鹅也要把它那些孩子向谁炫耀一下。因此它把这些小天鹅带到萨姆坐着的地方。它们全都从水里踏出来,站在他面前——只除了天鹅妈妈。它留在后面。

"咯—嗬!"雄天鹅说。

"你们好!"萨姆说,他根本没有想到会有这么回事,连气都不敢透。

第一只小天鹅看着萨姆,说:"毕。"第二只小天鹅看着萨姆,说:"毕。"第三只小天鹅也用同样的方式和萨姆打招呼。第四只也一样。只有第五只不同。它张开了嘴,但一声也不响。它拼命要说"毕",却没有声音发出来。于是它伸出了脖子,叼住萨姆的一根鞋带,用力一拉。它拉了一会儿鞋带。鞋带散开了。然后它放了口。这像是打招呼。萨姆咧开嘴笑了。

这时候雄天鹅看上去很担心。它把它的雪白长脖子拦在小天鹅们和这男孩之间,然后带领它那些小宝宝回到水上去,回到它们的妈妈那里。

"跟我来!"雄天鹅说。它带它们走了,一副神气的样子,非常自豪。

当天鹅妈妈觉得小天鹅们游够了,可能会冷的时候,它踏上沙岸,蹲下来叫它们。小天鹅们很快地跟着它离开池塘,钻到它的羽毛底下取暖。一下子,一只小天鹅也看不见了。

中午时候,萨姆站起来回营地去,满脑子想着他所看见的事情。

第二天,萨姆和他的爸爸听到了天上传来的飞机声,看到矮子的飞机飞来了。他们抓起他们的行李袋。"再见,帐篷!秋天见!"比弗先生说着关上帐篷门,还拍拍它。他和萨姆爬上飞机,很快就飞上天,回蒙大拿他们的家去了。

比弗先生一点不知道他的儿子看见了一只雌的吹号天鹅生下了它那些小天鹅。萨姆把这件事藏在了心里，只让自己知道。

"我活到一百岁也忘记不了，"萨姆想，"我的鞋带让一只天鹅小宝宝解开是一种什么感觉。"

萨姆和他爸爸回到牧场他们的家已经很晚，尽管很晚，萨姆在晚上上床睡觉之前还是拿出他的日记本。他写道：

> 一共有五只小天鹅。它们都是一律脏兮兮的棕灰色，不过非常可爱。它们的腿是黄的，像芥末的颜色。雄的老天鹅把它们一直带到了我的面前。这一点我根本没想到，可是我保持冷静，一动不动。四只小宝宝对我说"毕"。第五只想说说不出。它叼着我的一根鞋带，好像它是条虫子似的，然后这小天鹅把鞋带拉啊拉，直到它散开了。我在想：**我大起来会成个什么人呢？**

他熄了灯，把被单拉过头，想着他大起来会成个什么人，睡着了。

5.路易斯

几星期后的一个晚上,小天鹅都睡了,雌天鹅对雄天鹅说:"你注意到我们孩子当中有一只,我们叫它路易斯的,有什么两样吗?"

"两样?"雄天鹅回答说。"路易斯跟它的兄弟姐妹有什么两样?我觉得路易斯看上去很好。它长得好,游水潜水都很漂亮。它吃得也好。很快它就要长出它的飞羽,可以学飞了。"

"噢,它看上去很好,"雌天鹅说。"老天爷也知道它吃得饱饱的。它健康,机灵,是个游泳健将。可你听见路易斯发出过声音或者说过话吗?你听见它叫过一声'毕'或者叽里咕噜过吗?"

"这件事回过头想下来,我倒是从来没有听到过,"雄天鹅回答说,它那样子开始担心了。

"你听到路易斯像别的孩子那样对我们说过晚安吗?你听到它像别的孩子那样,用它们可爱的方式毕毕毕毕、叽里咕噜对我们说过早上好吗?"

"现在你这么提起来,我倒是从来没有听到过,"雄天鹅说。"天啊!你想要说什么?你是要我相信,我有一个儿子有什么缺陷吗?真有这么回事会让我痛苦万分。我只希望我的家庭生活一切顺顺当当,这样在我现在的壮年期可以快活平静地游来游去,不被担心和失望困扰。做爸爸本来就是个很大的负担。我不希望外加一个有缺陷的孩子,一个有麻烦的孩子。"

"不过,"它的妻子说"我近来一直在注意路易斯。我认为这小不点儿不会说话。我从来没有听见它发出过声音。我想它来到这个世界上缺少了嗓子。如果它有嗓子,它会使用它的,就像其他孩子那样。"

"噢,这太可怕了!"雄天鹅说。"这是无法形容的苦恼。这是非常严重的事情。"

它的妻子用好笑的眼光看着它。"现在还不太严重,"它说。"但是两三年后,等到路易斯谈恋爱,那就会严重了,到那时候它是一定要谈恋爱的。一只年轻的天鹅小伙子不能说咯—嗬,咯—嗬,或者不能对它选中的年轻天鹅小姐说出通常的表达爱情的话,那它找伴侣就有很大的障碍。"

"你断定是这样吗?"雄天鹅问道。

"我当然断定是这样,"雌天鹅回答说。"我还记得清清楚楚,那年春天,都许多年以前了,你和我谈恋爱,你开始追求我。你那时候是个什么样子,你那时候叽叽呱呱发出了多少叫声!那是在蒙大拿,你记得吗?"

"我当然记得,"雄天鹅说。

"对,你最吸引我的东西就是你的声音——你了不起的声音。"

"是吗?"雄天鹅说。

"是的。在蒙大拿州红石湖国家野生动物保护区里,你在所有年轻天鹅小伙子当中有最好、最响亮、最雄壮的嗓音。"

"我有吗?"雄天鹅说。

"你有,的确如此。每次我一听见你用你那深沉的嗓音说什么话,我已经准备好和你一起到任何地方去了。"

"你已经准备好了?"雄天鹅说。它听了妻子的赞美话显然非常高兴。这些话撩动它的虚荣心,使它觉得自己很伟大。它一直就在想像自己有一条好嗓子,现在听到妻子亲口说出来,这真叫它激动。在这快活的时刻,它完全忘掉了路易斯的事而只想着它自己。当然,它的确记得那个春天在蒙大拿的湖上,它坠入了情网。它记得这天鹅小姐有多么漂亮,有多么年轻和天真烂漫,有多么迷人,有多么可爱。现在它充分了解到,如果它当时不能说话,它就不可能追求它和赢得它。

"我们目前还不用为路易斯担心，"雌天鹅说。"它还太小。不过下一个冬天在蒙大拿过冬，我们就必须注意它了。我们必须一家待在一起，直到我们看到路易斯怎么对付过去。"

它走到小天鹅们在睡觉的地方，在它们旁边待下来。夜晚很冷。它举起一个翅膀，用它盖住那些小天鹅。它们在睡梦中动着，向妈妈紧靠过来。

雄天鹅静静地站着，想着它妻子就在刚才告诉它的话。它是一只勇敢、高贵的鸟，已经在开始为它的小儿子路易斯想办法了。

"万一路易斯真的不会发出声音，"雄天鹅心里说，"那么我要给它一个什么仪器，让它能发出许多声音。一定有什么办法可以走出困境的。再说，我儿子到底是一只吹号天鹅，它应该有一条像小号那样的嗓子。不过首先我要把它测试一下，看它妈妈说的话是不是真的。"

那天晚上雄天鹅没法入睡。它静静地用一条腿站着，但睡意始终不来。第二天早晨，在大家美美吃过早饭以后，它带路易斯离开大家。

"路易斯，"它说，"我想单独和你谈谈。让你和我两个游到池塘另一头去吧，到那里我们可以单独谈话，没有谁来打搅。"

路易斯听了这话大为奇怪。不过它点点头，紧跟着爸爸使劲地游水。它不明白它爸爸为什么要跟它单独谈话，没有它的哥哥姐姐在一起。

"好!"到了池塘上游那一头的时候，雄天鹅说。"我们到了，在这里优雅地浮着，轻松之至，离开大家远远的，周围环境无话可说——美好的早晨，池塘静悄悄，只有乌鸫的歌声，使得空气非常甜润。"

"我希望我爸爸能说到点子上，"路易斯想。

"这是我们谈话的理想地方，"雄天鹅说下去。"有一件事情，我觉得我应该和你非常坦率地谈谈——一件和你的未来有关的事情。我们不必涉及鸟类生活的整个范围，而只把我们的谈话限于一件非常重要的事情上，这件事情就是在这不寻常的场合摆在我们面前的。"

"噢，我希望我爸爸能谈到点子上，"路易斯想，它到这时候已经紧张极了。

"我已经注意到，路易斯，"雄天鹅说下去，"你难得说句话。事实上，我想不起来你曾经发过一次声音。我从来没有听你说过话，说'咯—嗬'，或者大叫，不管是害怕还是快活。对于一只小吹号天鹅来说，这是最最少有的。这很严重。路易斯，让我听听你说'毕'。说起来吧，说吧!说

35

'毕'!"

可怜的路易斯！在它爸爸看着的时候，它深深吸了口气，张开嘴，把气放出来，希望能发出"毕"的一声。但是没有声音出来。

"再试试，路易斯，"它爸爸说。"也许你用力不够。"

路易斯再试。没有用。没有声音从它的嗓子眼里出来。它难过地摇摇头。

"看着我！"雄天鹅说。它伸直脖子，"咯—嗬"叫得那么响，几英里内的每一只野兽都听见了。

"现在让我听听你说'毕'！"它继续说。"说'毕'，路易斯——说得响，说得清楚！"

路易斯试着说。它说不出"毕"。

"那么让我听你说'波'！说吧，'波'！像这样：波—波—波。"

路易斯试着说"波"。它说不出。没有声音出来。

"算了，"雄天鹅说，"我想没有用。我想你是哑的。"

路易斯一听"哑"这个字，觉得都要哭出来了。雄天鹅看到自己伤了路易斯的心。"你误会我的意思了，我的儿子，"它用安慰的口气说。"哑只是不会发出声音，是个缺陷，但是你并不笨。实际上我想，在我所有的小天鹅当中，你也许是最聪明、最棒、最机灵的。人看不见叫瞎。人听不见叫聋。人不会说话叫哑。这只是说他不会说话而已。现在你明白了吗?"

路易斯点点头。它觉得好受点,很感谢它的爸爸把这个字的两种意思解释给它听。不过它还是极其不快活。

"不要存有一种不正常的难过,路易斯,"雄天鹅说。"天鹅必须快活而不要难过,要优雅而不要笨拙,要勇敢而不要胆小。你要记住,世界上有障碍必须克服的年轻人多的是。你显然有说话方面的缺陷。我肯定你会及时克服它的。在你这种岁数,不能说话甚至还可能有点儿好处呢。这样就迫使你很好地听人家说话。世界上只管喋喋不休地自己说话的人太多了,肯听人家说话的人却难得找到。我告诉你,你在听人家说话的时候,比在自己说话的时候可以得到更多东西。"

"我爸爸自己就说话很多,"路易斯想。

"有些人,"雄天鹅说下去,"一辈子里喋喋不休,用他们的嘴发出许多喧闹声,他们从来不肯真正听听任何话——他们只忙着发表自己的意见,而这些意见常常是错误的,或者是根据道听途说得来的。因此,我的儿子,要开开心心!要享受生活,要学会飞!好好吃,好好喝!用你的耳朵,用你的眼睛!我保证有一天我一定使你能用上你的嗓子。有机械装置能把空气转化成美丽的声音。有一种东西叫做小号。在我的旅行中，有一次我见到过一把小号。我想你要过圆满生活的话就需要一把小号。我从来不知道有一只吹号天鹅会需要一把小号，但是你情况不同。我打算弄来你所需要的这个东西。我不知道我怎么能做到，但是时间长着，会做到的。现在我们的谈话该结束了，让我们愉快地回到池塘另一头去吧，你的妈妈和你的哥哥姐姐在等着我们呢！"

雄天鹅转身游走了。路易斯跟着。这是它的一个不愉快的上午。它和它的哥哥姐姐不同，它觉得吓坏了。它和大家不同使得它害怕。它不明白，为什么就是它来到这个世界上没有嗓子。其他人似乎个个都有。为什么就是它没有？"命运是残酷的，"它想。"命运对我是残酷的。"接着它想起爸爸答应过帮它的忙，这才觉得好过些。

很快它们回到了大伙儿那里，大家玩起了水上游戏，路易斯也参加进去了，浸水，泼水，潜水，打转。路易斯能把水泼得比任何一只天鹅远，但是它泼水的时候叫不出来。泼水的时候能大喊大叫，一半乐趣就在这里。

6. 去蒙大拿

夏天过完的时候，雄天鹅把一家叫到身边，向它们宣布。

"孩子们，"它开始了，"我有消息告诉你们。夏天要结束了。树叶在变红，变成淡红，变成灰黄。树叶很快就要掉下来。到了我们该离开这池塘的时候了。到了我们该走的时候了。"

"走?"所有的小天鹅大叫起来，除了路易斯。

"当然，"它们的爸爸回答说。"你们这些孩子已经足够大，该学会生活的事情了，而眼下生活的主要事情就是：我们再也不能留在这呱呱叫的地方。"

"为什么不能?"所有的小天鹅大叫，只除了路易斯。

"因为夏天已经结束，"它们的爸爸说，"照规矩，夏天结束，天鹅就要离开它们造窝的地方，迁移到南边更暖和的地方去，那儿食物也多。我知道你们都喜欢这漂亮的池塘，这了不起的沼泽地，这些芦苇岸和休养胜地。你们在这里找到了生活乐趣。你们学会了潜水和在水下游泳。你们喜欢我们每天的外出活动，我们排成一行，我优雅地游在前面，像个火车头，你们的妈妈游在最后，像货车守车。你们一整天听和学。你们避开了可恶的水獭和残忍的狼。你们倾听小猫头鹰叫'科—科—科—科'。你们听到了山鹑叫'奎—奎'。夜里你们在青蛙的叫声——夜之声——中入睡。但是这些乐趣和消遣，这些奇遇，这些游戏和欢乐，这些可爱的景物和声音必须告一段落。一切事情都到了结束时候。我们该走了。"

"我们去哪里呢?"所有的小天鹅大叫，除了路易斯。"我们去哪里呢，咯—嗬，咯—嗬?我们去哪里呢，咯—嗬，咯—嗬?"

"我们去南方，去蒙大拿，"天鹅爸爸回答。

"蒙大拿是什么?"所有的小天鹅大叫着问道，除了路易斯。"蒙大拿是什么?什么是蒙大拿?"

"蒙大拿，"它们的爸爸说，"是美国的一个州。在那里，在高山环绕着的一个可爱的山谷里有红石湖，是大自然专门给天鹅设计的。在这些湖里，你们可以享受到从隐蔽的源泉流出来的温泉。在那个地方，不管夜里怎么冷，水从来不结冰。在红石湖你们会找到其他吹号天鹅，还有较少的一些水禽——野鹅和野鸭。那里没有什么敌人。没有开枪的人。有许多麝鼠窠。麦粒随便吃。天天游玩。在漫长漫长的严冬,天鹅还能再要求什么呢?"

路易斯惊讶地听着所有这些话。它很想问问爸爸,它们怎么能学会飞呢,就算学会了飞,又怎么能找到路上蒙大拿去呢。它开始担心迷路。但是它没有办法问任何问题。它只能听着。

它的一个哥哥开了口。

"爸爸,"它说,"你和我们要飞到南方。可我不会飞。我从来没有上过天。"

"一点不错,"它们的爸爸回答。"不过飞主要是有个正确的姿势问题——自然,再加上好的翅膀羽毛。飞一共包括三个部分。第一是起飞,起飞时要忙乱喧闹一通,劈劈啪啪,快速地拍打翅膀。第二是上升,也就是增加高度——这需要花大力气和快速扇动翅膀。第三是平飞,在高空稳定地飞行,这时候翅膀拍打得慢一些了,但拍打得有力和均匀,翅膀轻快和稳当地把我们一路带走,我们叫着咯—嗬,咯—嗬,整个大地在我们下面展开。"

"听上去非常美,"这小天鹅说,"不过我说不准我是不是能做到。在那上面我可能头晕眼花——要是我朝下看的话。"

"不要朝下看!"它的爸爸说。"笔直朝前看。不要慌张。再说,天鹅从来不头晕眼花——它们在空中感觉非常好。

它们感到得意扬扬。"

"'得意扬扬'是什么意思?"这小天鹅问。

"它的意思是感到自己强大,高兴,坚定,神气,自豪,成功,满意,有力,出众——就像已经征服了生活,具有一个崇高的目标。"

路易斯极其专心地听着所有这些话。想到飞它觉得害怕。"我说不出咯—嗬,"它想,"我不知道天鹅发不出声音,说不出咯—嗬,是不是还能够飞。"

"我想,"天鹅爸爸说,"最好的办法是让我先飞给你们看看。你们看着,我来飞一下。把我做的一切动作仔细看好了!看我在起飞之前把我的脖子上下摆动!看我把我的头转过来转过去测试风向!起飞必须一下子飞到风里面——这样飞起来要容易得多。听我发出的吹号声音!看我怎样举起我两只大翅膀!看我怎样使劲地拍打翅膀,同时用我的两只脚在水上像发疯似的冲刺!这种发疯似的冲刺大概持续两百英尺,到了这当儿,我会忽然腾空,我的翅膀仍旧用惊人的力量拍打空气,可是我的两只脚已经不再碰到水面了!这时候你们看着我怎样把我细巧的雪白长脖子向前伸出去,直到伸得笔直!看着我怎样收起双脚,让它们向后伸得笔直,一直伸到尾巴后面!听我在占了上风开始叫时的叫声!看我拍打翅膀变得多么有力和均匀!然后看我侧着身子

42

拐弯,翅膀平展着滑翔下来!就在我重新到达池塘的时候,看我怎样把双脚撑到我前面,用它们来做溅落动作,好像它们是一副滑水板似的!看完了所有这些,你们可以跟我一起来,还有你们的妈妈,我们大家一起练习飞行,直到你们掌握了飞行技巧为止。然后我们明天再来,不过不再回到池塘,我们向南方,向蒙大拿飞去了。你们准备好看我飞行了吗?"

"准备好了!"所有的小天鹅大叫,只除了路易斯。

"很好,现在我飞了!"天鹅爸爸叫道。

大家就那么看着,它逆风游到池塘一头,转过身来,测试了一下风向,把脖子上下摇动,吹号似的叫着,冲刺了两百英尺,飞起来,开始往上升。它雪白的长脖子向前伸出。它的黑色大脚向后伸直。它的大翅膀有很大的力量。等到它进入持续飞行,翅膀的拍打慢下来了。所有的眼睛盯住了看。路易斯比以往任何时候更加紧张。"我不知道我是不是真能做到这样?"它想。"万一我做不到呢?那么大家都飞走了,就留下我一个孤零零地在这走空了的池塘上,冬天来了,没有爸爸,没有妈妈,没有姐姐,没有哥哥,池塘全结冰了,没有东西吃。我准得饿死。我怕。"

几分钟以后,天鹅爸爸从空中滑翔下来,在池塘上用脚刹住。大家欢呼。"咯—嗬,咯—嗬,毕毕,毕毕!"大家欢呼,只除了路易斯。它表达它的称赞只是拍动翅膀,把水溅到了它爸爸的脸上。

"很好,"天鹅爸爸说。"怎么飞,你们都看到了。跟我来,我们大家来试试看。你们尽量伸开,做所有的动作完全要按照规矩,一分钟也不要忘记你们是天鹅,因此是出色的飞行能手,我肯定一切会顺顺利利的。"

它们全都逆风游到池塘一头。它们把它们的脖子一上一下地摆动。路易斯摆得比其他任何一只小天鹅更起劲。它们把头转来转去测试风向。一下子,天鹅爸爸发出起飞的信号。于是吵声喧天——翅膀拍打,脚向前冲刺,池水打转,泡沫四溅。说时迟那时快,真是奇迹中的奇迹,空中飞着七只天鹅——两只雪白,五只灰不溜秋。起飞完成了,它们开始升高。

在所有的小天鹅中,路易斯第一只御风而行,飞在它的哥哥姐姐们前面。它的脚一离开水面,它就知道它能够飞了。它一下子大大放了心——同时感觉棒极了。

"乖乖!"它心里说。"我从来不知道飞起来那么好玩。真棒!这真刺激。这真妙不可言。我觉得得意洋洋,头一点不晕。我可以和全家一起到蒙大拿去了。我是有缺陷,但是至少我能飞。"

七只大鸟在空中飞了大约半小时,然后回到池塘上,天鹅爸爸依然带头。它们大家喝了点水庆贺飞行的成功。

第二天它们一早起来。这是个美丽的秋天早晨，池塘上升起迷雾，树木闪着缤纷五色。靠近傍晚，当太阳在天际降得很低的时候，天鹅们从池塘上飞起来，开始它们去蒙大拿的长途旅行。

"这边走！"天鹅爸爸叫道。它朝左转，笔直朝南飞去。其他天鹅跟着，一边飞一边吹起了它们的号。当它们飞过萨姆·比弗所在的帐篷时，萨姆听见了它们的叫声，跑了出来。他站在那里看着它们在远处越来越小，越来越小，最后不见了。

"什么东西？"萨姆回到帐篷里的时候，他爸爸问他。

"天鹅，"萨姆回答。"它们朝南飞去了。"

"我们最好也这么做，"比弗先生说。"我想矮子明天要来接我们走了。"

比弗先生在他的床上躺下来。"是些什么天鹅啊？"他问道。

"是吹号天鹅，"萨姆说。

"奇怪，"比弗先生说。"我还以为吹号天鹅已经走了。我以为它们整年在红石湖，在那里它们是受到保护的。"

"它们大多数是这样，"萨姆回答说。"但不是全部。"

这是上床时间。萨姆拿出他的日记本。这是他在记事

本上写的:

今天夜里我听到天鹅叫了。它们朝南方飞去。夜间飞行一定很棒。我不知道我还能不能看到它们当中的一只。**鸟怎么会知道,怎样从它所在的地方飞到它想去的地方呢?**

7. 上课的日子

　　天鹅们到达它们在红石湖的过冬的家几天以后，路易斯有了一个主意。它决定，既然它不能用它的嗓子，它应该学会读和写。"如果我在某一方面有缺陷，"它对自己说，"我应该让自己在其他方面发展。我要学会读和写。然后我在脖子上挂块小石板，带支石笔。这样，我就能够和随便哪一个会读的人书面交谈了。"

　　路易斯爱交朋友，它在湖上已经有了许多朋友。这地方是水鸟的保护区——有天鹅、野鹅、野鸭和其他水鸟。它们住在这里，因为这是个安全地方，因为水在冬天最冷的气候里也是温暖的。路易斯的游泳本领受到大家高度仰慕。它喜欢和别的小天鹅比赛，看谁在水下游得最远，待得最久。

　　当路易斯拿定主意要学会读和写以后，它决定去拜访萨姆·比弗，好得到他的帮助。"也许，"路易斯想，"萨姆会让我和他一起上学，老师会教我写字。"这个主意让它万分兴奋。它不知道小"人"的课堂里收不收小天鹅。它不

47

知道学会读和写是不是很难。最主要的是，它不知道是不是能找到萨姆。蒙大拿是一个很大的州，它甚至说不准萨姆是不是住在蒙大拿，不过它希望他住在这里。

第二天早晨趁爸爸妈妈不注意，路易斯飞上了天。它朝东北方向飞。当它来到黄石河的时候，它沿着这条河飞到甜草乡。它看到下面有个镇，就飞下来，降落到一所小学校旁边，等着男女小学生放学。路易斯一个一个男生看，希望能看到萨姆。但是萨姆不在他们当中。

"不是这个镇，不是这所小学校，"路易斯想。"我要再试试。"

它飞走了，找到另一个镇，降落到另一所小学校，但是所有的小学生都放学回家了。

"我就在周围看看吧，"路易斯想。它不敢沿着大街走，因为怕有人会开枪打它。它于是飞起来，飞得低低的，打着转仔细看碰到的每一个男孩。飞了大概十分钟，它看见有一座牧场房子，一个男孩正靠近厨房门在劈木柴。这男孩黑头发。路易斯滑翔下来。

"我真幸运，"它想。"这正好是萨姆。"

萨姆一看见来了只天鹅，放下斧子，站着一动不动。路易斯胆小地走上前去，然后低下头来解萨姆的鞋带。

"你好，"萨姆用友好的声音说。

路易斯想说"咯—嗬"，但是从它的喉咙里一点声音也发不出来。

"我认识你，"萨姆说。"你就是一声不响，拉我鞋带的那只小天鹅。"

路易斯点点头。

"我很高兴看到你，"萨姆说。"我能为你做什么事吗?"

路易斯只是向前直望着。

"你肚子饿吗?"萨姆问道。

路易斯摇摇头。

"你渴吗?"

路易斯摇摇头。

"你要在这里牧场和我们过夜吗?"萨姆问道。

路易斯点点头，蹦蹦跳跳。

"没问题，"萨姆说。"我们住的地方有的是。问题只是要得到我爸爸的同意。"

萨姆捡起斧子，把一块木柴放在木砧上，一斧子下去，把木柴正好劈成两半。他看着路易斯。

"你的嗓子有毛病，对吗?"他问道。

路易斯点点头，把脖子拼命地上下点动。它知道萨姆是它的朋友，虽然它不知道萨姆有一回还救过它妈妈

49

的性命。

过了几分钟,比弗先生骑着一匹牧牛的矮脚马走进院子。他下了马,把它拴在一根木桩上。"你弄到了什么啦?"他问萨姆。

"是小吹号天鹅,"萨姆说。"它只有几个月大。你能让我养它一阵子吗?"

"这个嘛,"比弗先生说,"我想,收养一只这种野禽是违反法律的。不过我可以打个电话问问渔猎法执行官,看看他怎么说。如果他说可以,你就可以收养它。"

"告诉执行官说这天鹅有点毛病,"萨姆在他爸爸朝房子走的时候对他叫着说。

"它怎么啦?"他的爸爸问。

"它有发不出声音的问题,"萨姆回答说。"它的喉咙有毛病。"

"你说什么?谁听说过一只天鹅会有发不出声音的问题?"

"不过,"萨姆说,"这是一只不能吹号的吹号天鹅。它有发声的缺陷。它一点声音也发不出来。"

比弗先生看着他的儿子,好像不知道相信他的话好还是不相信他的话好。不过他走进了屋子。几分钟后他回来。"执行官说了,如果你能帮助这小天鹅,你可以把它留在这里过一阵子。不过这小天鹅迟早要回到红石湖去的，它属于那里。执行官又说，他不会答应任何人留下一只小天鹅，但是他答应你留下它，因为他知道你懂得鸟类，他信任你。这是很高的评价，孩子。"

比弗先生看上去很高兴。萨姆看上去很快活。路易斯大大松了口气。过了一会儿，大伙儿走进牧场房子，在厨房里吃饭。比弗先生允许路易斯站在萨姆的椅子旁边，他们喂它吃一些玉米和麦子，它们很好吃。

萨姆准备上床的时候，想让路易斯睡在他的房间里，跟他在一起，但是比弗先生说不行。"它会把房间弄得一塌糊涂的。它不是金丝鸟，它太大了。把它放在谷仓吧。它可以睡在一个空马厩里，那些马不会在乎的。"

第二天早晨，萨姆带路易斯到学校。萨姆骑他的小马驹去，路易斯一路跟着飞。到了学校，其他孩子看到这只大鸟都很惊奇：它脖子长，眼睛亮，脚大。萨姆把它介绍给矮胖的一年级老师哈默博瑟姆太太。萨姆向她解释，说路易斯要学读和写，因为它的喉咙发不出声音。

哈默博瑟姆太太看着路易斯。接着她摇摇头。"鸟不能来！"她说。"我的麻烦已经够多了。"

萨姆很失望的样子。

"谢谢你，哈默博瑟姆太太，"他说。"谢谢你就让它站在你的班里学读和写吧。”

"一只鸟干吗要读要写呢?"老师回答。"只有人才需要和别人交流思想。"

"这话不完全对,哈默博瑟姆太太,"萨姆说,"如果你原谅我这么说的话。我已经观察了许多鸟和兽。所有的鸟和兽都相互交谈——它们的确得交谈,好相处下去。鸟兽妈妈得和它们的孩子交谈。雄的鸟兽得和雌的鸟兽交谈,特别是在一年的春天,那时候它们相爱了。"

"相爱?"哈默博瑟姆太太说,听了这话她似乎震动起来。"关于爱情你知道些什么?"

萨姆脸红了。

"它是只什么鸟?"老师问道。

"是只小吹号天鹅,"萨姆说。"眼下它是脏灰色,可到明年它将是你看到的最美丽的鸟——全身雪白,黑嘴黑脚。它是春天在加拿大孵出来的,如今住在红石湖,但是它不会像其他天鹅那样说'咯—嗬',这对它大大不利。"

"为什么?"老师问道。

"因为就是不利,"萨姆说。"万一你要说'咯—嗬',却又说不出一点声音,你会感到担心吗?"

"我不要说'咯—嗬',"老师回答说。"我甚至不知道那是什么意思。反正这都很傻,萨姆。你怎么会想到一只鸟能学会读和写呢?这是不可能的。"

"给它一个机会吧!"萨姆求老师说。"它很规矩,它很聪明,它就是得了这个非常严重的不会发音的毛病。"

"它叫什么名字?"

"我不知道,"萨姆回答。

"不过,"哈默博瑟姆太太说,"它要到我的班上来,它就得有个名字。也许我们可以问出它的名字来。"她看着小天鹅。"你是叫乔吗?"

路易斯摇摇头。

"叫乔纳森?"

路易斯摇摇头。

"叫唐纳德?"

路易斯还是摇摇头。

"你叫路易斯吧?"哈默博瑟姆太太问道。

路易斯使劲点头,双脚蹦蹦跳,拍着翅膀。

"见恺撒大帝的鬼!"老师叫道。"瞧它那对翅膀!那好,它的名字叫路易斯——这是没有问题的。好吧,路易斯,你可以进这个班。你就站在这儿黑板旁边。也不要把房间弄得乱七八糟!如果你有事要离开教室,你举起一只翅膀。"

路易斯点点头。所有一年级小学生都欢呼起来。他们喜欢这位新同学的样子,急着要看看它能做什么。

"肃静,同学们!"哈默博瑟姆太太严肃地说。"我们现在从字母A开始。"

她拿起一支粉笔,在黑板上写了一个很大的A字。"现在你来写写看,路易斯!"

路易斯用嘴叼起一支粉笔,就在老师写的这个字母下面写上一个方方正正的A字。

"你看到啦?"萨姆说。"它是一只不寻常的鸟。"

"不过,"哈默博瑟姆太太说,"A很容易写。我来个难一点的。"她说着在黑板上写上CAT[①]。"写这个词儿给我们看看吧,路易斯。"

路易斯写上了CAT。

"不过CAT还是容易写,"老师咕噜了一声。"CAT容易写因为它短。什么人能想出一个比CAT长的词儿来吗?"

"Catastrophe[②],"坐在第一排的查尔斯·内尔森说。

"好,"哈默博瑟姆太太说。"这是个很好的难词儿。但是谁知道它什么意思吗?什么是Catastrophe?"

"一场地震,"一个女生说。

"正确!"老师回答。"还有呢?"

"战争也是,"查尔斯·内尔森说。

"正确!"哈默博瑟姆太太回答。"还有呢?"

一个很小的红头发姑娘，叫珍妮的，举起了她的手。

"好，珍妮你说呢?什么是Catastrophe?"

珍妮用尖细的声音说："比方说要跟爸爸妈妈去野餐，做好了花生酱夹心面包和啫喱卷筒蛋糕，把它们放在保温箱里，保温箱里还放进了香蕉、苹果、葡萄饼干、纸巾、几瓶汽水、几个煮鸡蛋，然后把保温箱放上汽车。正要动身的时候，下起雨来了，于是爸爸妈妈说下雨天不能出去野餐，这就是Catastrophe。"

"非常好，珍妮，"哈默博瑟姆太太说。"这件事没有地震糟糕，这件事也没有战争可怕。但是正要去野餐却碰上了下雨，对于一个孩子来说，我想这就是Catastrophe。反正Catastrophe是个合适的词儿。没有鸟能写出那么一个词儿来。要是我能教会一只鸟写Catastrophe，这将是甜草乡一个大新闻。我的照片会登到《生活》杂志上去。我就出名了。"

她一边想着所有这些事，一边走到黑板旁边，用大字写上CATASTROPHE。

"好，路易斯，你把这个词儿写给我们看看吧。"

路易斯用嘴叼起另一支粉笔。它有点害怕。它仔细看看老师写的词儿。"一个长词儿，"它想，"其实不比一个短词儿难。我只要一个字母一个字母临摹下来就是了，很快就能写好。再说，我的生活就是Catastrophe，发不出声音就是Catastrophe。接着它开始写。CATASTROPHE，它写出来了，每一个字母都写得工整。当它写到最后一个字母的时候，小学生们拍手顿脚，拍他们的课桌，有一个男生很快折出了一只纸飞机，把它投向空中。哈默博瑟姆太太叫大家守秩序。

"非常好，路易斯，"她说。"萨姆，现在你该回你自己的教室去了——你不该在我的教室。你回五年级去吧。我会小心照顾你的朋友天鹅的。"

萨姆回到自己的教室去，坐在他的课桌椅上，觉得事情变得这么顺利，十分高兴。五年级正在上算术课，他们的老师安妮·斯纳格小姐看到萨姆来了，就向他提出一个问题。这位斯纳格小姐年轻漂亮。

"萨姆，如果一个人一小时能走三英里，四小时他能走多少英里？"

"这要看他走完第一个小时以后有多累，"萨姆回答说。

其他学生吵起来了。斯纳格小姐叫大家静下来。

"萨姆说得很对，"她说。"这个问题我以前倒没有这样考虑过。我一直认为那个人四小时可以走十二英里。不过萨姆说不定是对的：走完第一个小时以后，那个人可能不会觉得那么精神十足了。他可能拖着腿走。他可能慢下来。"

艾伯特·比奇洛举手。"我爸爸认识一个人,那人想走十二英里,结果心力衰竭死了,"艾伯特说。

"天啊!"老师说。"我也认为这是可能发生的。"

"四小时里什么事情都可能发生,"萨姆说。"脚后跟可能走出水泡。路边可能长着浆果,他停下来采浆果吃。这样他就算不累,或者脚后跟没走出水泡,也会让他慢了下来。"

"确实会这样,"老师说。"好了,孩子们,我想关于算术我们全都学会了很多东西,这都得感谢萨姆·比弗。现在还有一个问题要请教室里一位女生回答。用一个牛奶瓶喂一个婴孩喝牛奶,喂一顿是八盎司,那么,喂了两顿,那婴孩一共喝了多少盎司?"

琳达·斯特普尔斯举手。

"大约十五盎司,"她说。

"为什么?"斯纳格小姐问。"为什么那婴孩不是喝了十六盎司?"

"因为他每次都要洒掉一点儿,"琳达说。"牛奶从他嘴角流下来,流到他妈妈的围裙上了。"

这一回全班叫得那么响,算术课只好结束。但是每个人都学会了,跟数字打交道得多么小心。

---

① 英语的"猫"。
② 英语的"灾难"。

8. 爱情

　　路易斯的爸爸妈妈发现路易斯不见了,它们多么担心啊。湖上没有别的小天鹅不见过——只有路易斯。

　　"问题现在发生了,"雄天鹅对它的妻子说,"不管怎样,我得去找我的儿子。现在我真不想离开这些迷人的湖,在这一年的秋天,而冬天快到了。事实上我一直在盼望着这个安静的时刻,跟其他的水鸟在一起。我喜欢这里的生活。"

　　"除了你的个人舒适,还有一件小事情要考虑,"它的妻子说。"你想到吗,我们不知道路易斯离开的时候是朝哪一个方向飞的。它到底上哪儿去了,你知道的并不比我多。你要去找它,你朝哪个方向飞呢?"

　　"这个嘛,"雄天鹅说,"根据最后分析,我相信我可以朝南飞。"

　　"'根据最后分析',你这话是什么意思?"雌天鹅不耐烦地说。"你根本什么也没有分析。你为什么说'根据最后分析'?你为什么要朝南飞去找路易斯?还有别的方向啊。

有东，有西，有北。还有东北、东南、西南、西北。"

"不错，"雄天鹅回答。"还有那么些介于两者之间的方向：北东北、东东南、西西南。还有正北偏东，正东偏北。还有东南半偏东，正西半偏北。想起来，一只小天鹅会去的方向真是不计其数。"

因此得出结论，无法可找。"我们只能在这里等着，看到底出了什么事，"雄天鹅说。"我断定路易斯到时候会回来的。"

一个又一个月过去，冬天来到了红石湖。夜晚长，又黑又冷。白天短，很亮，但还是冷。有时候刮风。但是天鹅、野鹅、野鸭安全快活。注进这些湖的温泉使湖上不被冰覆盖——总是有水面露出。食物很多。有时候会有个人带来一袋麦子，把麦子撒在鸟能吃到的地方。

冬天过了春天到来，春天过了夏天到来。一年过去，又到了春天。还是没有路易斯的影子。然而有一天早晨，正当路易斯那些长大了的哥哥在玩水球的时候，其中一只抬起头，看到一只天鹅在天空中飞来。

"咯—嗬!"这小天鹅叫道。它跑到它的爸爸妈妈那里去。"瞧!瞧!瞧!"

湖上所有的水鸟转过身来，朝飞来的那只天鹅看。那天鹅在空中回环打转。

"是路易斯!"天鹅爸爸说。"但是用根绳子挂在它脖子上的古怪小东西是什么啊?那是什么?"

"等着瞧吧,"它的妻子说。"也许是个礼物。"

路易斯从天上朝下看,寻找像是它一家的天鹅。等到看准了,它滑翔下来,一下子刹住脚。它的妈妈冲上来拥抱它。它的爸爸漂亮地弓起了脖子,举起两只翅膀欢迎它。所有的天鹅叫道:"咯—嗬!""欢迎你回来,路易斯!"它们一家大喜过望。它出去了一年半——几乎十八个月。它看上去大多了,英俊多了。它的羽毛现在雪白,不再是脏兮兮的灰色。用一根带子挂在它脖子上的是一块小石板。用一根绳子拴在石板上的是一支白石笔。

等到大家见过面以后,路易斯用嘴叼住石笔在石板上写上:"你们好!"它很急地把石板拿着让大家看。

天鹅爸爸看着石板。天鹅妈妈看着石板。天鹅哥哥姐姐们看着石板。它们就那么站在那里看。石板上的字对它们来说一点意思也没有。它们不会读。它们一家以前从来没有见过石板,也没有见过石笔。路易斯向它们问好的打算落了空。它觉得好像白白浪费了一年半时间进学校去学写。它显然失望了。当然,它没有办法说话。石板上的话是它表达问好的唯一办法。

最后天鹅爸爸开腔了。

61

"路易斯,我的儿子,"它用它深沉洪亮的嗓音说起来,"这是我们等待了很久的一天——你回到我们红石湖保护区的一天。没有人能够想像,我们重新见到你有多么快活多么激动,你不在我们身边那么久,到了我们不知道的地方去,追求我们只能猜想的东西。重新看到你是多么好啊!我们只能希望你身体健康,当你在我们不知道的地方,追求我们只能猜想的东西……"

"这话你已经说过一遍了,"它的妻子说。"你在重复自己的话。路易斯长途旅行回来一定累了,不管它曾经在什么地方,曾经在做什么事。"

"一点不假,"天鹅爸爸说。"不过我必须把我的欢迎辞拖长一点,因为我的好奇心在于路易斯脖子上挂的那个奇怪小玩意儿,以及它用那根白色玩意儿一上一下画出来的奇怪的白条纹符号。"

"当然,"路易斯的妈妈说,"我们大家都对这个有兴趣。可是路易斯没有办法解释,因为它有缺陷不能说话。因此我们暂时只好把好奇心忘掉,让路易斯洗个澡,吃顿饭。"

大家一致同意,认为这个主意好。

路易斯游到岸边,把它的石板和石笔放在一丛矮树底下,洗了个澡。洗完了澡,它把一个翅膀的尖蘸上水,难过地擦掉石板上的字:"你们好!"接着它把石板重新挂在脖子上。回家和自家人在一起很愉快。在它和萨姆·比弗一起上学的这些月份里,它的一家"人数"增加了。现在又多了六只新的小天鹅。路易斯的爸爸妈妈夏天去加拿大旅行了一次,在那里造窝,孵出了这六只小天鹅,秋天它们全都回到蒙大拿的红石湖来团聚。

路易斯回来后不久,有一天,送麦子来的人又来了。他带着一袋麦子停在附近,路易斯向他游过去。那人把麦子撒在地上,路易斯拿下石板,在上面写道:"非常感谢!"它把石板举起来给那人看,那人惊奇极了。

"哎呀!"那人说。"你这天鹅真不简单!你是在哪儿学会写字的?"

路易斯擦掉石板上的字,又写:"在学校。"

"学校?"那人说。"什么学校?"

"公立学校,"路易斯写道。"哈默博瑟姆太太教我。"

"这个名字倒没听说过,"那人说。"不过她一定是一位好得要死的老师。"

"她是的,"路易斯写道。它能和一位陌生人对话真是高兴到极点。它明白了,石板尽管不能用来和别的鸟对话,和人说话它却能帮大忙,因为人会读。这一来,它心情好多了。它离开牧场的时候,萨姆·比弗给了它这块石板作为告别礼物。萨姆是用他积下的零花钱买来这石板和石笔的。路易斯决定,不管它到天涯海角,也要把它们一直带着。

那送来麦子的人简直不知道自己是在做梦,抑或当真看到一只天鹅在石板上写字。他决定不把这件事告诉任何人,生怕人们以为他脑子有毛病——疯了。

对于鸟类来说,春天是求偶的季节。春天的温暖甜蜜空气激起年轻天鹅一种奇怪的感觉。雄天鹅开始注意雌天鹅。它们在雌天鹅面前卖弄自己。雌天鹅也开始注意雄天鹅,不过它们装出根本什么也不注意的样子。它们羞答答的。

路易斯有一天觉得自己那么特别,于是知道自己一定爱上了谁了。它也知道它爱的是哪一只天鹅。每一次它游过这只天鹅身边,就能够感到自己心跳加快,心中充满爱和渴望的情思。它觉得它还从来没有见过那么美丽的一位天鹅小姐。这位天鹅小姐比其他天鹅小姐较为娇小,似乎比路易斯的其他朋友有更漂亮的脖子和更迷人的神态。它的名字叫塞蕾娜。路易斯希望能做点什么事吸引它的注意。它要塞蕾娜做它的伴侣,但是没法告诉它,因为路易斯发不出声音。它围着塞蕾娜绕圈圈,把脖子上下晃动,施展潜水本

64

领,在水下待着,要证明它比任何一只天鹅呼吸屏得更久。但这位天鹅小姐对路易斯的古怪举动一点也不注意。它装出一副路易斯根本不存在的样子。

等到路易斯的妈妈发现路易斯在追求一位天鹅小姐,它躲到一些灯心草后面去看是怎么回事。它可以断定,从路易斯的举动看,路易斯是爱上这位天鹅小姐了,不过它也看到,路易斯一无成就。

有一次,路易斯在毫无办法的情况下,游到它心爱的塞蕾娜面前,鞠了个躬。它的石板照旧挂在它的脖子上。它用嘴叼起石笔,在石板上写上"我爱你",把石板给塞蕾娜看。

塞蕾娜看了看石板,游过去了。它不会读,虽然它也很喜欢这只脖子上挂着个什么玩意儿的天鹅小伙子的长相,可是它不能对一只不能说句话的天鹅产生兴趣。一只吹号天鹅而不能吹号,依它看来是毫无价值的。

路易斯的妈妈看到这件事,就去找它丈夫,那位天鹅爸爸。

"我有个消息要告诉你,"它说,"你的儿子路易斯爱上一位天鹅小姐了,但是它爱的那位天鹅小姐不理它。正是我当初说的那样。路易斯不可能得到伴侣,只因为它没有嗓子。看到它在追求的那位天鹅小姐不把它放在眼里,我连脖子都痛了。不过我同样为路易斯难过。它以为这位小姐是湖上最伟大的'人物',但它不能说'咯—嗬,我爱你',而这正是这位小姐等着要听到的。"

"哎呀,这是最可怕的消息,"天鹅爸爸说,"这是最不得了的消息。我知道爱上谁是怎么回事。我记得很清楚恋爱会是多么苦恼,多么兴奋,碰到失恋又会是怎样日夜伤心失望。不过我是路易斯的爸爸,我不能坐视不管。我要行动。路易斯是一只吹号天鹅,是所有水鸟中最高贵的鸟。它快活,欢乐,强壮,有力,生气勃勃,善良,勇敢,英俊,可靠,信得过,飞行高手,了不起的游泳健将,无畏,耐苦,忠厚,诚实,有雄心大志……"

"等一等,"它的妻子说。"你用不着告诉我所有这些。问题是:你打算怎样帮助路易斯找到一个伴侣。"

"我要用我漂亮的方式达到这个目的,"天鹅爸爸回答说。"你说这位天鹅小姐要的是听到路易斯说'咯—嗬,我爱你',对不对?'

"一点不错。"

"那么它会听到的!"天鹅爸爸说。"人类做出了这些东西——喇叭,小号,各种各样乐器。这些乐器能够发出类似我们自然的叫声。我要开始物色这样一种乐器,为了给我们的年轻儿子找到一把小号,哪怕要我走到天涯海角,我最

66

终也会把它找到，并且带回家来给路易斯的。"

"好，如果我可以提个建议，"它的妻子说，"那么不用到天涯海角，就到蒙大拿州的比林斯吧。那儿近一点。"

"非常好。我一定去比林斯试试。我要在比林斯找到一把小号。现在不用再啰唆了，我去。一点时间也不能耽搁了。春天不会永存。爱情在飞逝。每一分钟都至关重要。我这就上蒙大拿的比林斯市去。那是个生机勃勃、充满了人类制造的东西的城市。再见，我的爱人！我会回来的！"

"你哪来的钱?"它那讲究实际的妻子问道。"小号是要钱买的。"

"这件事就留给我来办吧，"它丈夫回答说。它说着飞上了天。它像架喷气式飞机那样陡直地上升，接着平飞，高高地向东北方向疾速前进。它的妻子盯着看，直到它看不见了为止。

"一只怎么样的天鹅啊！"它嘟囔说。"我只希望它知道它在干什么。"

9．小号

当天鹅爸爸拍打着有力的白翅膀朝比林斯飞去的时候,它的脑袋瓜里旋转着各种各样伤脑筋的念头。天鹅爸爸以前从来没有去访求过小号。它也没有钱买小号。它也担心飞到那里的时候,商店已经停止营业了。它知道在整个北美洲,它是一路飞到城里去要弄到一把小号的唯一一只吹号天鹅。

"这是一次奇怪的冒险,"它对自己说。"然而这是一次崇高的冒险。我要尽一切力量帮助我的儿子路易斯——哪怕我卷进真正的麻烦。"

靠近傍晚时分,天鹅爸爸向前一看,看到了远处比林斯的教堂、工厂、商店和住家。它决定迅速果敢地行动。它把这座城市绕了一遍,要寻找一家音乐商店。一下子它看到了一家。它有一个宽大的橱窗,橱窗的玻璃厚厚的。天鹅爸爸飞得低一些,打着转,好看得清楚些。它向商店里面看。它看到了一个漆成金色的鼓。它看到了一个漂亮的吉他,带着电线的。它看到了一架小钢琴。它看到了班卓琴、

69

号、小提琴、曼陀林、钹、萨克斯管、木琴、大提琴和许多别的乐器。接着它看到了它所要的东西，它看到了一把铜的小号，用一根红带子挂在那里。

"现在我行动的时刻到了！"它对自己说。"现在我孤注一掷的时刻到了，不管它对我的感情会是怎么样的打击，不管它和支配人类生活的法律会如何抵触。我这就干！愿我好运！"

天鹅爸爸这么想着，振翅飞下去。它瞄准了那大橱窗。它把脖子伸直了，绷得紧紧的，准备着哗啦一声。它飞快地下潜，全速冲击那橱窗。玻璃哗啦一声破了。那响声是惊人的。整个商店都震动了。乐器纷纷落到地板上。玻璃碎片四溅。一位女营业员昏倒过去。天鹅爸爸感到一阵刺痛，一块玻璃碎片割伤了它的肩，但是它用嘴叼起那把小号，在空中猛一转身，飞出了橱窗玻璃上的大洞，开始飞快地升到比林斯那些屋顶上空。几滴血落到了下面地上。它的肩膀受伤了。但是它成功地得到了它所为而来的东西。它嘴里牢牢叼住，在红带子上晃来晃去的是一把漂亮的铜的小号。

你可以想像天鹅爸爸冲过橱窗时音乐商店里那一声哗啦。就在玻璃撞破的时候，一位店员正在给一位顾客看一个低音鼓，他只见一只白色大鸟撞破玻璃飞进橱窗，吓得拼命狠狠地敲鼓。

"咚咚咚!"鼓响了。

"哗啦!"玻璃给撞破的响了。

女营业员晕倒的时候,她倒在钢琴的琴键上。

"叮叮咚—叮叮咚—叮叮咚!"钢琴响了。

店老板一把抓起他的猎枪,可是没打中,一枪在天花板上打了个窟窿,石灰纷纷扬扬地洒下来。所有的东西飞起落下,响起了喧闹声。

"咚!"鼓响。

"砰!"班卓琴响。

"叮叮咚—叮叮咚—叮叮咚!"钢琴响。

"崩!"小提琴响。

"救命啊!"一个店员大叫。"我们遭抢劫了。"

"让开!"店老板大叫着向门口奔去,走到外面,朝飞走的天鹅又开了一枪——砰!他这一枪开得太晚了。天鹅爸爸早已在天上射程之外,十分安全。它高高地飞在比林斯的屋顶和尖塔上空,朝着西南方向飞回家。在它的嘴上叼着那把小号,在它的心里是犯了罪的痛苦感觉。

"我抢了一家商店,"它对自己说。"我成了一个贼。对于一只像我这样具有高尚品格和崇高理想的天鹅来说,这是多么悲惨的命运啊!我为什么这样做呢?是什么事使我犯这个罪呢?我的过去一生是无懈可击的——良好行为和端正品德的典范。我天生是守法的。为什么,噢,为什么我做这件事呢?"

可是在它稳稳地在傍晚天空中飞行时,答案来了。"我做这件事是要帮助我的儿子。我做这件事是出于对我儿子路易斯的爱。"

回头说比林斯吧,那儿消息很快传开了。这是开天辟地以来第一次,天鹅竟闯入一家音乐商店叼走了一把小号。许多人不肯相信有这等事。报社编辑派了一名记者去这家商店看看。记者采访了店老板,为报纸写了一篇报道。这篇报道的标题是:

大鸟破窗闯进音乐商店

一只白天鹅撞破橱窗闯入,

叼走了一把价格昂贵的小号

在比林斯,人人买了这份报,细读这一桩异乎寻常的事件。满城都在谈论这件事。有人相信,也有人说这根本不可能。他们说,这不过是店老板想出这么个花招,要给他的店做广告罢了。不过店里的店员们说这件事的确发生了。他们指着地板上一滴滴的血。

警方来查看损坏情况,估计损失约为九百元。警方答应设法找到窃贼并逮捕归案,不过警方听到窃贼竟是一只鸟时,觉得十分抱歉。"鸟类是特殊问题,"他们说。"鸟类很难对付。"

又回过头来讲红石湖。路易斯的妈妈心急如焚地等着它的丈夫回来。当天鹅爸爸终于在夜空中出现的时候,天鹅妈妈看到它带着一把小号。它由一条带子挂在天鹅爸爸的脖子上。

"好,"当天鹅爸爸滑翔下来,在水面上停住的时候,天鹅妈妈说,"我看到你办成了。"

"我办成了,我亲爱的,"天鹅爸爸说。"我飞得又快又远,牺牲了我的名誉,现在回来了。路易斯在哪里?我这就要把它的小号交给它。"

"它正坐在那边麝鼠窝上,梦想着它想得发疯了的那位天鹅傻小姐。"

天鹅爸爸向它的儿子游过去,发表了一番赠送演讲。

"路易斯,"它说,"我走远路去了人们常去的地方。我访问了一个生活沸腾、生意兴隆的大城市。就在那儿,我给你捎来了一件礼物,现在我充满爱心和祝福把它送给你。喏,路易斯,这儿是一把小号。它将成为你的嗓子——代替上帝没能给你的嗓子。学会吹它吧,路易斯,这样生活对你就将顺利些,容易些,丰富些,愉快些!有了这小号的帮助,你终于能够像所有其他天鹅那样说'咯—嗬'。音乐之声将传到我们的耳朵里。你将能吸引迷人的小姐们注意。掌握这小号吧,你将能为这些小姐们演奏情歌,使它们充满热情、惊奇和向往。我希望这小号将带给你快乐,路易斯,将带给你新的更好的生活。我得到它是作出了一些我的个人牺牲,损失了一些我的自尊心的,不过我们现在不去谈这个。说来说去都只为我没有钱,我没有付钱就拿走了这小号。这是一个遗憾。不过更重要的是你学会演奏乐器。"

天鹅爸爸说着,从自己的脖子上拿下小号,挂到路易斯的脖子上,让它和石板跟石笔挂在一起。

"健康地挂着它吧!"它说。"快乐地吹奏它吧!让森林、群山、沼泽地回响起你青春渴望的声音吧!"

路易斯想对它的爸爸说一声谢谢,但是它说不出一个字来。它知道在石板上写"谢谢你"也没用,因为它的爸爸从来没有受过教育,不会读。因此路易斯只是拼命上下点它的头,摇它的尾巴,拍它的翅膀。天鹅爸爸从这些动作知道,它的儿子感谢它,接受了自己送给它的这把小号。

10. 金钱烦恼

路易斯是上红石湖最受大家喜欢的天鹅小伙子,而且它的装备也最好。它的脖子上不但挂着一块石板和一支石笔,还用红带子挂着一把铜小号。天鹅小姐们开始注意它了,因为它看上去和其他天鹅小伙子完全两样。它在群中出众。其他天鹅都没带着什么东西。

路易斯很喜欢它那把新小号。从第一天拿到起,它整天试着使它发出声音来。抓住小号很不容易。它试过好几种不同姿势,弯曲着它的脖子去吹。起先没吹出声音。它吹得越来越用力,脸颊都鼓了起来,脸都涨红了。

"这可不好办了,"它想。

但后来它发现,只要把舌头保持在一定位置,它能让小号发出一个很小的、喘气似的声音。这声音不太好听,但总算是个声音。它听上去有点像热气从取暖器里出来。

"卜,卜,卜,"小号响着。

路易斯继续吹。最后,到试吹的第二天,它终于使小号吹出了一个音—— 一个清楚的音。

"咯!"小号响起来。

路易斯听到这声音,心怦地跳了一下。一只正好游过的野鸭停下来听。

"咯!咯—衣—呜—呜,"小号响着。

"这要时间,"路易斯想。"我不能一天就成为小号手,这是没有疑问的。不过罗马城也不是一天造起来的啊,哪怕需要一整个夏天,我也要学会吹这小号。"

路易斯除了学吹小号,还有别的问题。问题之一,它知道它的小号没有付钱——它是偷来的。它根本不愿意这样。问题之二,塞蕾娜,它爱上的天鹅,已经走了。它和几只年轻天鹅小姐离开了这个湖,朝北飞到蛇河去。路易斯很怕再也见不到塞蕾娜。因此它觉得心都碎了,就算有一把偷来的小号,又没有谁教它吹。

什么时候路易斯有麻烦,它就想到萨姆·比弗。萨姆以前帮助过它,也许再能帮助它。再说春天弄得它心神不定:它觉得有什么在怂恿它离开这湖,飞到什么地方去。因此有一天早晨,它动身了,笔直朝萨姆居住的甜草乡那个牧场飞去。

这一回飞去不像上一回容易。如果你试过像它那样一路飞,脖子下面有一个小号晃来晃去,还有一块石板在风中劈劈啪啪,再有一支石笔在绳子头上一跳一跳,那你就知道这有多么费劲了。路易斯明白,轻身上路,不带那么多东西,那要好得多。不过它是一位坚强的飞行者,石板、石笔和小号对它至关重要。

当它来到萨姆居住的牧场时,它转了个圈,然后滑翔下来,走进谷仓。它找到了,萨姆正在刷洗他的小马驹。

"哈,瞧谁来了,"萨姆叫道。"你脖子上挂着那么多东西,活像一位旅行推销员。看到你我很高兴。"

路易斯把石板按在小马驹的马栏上,在上面写上:"我有麻烦了。"

"怎么回事?"萨姆问。"这小号你是从哪儿弄来的?"

"麻烦就在这儿,"路易斯写道。"是我爸爸偷来的。它给我小号,因为我没有嗓子。小号还没付钱。"

萨姆吹了声口哨。然后他把小马驹牵进马栏,拴好,走出来,坐在一捆干草上。好一会儿他就那么看着路易斯。最后他说:"你有钱的问题。不过这不是什么不寻常的事情。几乎每一个人都有钱的问题。你需要的是一个工作。这样,你就可以把挣到的钱积蓄起来,钱积够了,你爸爸就可以去把钱还给它偷了小号的那个人。你真能演奏什么东西吗?"

路易斯点点头。它把小号举到它的嘴上。

"咯!"小号响了。小马驹跳了起来。

"嘿!"萨姆说。"非常好。你还会吹别的音吗?"

路易斯摇摇头。

"我有主意了,"萨姆说。"今年夏天我有一个工作,在安大略省一个儿童夏令营担任少年辅导员。那是在加拿大。我敢打赌,只要你能再学会吹几个音,我可以给你找一个工作担任夏令营的号手。夏令营正好需要一个会吹号的人。这主意就是,你一早吹起一连串很响很快的号音,把孩子们叫起来。那叫做起床号。然后吹几个别的号音叫营员们吃饭。那叫做就餐号。到了晚上,大家都上床了,天空的亮光消退了,湖上静悄悄的,蚊子在帐篷里开始大肆活动,叮孩子们,而孩子们在床上睡意正浓,这时候你吹起了别的号音,非常柔和,甜蜜,伤感。那叫做熄灯号。你愿意和我一起去夏令营试试看吗?"

"我什么都愿意试,"路易斯说。"我急着要钱。"

萨姆格格笑。"那好,"他说。"夏令营大概三星期以后开始。这样你有时间学吹这几种号。我会给你买本音乐书,它会告诉你吹一些什么音。"

萨姆办到了。他找到了一本讲解吹各种号的书,是军队里吹的号。他把说明读给路易斯听。"立正。把号对着前面。不要把它朝向地上,因为这个姿势束缚肺部,而且使号手的样子极其难看。乐器应该一星期擦洗一次,去掉

78

口水。"

每天下午，当比弗先生牧场的客人背着背包进山旅行，路易斯就练习吹它那个号。很快它就能吹起床号、就餐号和熄灯号了。它特别喜欢熄灯号的声音。路易斯有音乐天赋，它渴望成为一名真正的好号手。它想："一只吹号天鹅应该吹一口好小号。"它也很高兴找个工作的主意，好挣到点钱。它正到了工作的合适岁数。它几乎已经两岁了。

在去夏令营的头天晚上，萨姆把他所有去夏令营的东西塞进行李袋。他塞进运动鞋和软帮鞋。他塞进前面写着"库库斯库斯夏令营"的运动衫。他用一条毛巾包起照相机也塞了进去。他把钓鱼竿、牙刷、梳子、刷子、羊毛衫、雨披和网球拍也塞了进去。他塞进去拍纸簿、铅笔、邮票簿、一套急救用品和鸟类鉴别手册。他上床前打开记事本写道：

> 明天是六月最后一天。爸爸要开车送路易斯和我到库库斯库斯夏令营去。我可以打赌，这是天底下独一无二的男生夏令营，竟有一只吹号天鹅当它的号手的。我喜欢有工作。我希望知道我长大后将成个什么人。**狗为什么醒来时总要伸懒腰呢？**

萨姆合上记事本，也把它塞进了行李袋和其他杂七杂八的东西在一起，然后上床，关了灯，躺在那里想，狗为什么醒来的时候总要伸懒腰。过了两分钟他就睡着了。路易斯在外面谷仓里早就睡觉了。

第二天大清早天一亮，路易斯把它的石板、石笔和小号端正地挂在脖子上，爬到比弗先生的汽车后座。汽车是辆折篷车，因此比弗先生把车篷放下来。萨姆和他爸爸坐在前面。路易斯站在后座上，高高的，浑身雪白，漂漂亮亮。比弗太太和萨姆亲吻告别。她叫他乖乖的，当心自己，不要在湖里淹了，不要和别的男孩打架，下雨天不要外出，弄湿了身，又不穿羊毛衫坐在冷风里，不要在森林中迷路，糖不要吃得太多，汽水也不要喝得太多，不要忘记过几天就写一次信回家，湖上刮风的时候不要坐小艇出去，等等等等。

萨姆一一答应了。

"好啊！"比弗先生叫道。"我们敞开了车篷，在明媚的阳光里出发去安大略了！"他发动汽车，按响喇叭。

"再见，妈妈！"萨姆叫道。

"再见，孩子！"他的妈妈叫道。

汽车向着牧场的正大门飞快地开去。一到牧场看不见，路易斯就在它的座位上转过身来，把它那把小号放到嘴上。

"咯—嗬！"它吹道。"咯—嗬，咯—嗬！"

小号声响个不停——一种狂野、清晰、震耳的声音。后面牧场的每个人听到了它,这小号声使他们感到心惊。它和他们听到过的声音全都不同。它使他们想起了他们知道的所有大自然奇特的东西和地方:日落和月出,山峰和山谷,寂静的小溪和深邃的森林。

"咯—嗬!咯—嗬!咯—嗬!"路易斯吹着。

小号声渐渐消失了。牧场的人接着吃他们的早饭。路易斯一路去迎接它的第一个工作,觉得就像有生以来第一次学飞那天同样兴奋。

11. 库库斯库斯夏令营

库库斯库斯夏令营位于安大略森林深处一个小湖那里。这里没有避暑的小屋,没有带发动机的汽艇,没有汽车穿来穿去的大路。这是一个荒凉的湖,对男孩们正合适。比弗先生把萨姆和路易斯留在泥路头上,他们接下来坐小划子到营地。萨姆坐在小划子船尾划桨,路易斯站在小划子船头直望前方。

营地有一座大木屋,是大家吃饭的地方。另有七个帐篷,孩子们和辅导员们在那里睡觉,前面有个码头,后面有个厕所。周围都是森林,有一块空地用作网球场;营地有许多小划子,坐着它们上别的湖去。全营约有四十个男孩。

萨姆的小划子靠到营地码头旁边的沙滩上,路易斯挂着它的石板、石笔和小号跳上了岸。二十来个男孩冲到码头上来看是怎么回事。他们简直难以相信自己的眼睛。

"嘻,看是什么东西来了!"一个男孩大叫。

"一只鸟!"另一个喊道。"瞧它多大!"

所有人围住路易斯,要仔细看看这位新营员。萨姆得把一些男孩推开，好不让路易斯给挤着。

"别急，好吗?"萨姆求大家。

那天晚上吃过晚饭以后，营主任布里克尔先生在主屋前面生起了营火。男孩们围聚在一起。他们唱歌，大吃果汁软糖，拍蚊子。有时候也不知歌里唱些什么，因为孩子们唱歌的时候嘴里塞着软糖。路易斯不跟大家在一起。它独个儿离开一点儿站着。

过了一会儿，布里克尔先生站起来对男孩和辅导员们讲话。

"我要请大家注意我们中间一位新营员——天鹅路易斯，"他说。"它是一只吹号天鹅，一种稀有的珍禽。我们很幸运有它在一起。我用聘请少年辅导员的同样工资聘请了它：一个季度一百元。它性情温和，只是发不出声音。它是和萨姆·比弗一起从蒙大拿来的。路易斯是一位乐师。和大多数乐师一样，它需要钱。它早晨将吹号叫醒你们；它将吹号叫你们就餐；晚上，当你们昏昏欲睡的时候，它给你们吹熄灯号，这样一天就结束了。我请你们注意，要平等地对待它，要尊重它——它一只翅膀就有惊人的力量。为了让大家饱饱耳福，我现在向你们介绍天鹅路易斯。鞠个躬吧，路易斯!"

路易斯很尴尬，但是它走上前来鞠了个躬。接着它把

84

小号举到嘴上，吹了很长的一声"咯"。它刚吹完，湖对岸响起了回声：咯—。

孩子们拍手。路易斯又鞠了一个躬。萨姆·比弗，他跟其他孩子坐在一起，嘴里塞满了果汁软糖，这时因为他的计划实现了，心里很高兴。到夏天结束，路易斯可以有一百块钱了。

一个叫平果·斯金纳的孩子站起来。

"布里克尔先生，"他说，"我怎么办？我不喜欢鸟。我从来不喜欢鸟。"

"好吧，平果，"布里克尔先生说。"你不用喜欢鸟。如果这是你的想法，你就继续不喜欢鸟好了。每个人都有他喜欢或不喜欢的权利，有保持他的偏见的权利。试想一想，我不喜欢吃冰淇淋。我不知道我为什么不喜欢吃，可我就是不喜欢吃。但不要忘了，路易斯是你的辅导员之一。不管你喜欢它不喜欢它，你都必须尊重它。"

一个以前从来没有参加过夏令营的新营员站起来。

"布里克尔先生，"他说，"为什么这个夏令营叫做'库库斯库斯夏令营'呢？'库库斯库斯'是什么意思？"

"这是'大角号鸟'的印第安语叫法，"布里克尔先生回答。

这新营员把这话想了一会儿。

"那为什么不就叫'大角号鸟夏令营',却要叫'库库斯库斯夏令营'呢?"

"因为,"布里克尔先生回答,"一个儿童夏令营应该有个古怪的名字,要不然听上去就不有趣了。'库库斯库斯'是个可怕的名称。它很长,但是只有'库''斯'两个音节。像这样古怪的名称你找不到很多。夏令营名称越古怪越好。总而言之,欢迎到'库库斯库斯夏令营'来。

"好,现在大家该上床去睡觉了。明天吃早饭以前,你们可以去游泳,不用穿游泳裤。听到天鹅的吹号声,你们跳下床,脱掉睡衣,跑到码头,跳下水就行了。我会比你们先到那里,从跳台做我拿手的后空翻。这使我精神起来去对付接下来的费劲一天。晚安,路易斯!晚安,萨姆!晚安,阿普尔盖特!晚安,大伙儿们!"

火光暗下来了。孩子们在黑地里三三两两地离开,回自己的帐篷去。大人辅导员们一起坐在帐篷门口抽最后一斗烟。

萨姆钻进他第三号帐篷的毯子底下。路易斯登上岸边一块平坦的高岩石,站在那里等着。等到天全黑齐,它面对营地,把小号举到嘴上,吹起了熄灯号。

最后一个音符像在平静的湖水上逗留不去。孩子们从他们的床上听着美丽的号声。他们觉得迷迷糊糊,安安心

86

心，快快活活——只除了平果·斯金纳，他睡觉时不喜欢鸟。不过连平果也和其他孩子一起很快就睡着了。他睡着了，还打着呼噜。不喜欢鸟的人常常打呼噜。

深深的宁静气氛笼罩着库库斯库斯夏令营。

12. 抢救

路易斯喜欢在湖上睡觉。夜里吹过熄灯号以后,它会走到码头旁边的沙滩。它在那里摘下石板、石笔和小号,把它们藏在一丛矮树底下。接着它跳进水里。等到浮上来,它把它的头塞到一只翅膀下面。它会打会儿盹,想到家,想到爸爸妈妈。然后它会想到塞蕾娜——塞蕾娜是多么美丽,它多么爱塞蕾娜啊。很快它就睡着了。等到天刚亮,它游上了岸,简单地吃点水生植物做早饭。接下来它又挂上它那些东西,爬上那块平坦的岩石,吹起了起床号。孩子们一听见号声,马上醒来,冲到码头上去,在吃早饭前游一会儿泳。

晚上,营员们吃过了晚饭常打排球。路易斯爱这游戏。跳它没有孩子们快,但它能用它那长脖子远远够到球,把球顶到空中,顶过了网。很难让路易斯漏过一个球——它几乎能够把每一个球打回去。球赛开始前选队员的时候,路易斯总是第一个被选上。

孩子们爱安大略的夏令营生活。他们学习划小划子。

他们学习游泳。萨姆·比弗带他们去大自然中远足,教他们静静地坐在大木头上观察野兽和鸟类。他教他们怎样在林中走而不发出太多的响声。萨姆指给他们看翠鸟做窝的地方,在小溪岸边一个洞里。他指给他们看山鹬和它的幼雏。当孩子们听到轻轻的"科科科科"声音时,萨姆告诉他们,他们听到的是棕榈鬼号鸟的叫声,这是猫头鹰中最小的一种,不比人的巴掌大。有时候半夜里全营会让一只野猫的尖叫声惊醒。整个夏令营没有人见过野猫,但夜里总是听到它的尖叫声。

一天早上,萨姆正跟平果·斯金纳在打网球,他听到哐当一声。回头一看,是一只臭鼬正从森林里走出来。臭鼬的头钻进了一个洋铁罐头,于是它分不出南北东西,看不见自己在往哪儿走。它老是撞上树木和岩石,罐头也就一个劲儿哐当哐当响。

"那臭鼬遇到麻烦了,"萨姆放下球拍说。"它本要到垃圾堆去找东西吃,结果把头钻进了那空罐头,现在它没法把罐头甩掉。"

一只臭鼬到营地来了,这个消息很快传遍了全营。孩子们纷纷跑来看热闹。布里克尔先生警告大家不要走得太近——臭鼬会放臭气喷射他们。孩子们于是在周围蹦蹦跳跳,保持着距离,捂住了鼻子。

如今的大问题是,怎样把罐头从臭鼬的脑袋上拿下来,又不让它的臭气喷到自己身上。

"它需要帮忙,"萨姆说。"要是我们不把那罐头拿下来,那臭鼬会饿死的。"

所有的孩子各有各的主意。

一个孩子说要做弓箭,箭上拴一根绳子,然后把箭射到罐头上去。箭射中了罐头以后,他们可以拉绳子,罐头自然从臭鼬的脑袋上拉出来了。这个主意没人怎么考虑——听上去它似乎太麻烦了。

另一个孩子建议两个人爬上树,一个孩子双手抓住另一个孩子的双脚让他倒挂着,等到臭鼬走到这棵树下,给抓住脚倒挂着的孩子可以往下伸出手把罐头拉掉,万一臭鼬放臭气,臭气不会喷到那孩子,因为他悬在空中。这个主意更没有人考虑了。布里克尔先生根本不赞成这个主意。他认为这个主意一点不实际,再说他不会允许这么干。

再有一个孩子建议弄来一块木头,涂上胶水,臭鼬一碰到它,罐头自然被木头粘住。这个主意也没有人考虑。布里克尔先生说他根本就没有胶水。

正当大家在那里纷纷出主意的时候,萨姆悄悄地回到他的帐篷。几分钟后他回来,手里拿着一根长竿和一根长钓鱼丝。萨姆把钓鱼丝的一头拴在竿上。接着他在钓鱼丝的另一头打上一个活结，做成一个套索。然后他爬到帐篷门顶上，同时请其他孩子不要靠臭鼬太近。

这段时间里，那臭鼬一直在四处乱闯，在各种东西上面瞎撞。看上去真惨。

萨姆在帐篷门顶上，握住他那根竿子耐心地等待。他看着就像个钓鱼的在等鱼咬钓饵。等到臭鼬走近帐篷，萨姆把身子探出去，让套索在臭鼬前面一上一下移动，一点一点让套索套住罐头，然后狠狠一拉。套索一下子套紧，罐头拉下来了。罐头一拉下来，那臭鼬转过身子就放臭气——对准了布里克尔先生。布里克尔先生赶紧往后跳，绊了一下，摔了一跤。所有的孩子捏住鼻子在周围蹦蹦跳跳。那臭鼬逃进森林里去了。布里克尔先生站起来，拍掉身上的灰尘。空气里只闻到臭鼬的强烈臭气。布里克尔先生也闻到了。

"恭喜你，萨姆！"布里克尔先生说。"你救了一只野兽，又给了库库斯库斯夏令营一顿香喷喷的臭气。我断定我们大家都会久久记住这一个臭气熏天的事件。我想不出我们怎么能够一下子忘记它。"

"咯——嘀！"路易斯举起它的小号吹了一声。湖上响起了回声。空气里臭鼬的强烈麝香气味很浓。孩子们捂住鼻子跳了又跳。有些人捧着肚子假装呕吐。接着布里克尔先生宣布该去洗个早晨澡了。

"洗个澡会让空气清爽一些，"他说着走开，到他的小屋去换衣服。

　　每天吃过中饭，营员们到各自的帐篷去休息。有人读书，有人写信回家，告诉他们的爸爸妈妈菜有多糟。有人就躺在行军床上讲话。有一天下午在休息时间里，平果那帐篷里的孩子们开始取笑他的名字。

"平果·斯金纳，"一个孩子说。"你是打哪儿弄来这么傻一个名字的，平果？"

"是我爸爸给我取的，"平果回答说。

"我知道他的名字是怎么回事了，"另一个孩子说。"酸苹果！酸苹果·斯金纳。"孩子们一听都叫嚷起来，开始唱："酸苹果，酸苹果，酸苹果。"

"安静！"这个帐篷的帐篷长大叫。"我要求这帐篷安静。不要去烦平果！"

"不要烦烂苹果！"另一个孩子悄悄说。有几个孩子得把他们的枕头拉到他们的头上，好不让他们的偷笑声给听见。

平果很生气。等到休息时间结束，他一个人荡到码头上去。他不高兴让人取笑，他要做点什么事情来回敬他们。

他对谁也没说，把一条小划子放到水上，就划到湖里去，对着一英里远的对岸划。没有人注意到他。

平果不该一个人划小划子。他还没有通过他的游泳测验。他也没有通过他的划小划子测验。他这是违反了营规。当他离岸三分之一英里，到了深水地方的时候，风大起来了。浪头高起来了。小划子很难掌握。平果害怕起来。忽然之间，一个大浪抓住了小划子让它团团转。平果拼命靠在桨上。他的手一滑，身体失去了平衡。小划子翻了过来。平果落到了水里。他的衣服湿得厉害，重得可怕。他的鞋子把他往下拽，他好容易挣扎着把头伸出水面。他不是去抓住小划子，却开始向岸上游——这样做真是发疯了。一个浪迎面打来，他喝了一大口水。

"救命啊！"他尖声大叫。"救救我啊！我要淹死了。我淹死了会给夏令营带来坏名声的。救命啊！救命啊！"

辅导员们拼命跑到湖边。他们跳上小划子和小艇，赶紧去救那落水的男孩。一位辅导员踢掉他的软帮鞋，跳到水里，开始向平果游去。布里克尔先生飞奔到码头，爬上跳水台，用喇叭筒大叫着指挥救援行动。

"平果，你抓住小划子！"他叫道。"不要放开小划子！"

可是平果已经离开小划子。他孤零零一个人，两手乱划，白白浪费了他的力气。他觉得自己一定很快就沉到水底淹死了。他觉得已经没有力气,吓得要命。水已经进入他的肺部。他支持不了多久了。

第一条离开码头的小艇是萨姆·比弗划的,他用尽了力气划桨。但是平果看来情况不妙。所有的小艇离开他还有很大一段路。

当叫救命的第一声传到营地时,路易斯正绕过主屋的角落过来,它马上看到了平果,马上对这声呼唤作出反应。

"我没有办法飞到那里去,"路易斯想,"因为我的飞羽最近刚掉了。不过我一定可以比那些小艇去得快。"

它扔下它的石板、石笔和小号,扑到水里,拍动它的翅膀,踢着它的大蹼足,拼命游过去。路易斯有力的翅膀拍打着空气。它的脚搅动着波浪,像是在水面上奔跑一样。一转眼工夫,它已经超过了所有的小艇。当它来到平果身边时,它很快地潜到水里,把它的长脖子钻到平果的两腿之间,然后一下子浮出水面,平果已经骑在它的背上。

岸上和小艇上的人发出欢呼声。平果抱住路易斯的脖子。在千钧一发的时刻,他得救了。再晚一分钟,他就要沉下水底。水会灌满他的肺部。他也就完了。

"谢谢老天爷!"布里克尔透过他的喇叭筒叫道。"了不起,路易斯!库库斯库斯夏令营永远不会忘记这一天!夏令营的名声保住了。我们的安全纪录依旧保持着。"

路易斯对所有的欢呼叫喊没怎么注意。它很小心地游到萨姆的小艇旁边,萨姆把平果拉上了小艇,扶他坐在船尾的座位上。

"你骑着天鹅真好玩,"萨姆说。"你能活着够幸运的。你不该一个人划小划子出来。"

平果吓得太厉害,又是浑身水淋淋,话也说不出口。他只是坐在那里眼定定地看着前方,吐着嘴里的水,拼命喘气。

那天晚上吃晚饭的时候,布里克尔先生让路易斯坐在他右边的荣誉席上。等到饭吃完,他站起来发表讲话。

"今天湖上发生了什么事,大家都看到了。平果违反了营规,一个人划小划子出去,小划子翻了。他已经淹在水里,这时天鹅路易斯飞快地赶过其他营员,一直来到他身边,把他托起来,挽救了他的性命。让我们大家起立给路易斯热烈鼓掌欢呼吧!"

所有的孩子和顾问一起站起来。他们欢呼,鼓掌,用勺子敲打洋铁盆子。接着他们坐下。路易斯看上去不知所措。

"现在,平果,"布里克尔先生说,"我希望这次救援已经让你改变了对鸟类的看法。你第一天来到营地的时候对我们说过,你不喜欢鸟类。你现在又是怎么想的呢?"

"我觉得我的胃难过，"平果回答。"几乎淹死的处境让人的胃难过死了。我的胃里还积着许多湖水。"

"对，可是对于鸟类你觉得怎么样呢?"布里克尔先生问道。

平果苦苦思索了一阵。"这个嘛，"他说，"我感激路易斯救了我的命。不过我还是不喜欢鸟。"

"真的?"布里克尔先生说。"那是十分特别的。甚至在一只鸟当你快淹死的时候救了你的命以后，你依然不喜欢鸟?你有什么原因反对鸟类呢?"

"没有原因，"平果回答说。"我没有任何原因要反对它们。我只是不喜欢它们。"

"好吧，"布里克尔先生说。"我想我们只好谈到这里为止了。不过夏令营为路易斯而自豪。它是我们最杰出的辅导员——一位伟大的号手，一只伟大的鸟，一位强有力的游泳健将，而且是一位好朋友。它理应得到一枚奖章。事实上我已经打算写一封信推荐，授予它一枚'救生奖章'。"

布里克尔先生照他说的做了。他把信写了出去。几天以后，一个人从华盛顿带来了这枚"救生奖章"，当着全体营员的面，把奖章挂在路易斯的脖子上，和小号、石板、石笔在一起。这是一枚美丽的奖章。奖章上镌刻着如下的字:

授予天鹅路易斯，

它以它的非凡勇气和全然舍己忘生的精神

救了平果·斯金纳的性命。

路易斯拿下石板来写上："谢谢你授予我这枚奖章。这是极大的荣誉。"

但是它心里想："我脖子上的东西开始要过重了。我有一把小号。我有一块石板。我有一支石笔。现在我又有了一枚奖章。我开始看上去像一个嬉皮士。我希望我的飞羽重新长出来以后我还能飞。"

那天晚上天黑以后，路易斯吹起了它从吹号以来吹得最漂亮的一次熄灯号。那位送奖章来的人细细地听着，看着。他很难相信自己的耳朵和眼睛。他回到华盛顿以后，把他听到的和看到的讲给人们听。路易斯的名声越来越大。它的名字传开了。人们到处开始谈论一只会吹小号的天鹅。

13. 夏末

　　一个小号有三个小活瓣。它们是让演奏者用手指按的。它们看上去是这个样子：

　　只要按照正确的方式把它们按下去，演奏者就能奏出音阶上所有的音符。路易斯常常察看它那把小号上这三个小活瓣，但一直不会使用它们。路易斯每只脚有三个前趾，但它是只水鸟，它的脚是蹼足。蹼足妨碍路易斯分别使用这三个脚趾。幸亏吹营号不需要小号上的活瓣，因为营号只有"朵""米""索"几个音，号手不用按下任何一个活瓣就可以吹出"朵""米""索"来。

　　"如果我能用我的三个脚趾按这三个活瓣，"它对自己说，"我就能吹出各种音乐，而不只是吹营号了。我可以吹奏爵士乐。我可以吹奏乡村音乐和西部音乐。我可以吹奏摇滚乐。我可以吹奏巴赫、贝多芬、莫扎特、西贝柳斯、格什温、欧文·伯林、勃拉姆斯等等等等的伟大音乐。我可以当真成为一名小号演奏家，而不只是一名夏令营的号手。我甚至可以在乐队里找到一个工作呢。"这个想法使它充满了雄心大志。路易斯爱音乐,而且它已经在想办法,等到夏令营结束以后去挣钱了。

路易斯虽然很喜欢库库斯库斯夏令营的生活,但是常常怀念它在蒙大拿上红石湖的家。它怀念它的爸爸妈妈、它的兄弟姐妹以及塞蕾娜。它热爱着塞蕾娜,常常想它这会儿怎么样了。深夜里它会抬头看着星星想着塞蕾娜。晚上大牛蛙在静悄悄的湖上呱呱叫的时候,它也想着塞蕾娜。有时候它感到难过,孤独,想家。音乐对它到底是一种安慰。它爱它自己那小号的声音。

夏天过得太快了。在夏令营的最后一天,布里克尔先生把他所有的辅导员请到一起,分发给他们他该付的钱。路易斯得到了一百块钱——它挣到的第一笔钱。它没有皮夹子也没有口袋,因此布里克尔先生把钱放进一个有束带的防水小袋。他把这小钱袋挂在路易斯的脖子上跟小号、石板、石笔和"救生奖章"在一起。

路易斯来到萨姆·比弗的帐篷,看到萨姆正在收拾行李。路易斯拿下它的石板和石笔。

"我需要另外一个工作,"它在石板上写道。"我该上哪儿去呢?"

萨姆在床上坐下,想了一会儿。接着他说:"上波士顿去吧。也许你能在天鹅游船上找到个工作。"

路易斯从来没有去过波士顿，也不知道天鹅游船是什么玩意儿，不过它点了点头。接着它又在石板上写："你能帮我个忙吗？"

"当然，"萨姆说。

"用把剃刀片把我右脚的蹼割开，这样我就能活动我的脚趾了。"它伸出它的右脚。

"你为什么要活动你的脚趾呢？"萨姆问道。

"你会知道的，"路易斯写道。"我有事情需要我的脚趾来做。"

萨姆犹豫了一下。最后他还是向一位大人辅导员借来一块剃刀片。他在路易斯里面的脚趾和中趾之间整齐地长长割了一道。接着他又在路易斯的中趾和外面的脚趾之间割了一道。

"痛吗？"

路易斯摇摇头。它把小号举起来，把三个脚趾放在三个活瓣上，吹出了：朵、来、米、法、索、拉、梯、朵。朵、梯、拉、索、法、米、来、朵。咯—嗬！

萨姆咧开嘴笑。"天鹅游船会雇用你的，没问题，"他说。"现在你是真正的小号手了。不过你的蹼割开了，你游起水来要困难一点。你游起来会打转转，因为你的左脚划水比右脚有力。"

"我能对付的，"路易斯在石板上写道。"非常感谢你的外科手术。"

第二天营员离开了。小划子都架在停船棚屋的船架上，浮码头拖到了岸上，屋子的窗都钉上了木板不让狗熊和松鼠进去，垫子都装到了拉链袋里，对一切东西都做好了保温措施，好准备度过漫长寂静的冬季。在所有营员中，只剩下了路易斯一个。它的飞羽长得很快，但它依然不能飞。它决定独自一个留在营地，直到能够飞上天空，到那时，它将直飞波士顿。

没有了孩子们，湖上很寂寞，不过路易斯不怕孤单。接下来三星期它过得很轻松。它让飞羽生长，它日夜想着塞蕾娜，还练习它的小号。它听了一个夏天的音乐——有几个孩子带来了收音机和录音机——现在它用它的小号练习这些曲子。它吹得一天比一天好。有一天它为塞蕾娜作了一首情歌，把歌词和歌谱写在它的石板上：

它其实想的是塞蕾娜，但它没有把塞蕾娜的名字写出来，让歌词不专指某一个。

它的羽毛现在很漂亮，它觉得很棒。9月21日，它试了试它的翅膀。它们托起了它，于是它大为放心。路易斯飞上了天空。小号碰着石板，石板碰着小钱袋，"救生奖章"丁丁丁碰着石笔——但是路易斯又乘风飞行了。它越

102

飞越高,越飞越高,一直向着波士顿。重新飞在空中真是太好了。

"跟我有了所有这些东西以前相比,飞起来费力多了,"路易斯想。"旅行的确是轻装好。反过来说,这些东西又是我非有不可的。如果我要赢得塞蕾娜做妻子,我必须有小号;我得带着这钱袋好去还我爸爸欠下的债;我和人类交谈又不能没有石板和石笔;奖章我应该带着,因为我确实救了一个人,如果我不带着它,人们要认为我不领情了。"

它向着波士顿飞啊飞。波士顿是马萨诸塞州的首府,它出名的是它的豆①、它的鳕鱼、它的茶会、它的卡伯特家族、它那几位鲍威尔和几位索顿斯托尔,还有就是它的天鹅游船。

---

① 这种豆是用黄豆加肉、糖浆、番茄酱制成的。

14. 波士顿

路易斯从空中一看到波士顿，就喜欢上它了。在它底下远远的是条河。靠近河是个公园。公园里是个湖。湖里是个小岛。岸边是个码头。码头上拴着一条船，形状是只天鹅。这地方看上去很理想。附近甚至有一座十分漂亮的旅馆。

路易斯打了两个转，然后滑翔下去，在湖上停下，溅起了水花。几只鸭子游过来看它。这公园叫大公园。波士顿人人知道它，到这里来坐在长椅子上晒太阳，散步，喂鸽子和松鼠，乘那种天鹅游船。乘一次船，成人二十五美分，儿童十五美分。

路易斯休息了一下，吃了点东西以后，游到码头上岸。那正在收天鹅游船船票的人看到，一只巨大的白天鹅在脖子上竟挂了那么多东西，似乎十分惊讶。

"你好！"那人说。

路易斯举起它的小号回答："咯—嘀！"

一听到这声音，公园里所有的鸟都抬起头来。那船老板跳起来。连一英里外的波士顿市民也一下子抬起头来问："那是什么声音?"波士顿没有人听到过吹号天鹅的叫声。这声音引起极大的反响。很晚在阿林顿街里茨饭店吃着早餐的人从食物上抬起了头。服务员和侍仔说："那是什么声音?"

不过最吃惊的恐怕是天鹅游船那位船老板了。他看了路易斯的小号、钱袋、"救生奖章"、石板和石笔。接着他问路易斯要什么。路易斯在它的石板上写上："我有小号。我要工作。"

"没问题,"船老板说。"你得到工作了。一条船要在五分钟内开出去环湖一周。你的工作就是游在船的前面,吹着小号领头。"

"我的工资多少?"路易斯在石板上问。

"等我们看你做得怎么样以后会定下来的,"船老板说。"这只是一次试验。"

路易斯点点头。它把脖子上的东西理理好,安详地下水,在船前面几码占好了位置等着。它暗想,是什么让这船走呢。它看不见任何舷外的发动机,也没有船桨。船的前部有一张张供游客坐的长椅。船的尾部是一个天鹅形状的房间。它是空的,里面是一个座位,像自行车的座位。有两个踏板,也像自行车的踏板。

等到乘客都上了船，出现了一个年轻人。他爬到船的尾部，在天鹅形状空房间里的座位上坐下来，开始用双脚踏动踏板，就像蹬自行车一样。一个脚踏轮开始转动了。船老板把船缆解开，年轻人蹬动脚板，天鹅游船就慢慢地向湖里移动。路易斯带头，用左脚游水，用右脚举起它的小号。

"咯—嗬！"路易斯的小号响了。这狂放的声音响亮，清脆，激动着每个人的热血。接着路易斯明白，它该吹奏点什么合适的东西，于是它吹起了它在营地里听孩子们唱过的一支歌：

> 摇摇，摇你的船，
> 荡漾在河中，
> 真快活，真快活，真快活，真快活，
> 生活如做梦。

天鹅游船的乘客们高兴激动得忘乎所以。一只真正的活天鹅，还吹奏起小号来！生活如做梦，一点不假。多么有趣啊！多么好玩啊！多么快乐啊！

"吹得真出色！"前面座位上一个男孩叫道。"那天鹅和路易斯·阿姆斯特朗，那位大名鼎鼎的小号演奏家一样棒。我要称它作路易斯。"

路易斯听了这话，它游到船边，用嘴叼起石笔写道："那正好是我的名字。"

"嘿，怎么回事?"那男孩大叫。"这天鹅还会写字。路易斯会写字。让我们给它一个欢呼! "

游客们大声欢呼。路易斯重新游到前面去带头。船慢慢地、优雅地环绕小岛，一路上路易斯用它的小号吹奏着《我心温柔》。这是一个可爱的 9 月早晨，舒服温暖。树木开始显示它们秋天的色彩。路易斯吹起了《老人河》。

当天鹅游船靠在码头上，乘客们纷纷下船的时候，岸上排起了长队等着上船乘下一班。生意兴隆。于是再准备一条船好接待这些拥挤的人群。人人都想乘乘天鹅游船，跟在一只会吹小号的真正活天鹅后面。这是波士顿好长时间以来最大的一件事。人都是喜欢奇怪的新鲜花样的，有路易斯开道的天鹅游船一下子成了波士顿最轰动、最吸引人的事。

"你受雇了，"路易斯一上岸，那船老板就说。"有你吹小号，我的生意可以大一倍，大两倍，大三倍，大四倍，大五倍。可以大……大……大六倍。反正我要给你一个固定工作。"

路易斯举起它的石板。"工钱多少?"它问道。

那船老板看看周围等着乘船的人群。

"一星期一百美元，"他说。"只要你游在船前面吹你的小号，我每星期六付给你一百美元。就这样定了吗？"

路易斯点点头。那人似乎很高兴，但又大惑不解。"如果不怪我问得太多，"船老板说，"你能告诉我，你为什么对钱那么感兴趣吗？"

"人人都感兴趣，"路易斯在石板上回答。

"对，这我知道，"船老板说。"人人喜欢钱。这是一个疯狂世界。不过，我是说，为什么一只天鹅会需要钱呢？你只要把头钻下去叨起湖底美味的植物就能吃饱肚子。你要钱来干什么呢？"

路易斯擦干净石板。"我欠了债，"它写道。于是它想到偷了小号的可怜父亲，想到比林斯城那位挨了抢、店也被损坏了的可怜店老板。路易斯知道它必须挣到足够的钱来还清它欠下的债。

"好吧，"船老板招呼围着的人说，"这天鹅说它欠了债。大家请乘下一班船！"他开始卖票。这船老板有好几条船，全都做成天鹅的形状。很快每条船都坐满了人，钱源源而来。

这些天鹅游船整天绕着小岛转，载着它们快乐的乘客，其中大多数是儿童。路易斯吹着它的小号，它还从来没有这样吹奏过。它喜欢这个工作。它喜欢给人们娱乐。它喜

109

欢音乐。船老板真是高兴得不能再高兴了。

一天过去，这些船走完了最后一班，船老板走到站在岸上正在整理它那些东西的路易斯面前。

"你干得棒极了，"船老板说。"你是一只好天鹅。我真希望我早就得到了你。现在……你打算上哪儿去过夜呢?"

"在这湖上，"路易斯写道。

"这个嘛，我说不准，"那人不放心地说。"很多人对你感到好奇。他们会给你制造麻烦。坏孩子会骚扰你。我不信任那些夜里在公园里转来转去的人。你会被绑架的。我不愿失去你。我想我可以带你去里茨·卡尔顿饭店，给你要一个房间过夜。它干净，吃的东西好。那里会安全一些。这样我可以有把握你早晨会来工作。"

对这个主意路易斯没有多作考虑，它答应了上那里去。它想："好吧，我还从来没有在饭店里过过夜——这也许很有趣。"于是它和船老板一起走。

他们离开了公园，穿过阿林顿街，走进里茨饭店的大堂。对于路易斯来说，这是一个很累的漫长日子，但是它知道，它有了一份好工作，能够在波士顿当上一名乐手挣钱，因此它感到心中的石头落地了。

15. 里茨饭店之夜

　　当里茨饭店的服务台接待员看见船老板走进大堂，后面跟着一只黑嘴的雪白大天鹅时，他一点也不高兴。这接待员穿得很严谨——非常整齐，他的头发梳得很光滑。船老板大踏步走到服务台前面。

　　"我今天晚上要一个单人房间给我这位朋友过夜，"船老板说。

　　接待员摇摇他的头。

　　"鸟住不行，"他说。"里茨饭店不接待鸟。"

　　"你们接待名人，对吗？"船老板问道。

　　"当然，"接待员回答。

　　"如果理查德·伯顿和伊丽莎白·泰勒[①]要在这里过夜，你们接待他们，对吗？"

　　"那还用说，"接待员回答。

　　"你们接待伊丽莎白女王，对吗？"

　　"当然。"

　　"那好，"船老板说。"我这里这位朋友是名人。它是一

111

位著名音乐家。今天下午它在大公园引起了轰动。你一定已经听到这轰动事件了。它是一只吹号天鹅，小号吹奏得跟伟大的阿姆斯特朗一样。"

接待员怀疑地看着路易斯。

"它有行李吗?"接待员问道。

"行李?"船老板叫道。"你看看它! 看它带着的东西! "

"这个嘛，我不懂，"接待员看着路易斯那些东西——它的小号、它的钱袋、它的石板、它的石笔、它的"救生奖章"——说。"一只鸟就是一只鸟。我怎么知道它身上没有虱子呢?鸟身上常常有虱子的。里茨饭店不接待任何身上有虱子的客人。"

"虱子?"船老板大发雷霆。"你一辈子里见过一位更清洁的客人吗?你看它! 它雪白纯洁! "

听到这话，路易斯举起石板给接待员看。它写的是:"没有虱子。"

接待员吃惊地看石板。他开始软下来了。

"这个嘛，我必须小心，"他对船老板说。"你说它是名人。我怎么知道它有名呢?这话你也可能只是骗我。"

正好这时候，三个年轻姑娘走进大堂。她们在格格笑，还唧唧喳喳的。其中一个忽然指住路易斯。

"那是它! "她尖叫道。"那是它! 我要得到它的签名。"

三个姑娘一下子向路易斯扑上来。第一个姑娘递上来一个本子和一支铅笔。

"我可以请你签个名吗?"她问道。

路易斯接过铅笔。它很优雅地在本子上签上了:"路易斯"。

叽叽喳喳得更厉害,格格笑得更厉害,三个姑娘跑掉了。接待员静静地看着。

"你看到了!"船老板说。"它是一位名人不是?"

接待员犹豫了一下。他开始想,他该给路易斯一个房间。

这时候路易斯有了一个主意。它举起小号,开始吹奏一支老歌,它叫做《有家小旅馆》。

它吹的调子非常好听。经过大堂的客人们都停下来倾听。接待员把他的双肘撑在服务台上听得入了神。报架后面那个人抬起头来听。坐在楼上休息厅的人们放下他们的鸡尾酒来听。侍仔们看着,听着。好几分钟,当路易斯在吹奏的时候,大堂里一切都静止了。它迷住了所有听得见的人。在卧室里整理房间的那些女服务员也停下了活儿来听这小号声。这是十足魔幻的时刻。当这歌临近结束的时候,知道歌词的人都轻轻跟着曲子唱起来。

教堂钟声响：

"睡觉吧，晚安！"

我们全都感谢小旅馆。

"怎么样？"船老板笑着问接待员。"这天鹅是不是音乐家？"

"它小号吹奏得真甜，"接待员说。"我再没有什么犹豫不决要提出的问题了。它的个人习惯怎么样？它会把房间弄得一塌糊涂吗？演员都是够糟的。音乐家就更糟。我不能答应让一只大鸟睡我们的床——它会让我们做不成生意的。别的客人会抱怨。"

"我睡浴缸，"路易斯在石板上写道。"不睡床。"

接待员把重心从一只脚移到另一只脚。"谁付账单？"他问道。

"我付，"船老板回答说。"明天一早我到这里来，那时候路易斯退房。"

接待员再想不出理由来不让天鹅有一个房间了。

"那很好，"他说。"请登记吧！"他递给路易斯一支钢笔和一张卡片。

路易斯写道：

天鹅路易斯

上红石湖

蒙大拿

接待员把卡片看了。最后他似乎很满意。他叫来一个侍仔，交给他一把钥匙。"带这位先生到他的房间，"他吩咐说。

路易斯拿下它的奖章、它的小号、它的石板、它的石笔、它的钱袋，把它们全交给侍仔。他们一起走到电梯那里。船老板说再见。

"睡个好觉，路易斯！"船老板叫道。"准备好早晨来轻快地工作！"

路易斯点点头。电梯门打开了。"请进，先生！"侍仔说。他们进了电梯，等门关上。一股浓烈的香水味笼罩着整个电梯。路易斯站着一动不动。这时候它觉得自己在上升。电梯在七楼停下，侍仔把路易斯带到一个房间，用钥匙打开门，领它进去。

"到了，先生！"他说。"你要打开窗子吗？"

侍仔放下路易斯的行李，开亮了几盏灯，打开一个窗子，把门钥匙放在梳妆台上。然后他等着。

"我猜想他要小费，"路易斯想。因此它走到钱袋那里，解开束带，拿出一块钱来。

"非常感谢，先生，"侍仔接过那块钱说。他走出房间，轻轻关上门。路易斯终于独自一个留下了——独自一个在里茨饭店一个房间里。

路易斯从来没有独自一个在饭店里过过夜。起先它在房间里转来转去，把灯关了又开，检查各种东西。在写字台上它找到几张信纸，信纸上印着：

里茨·卡尔顿饭店
波士顿

它觉得身上脏，于是走进浴室，爬进浴缸，拉上浴帘，洗了一个淋浴。这让它顿时感到舒服，也使它想起过去经常跟哥哥姐姐们打的水仗。它很小心不让水溅出浴缸。它洗完以后，站了一会儿，很喜欢那张浴室地垫，它整理了它的羽毛。这时候它感到饿了。

在卧室墙上它找到了一颗按钮，上面写着：服务员。路易斯把嘴顶住了按钮，狠狠地一按。几分钟就听见敲房门的声音，一个服务员走进来。他穿得笔挺，发现房间里是一只天鹅，他尽力不露出惊讶的神色。

"我能给你拿来什么吗?"他问道。

路易斯拿起石笔,在石板上写道:"请给我十二个水田芥叶三明治。"

服务员想了一下。"你是在等客人吗?"他问道。

路易斯摇摇头。

"你是要十二个水田芥叶三明治?"

路易斯点点头。

"好的,先生,"服务员说。"要涂上蛋黄酱吗?"

路易斯不知道蛋黄酱味道怎么样,但它脑子动得快。它擦干净石板写道:"一个要,十一个不要。"

服务员弯腰离开了房间。半小时后他回来了。他把一张桌子推进房间,上面放着一大盘水田芥叶三明治,还有一只盆子、一把餐刀、一把餐叉、一把羹匙,以及盐和胡椒、一杯水、一条折得很好的布餐巾。此外,还有一碟牛油,几片牛油上撒着碎冰。服务员把一切仔细安排妥当以后,把一张账单递给路易斯请它签字。账单上写着:

12个水田芥叶三明治: 18.00元

"天啊!"路易斯想。"这是一个昂贵的地方。但愿明天早上船老板看到账单上这顿晚饭开销不要发疯。"

117

它从服务员那里借来铅笔，在账单上签上了："天鹅路易斯"。

服务员接过账单，站在那里等着。

"我想他是等小费，"路易斯想。于是它又打开钱袋，叼出两块钱，把它给了服务员，服务员千谢万谢，鞠了个躬，走了。

由于天鹅脖子那么长，桌子对路易斯来说高度正好。它不用椅子，站着吃它这顿晚饭。它尝了涂上蛋黄酱的那个三明治，决定自己不喜欢蛋黄酱。接着它把每一个三明治仔细打开。它实际想吃的是水田芥叶。它把一片片面包堆成整齐的两堆，把所有的水田芥叶扒拉在盆子上，这样就有了一顿丰盛的晚餐。它没有碰牛油。它渴了不是喝玻璃杯里的水，而是走进浴室，放了一面盆凉水来喝。接着它叼起餐巾擦擦嘴，把桌子推开不让它挡道。吃饱了，它觉得好多了。

独自一个待在一个饭店房间里，这给人一种舒适和了不起的感觉。路易斯觉得棒极了。不过很快它也就开始感到孤独。它想到萨姆·比弗。它想到库库斯库斯夏令营。它想到它远在蒙大拿老家的爸爸妈妈和兄弟姐妹。它想到它心爱的天鹅小姐塞蕾娜，不知道它怎么样了。它在大堂吹奏的那支歌的歌词回到了它心头：

118

有家小旅馆，

叫人真喜欢；

希望大家那里重相见。

　　它想，要是塞蕾娜能在这里，在里茨饭店，和它一起共享这家饭店的乐趣，那该多好啊！

　　服务员在桌子上留下了一份晚报。路易斯看看第一版。使它吃惊的是，它看到了自己在大公园和天鹅游船在一起的照片。大标题写着：

吹小号的天鹅
使波士顿欣喜若狂

报道的开头是这样的：

　　市里来了一只新的鸟。它的名字叫路易斯。它是一只吹号天鹅，它当真会吹奏小号。虽然似乎叫人无法相信，但这只稀有和美丽的水鸟接受了大公园天鹅游船管理处的聘用，用它圆润的小号声娱乐船上乘客。今天下午它到来以后，湖边人山人海，它甜美的小号声在波士顿许多地方都能听到……

路易斯把这篇报道从头看到尾，然后把它从报上撕下来。"萨姆·比弗应该知道这件事，"它想。于是它从房间里的写字台拿了一支钢笔和一张信纸。这是它写的信：

亲爱的萨姆：

　　我正在里茨饭店时髦的环境里过夜。关于波士顿，你的话是对的——它非常使人赏心悦目。我一到这里就找到了工作。我和天鹅游船商定，工资是一星期一百美元。你可能对信中附上的今天报纸剪报感兴趣。如果一切顺利，我很快能有足够的钱还清我爸爸欠音乐商店的债了，这样我就可以自由自在、清清白白地拥有那小号，并希望通过热情吹奏，我能够给我热爱的天鹅小姐一个良好的印象。那就皆大欢喜了：我爸爸的名誉得到恢复，比林斯的音乐商店将得到修理，我能得到一位妻子。我希望你平安，我想念你。一个饭店房间，尽管样样方便，却也会是个让人觉得孤单寂寞的地方。

　　　　　　　　　　　　　你的朋友
　　　　　　　　　　　　　路易斯

路易斯在信封上写明寄给萨姆，把信折好，连同剪报放进信封，在钱袋里找到一张六美分的邮票。它封好了信，贴上邮票，把信投进房门外一个滑槽邮筒里。"现在我要去睡觉了，"它想。

它走进浴室，用过厕所，然后放了满满一浴缸凉水。它没法把塞蕾娜从心中抛开。如果塞蕾娜在这里，那该多么好啊！在安息之前，它拿出它的小号，吹奏它在安大略的时候为塞蕾娜作的曲子：

噢，到了发绿的春天，
在岸边树旁歇着，
我将为爱情而悲伤，
为我想念的天鹅。

它极力要吹得轻一点，可是它房间里的电话还是马上响了起来。路易斯拿起电话听筒，放到耳边。

"很对不起，先生，"一个声音说，"不过我还是只好请你不要发出那么大的吵声。里茨饭店是不让它的客人在卧室里吹铜管乐器的。"

路易斯挂上电话，把小号放好。接着它关了灯，爬进浴缸,把长脖子向右弯过来,把头靠在背上,把嘴塞到翅膀底下,浮在水上睡觉,头轻轻地枕着羽毛。很快它就睡着,梦见了春天北方的小湖,梦见了塞蕾娜,它真正的爱人。

---

① 他们是好莱坞著名影星。

16. 费城

9月份的整个最后一周,路易斯都在为波士顿大公园那位天鹅游船老板工作。它大获成功,变得非常有名。星期六,船老板付给它一百美元现钞,路易斯把钱小心地放进它的钱袋。船老板付了里茨·卡尔顿饭店的第一夜账单以后,决定让路易斯睡在湖上而不是睡在饭店里,这更合路易斯的口味。它同鸭子和鹅一起睡在湖上,姿势优美地浮在水面上,头塞在翅膀底下。

路易斯小心保护它的小号。它把它擦得亮亮的,一星期把活瓣拔出来洗一次。一有机会它就听人们的无线电和进音乐会学新歌。记住听到的歌它非常有本领。它真是一位天生的音乐家——或者照它的情况说,一只天孵的音乐家。

有一支它喜欢的歌叫《入梦的美人,给我醒来吧》[①]。这支歌一吹,它就要想到塞蕾娜,这支歌一吹完,天鹅游船的乘客就大声拍手叫好。路易斯喜欢人拍手叫好。这让它感到轻松快活。

在下午结束的时候，路易斯有时候吹奏《现在一天已经过去》。它把它吹得甜蜜而忧伤。有一天下午，它带头走最后一班时，它吹起了勃拉姆斯的《摇篮曲》。乘客们随着曲调唱起了歌词：

坐在前面的一个男孩从他的外套里掏出一把气枪，向路易斯的小号开枪。枪弹一射中小号就发出砰的一声。因此《摇篮曲》听上去就是这个样子：

小宝贝（砰）

睡好觉（砰）

做个美梦真正好（砰）

听到这个样子，船上的孩子们都哈哈大笑，可是大人生气了。他们有一个抓住那男孩的枪。另一个回家，当天晚上给《波士顿环球报》写了一封信，要求加强枪支管理法。

有些下午，在一天结束的时候，人们聚集到湖边来听路易斯吹熄灯号。这是一个和平的场面，值得回忆的时刻。天鹅游船从来没享有过那么大的声誉，也没有给老板挣来过那么多钱。但是路易斯知道，这些游船不能整个冬天行驶。再过几天,它们就要从湖上给拉上岸来过冬,静静地等待明年春天降临。

有一天,当路易斯正在等候乘客们上船的时候,一名西部联合电信公司的电报投递员蹬自行车来了。

"我有个电报给天鹅,"他说。

船老板很奇怪,但他接过了电报交给路易斯。路易斯赶紧打开它。是费城一个人拍来的。电报上说:

夜总会可以出一周五百美元的工资聘请你。预定十周。请复。

阿贝·("幸运")·路卡斯(签名)

尼莫饭店

路易斯很快地一算。五百美元一周,十周就是五千美元。五千美元付它爸爸欠音乐商店的债就没问题了。

它拿起石板写道:

接受聘请。明天抵达。在动物园的鸟湖接我。下午四时五十二分降落。希望这时间对你方便。

路易斯把这内容给西部联合电信公司的电报投递员

看，他把它抄在空白电报纸上。

"由收报人付费，"路易斯写道。

电报投递员点点头，蹬着自行车走了。路易斯回到水上，船缆解开，路易斯带领着游船走。它知道这是它最后一次和天鹅游船在一起了，觉得有点伤感。这是一个温暖、安静的星期日下午，是9月份最后一个星期日。路易斯吹奏了它所有心爱的曲子：《懒惰河》、《入梦的美人……》、《噢，在发绿的春天里有过的事》、《现在一天已经过去》，最后，当船靠码头的时候，它举起它的小号吹熄灯号。

最后一个音符在里茨饭店的墙上响起回音，盘旋在大公园上空。这是一声伤心的再见。对于波士顿人来说，它意味着夏天结束了。对于船老板来说，这意味着生意最好的这星期结束了。对于路易斯来说，这意味着为了挣够钱让它爸爸和它自己摆脱困境而在大世界里冒险的生活中，又是一章结束了。

这天夜里它睡得很安静，也很小心地保护着它的钱袋。第二天它遵守同发来电报的路卡斯先生的协约，动身飞到费城去。

路易斯找到费城一点不费事。谁想要找费城几乎都能找到。路易斯就那么带着它脖子上所有那些东西飞上天

126

空,当它飞到大约一千英尺高的时候,它顺着铁路飞到普罗维登斯、新伦敦、纽黑文、布里奇波特、斯坦福德、科斯科布、格林尼治、切斯特港、拉伊、马马罗内克、纽罗彻尔、佩勒姆、弗农山和布朗克斯。当它看到纽约帝国大厦的时候,它转向右边,越过哈得孙河,再沿着铁路到纽瓦克和特伦顿,一直朝南飞。四点半它到达斯凯基尔河。就在那儿过去一点,它看到了费城动物园。从空中看下去,鸟湖十分吸引人。它挤满了各种各样的水鸟——最多的是鸭子和鹅。路易斯觉得它也看到了两三只天鹅。

它在空中打转,找到一块开阔地,准时在四点五十二分啪啦降落到水面。它的小号砰地碰着石板,石板碰着奖章,奖章碰着石笔,绳子拴住的石笔绕在钱袋上。一句话,这场降落引起了一场大乱。鸭子和鹅没想到会有这种事——一只雪白的吹号天鹅竟带着那么多私人东西从天而降。

路易斯一点不注意其他鸟。它有个约会。它看到一个人靠在鸟馆前面的宽阔栏杆上。那人穿一套紫色西装,戴一顶蒂罗尔式帽子。他那张脸看上去机灵聪明,好像他知道许多事情,其中有不少简直是不值得知道的。

"他一定就是阿贝·('幸运')·路卡斯了,"路易斯想。

它很快地游过去。

"咯—嗬!"它用小号说。

"很高兴见到你，"路卡斯先生回答。"你完全准时。这降落场面十分动人。欢迎光临费城动物园，这里有稀有的哺乳动物、爬行动物，还有鸟类、两栖动物、鱼类，包括鲨鱼、鳐和其他像鱼的脊椎动物。小心野兽什么的——这地方到处有它们：蛇、斑马、猴子、大象、狮子、老虎、狼、狐狸、狗熊、河马、犀牛、旱獭、臭鼬、老鹰、猫头鹰。我难得上这儿来，我的工作把我限制在城市跳动的心脏内，在钱商之间。我一直在我工作的巨大压力下。你从波士顿一路来怎么样？"

"很顺利，"路易斯在黑板上写道。"我一路上很好。我的工作怎么样？"

"一个愉快的问题，"路卡斯先生回答说。"工作从10月15日开始。合同已经订好。你的工作地方是一家非常有名的夜总会，在河对面——这个地方是最时兴、收费低的一家爵士乐夜总会。你每天晚上出场，除掉星期日，为快活的顾客们演奏你的小号。偶尔你可以参加一个爵士乐团：'吹小号的天鹅路易斯'。报酬十分优厚。想到报酬，我的情绪就高涨了。财富和快乐都在等着天鹅路易斯和幸运的路卡斯，一个心肠极好的人。我的佣金是百分之十，这真是小意思。"

"我怎么上夜总会去呢?"路卡斯先生的话只听懂一半的路易斯问道。

"坐出租汽车,"路卡斯先生回答说。"到动物园北门,吉拉德街和三十四街之间,10月15日晚九点,这将是一个永远也忘不了的夜晚。一辆出租汽车将等着你的光临,把你带到夜总会去。司机是我的朋友。他也承受着工作的压力。"

"出租汽车费谁付?"路易斯在石板上问。

"我付,"路卡斯先生回答说。"幸运路卡斯,慷慨大方的人,为天鹅路易斯付车费。再说我看到你挂着一个钱袋,里面的钞票胀鼓鼓的。从我伟大的心的好意出发,我建议当你逗留在费城这个强盗和扒手横行的地方时,把钱袋交给我保管。"

"不,谢谢你,"路易斯写道。"钱袋我还是自己保管好。"

"很好,"路卡斯先生说。"现在还有一件小小的事情我必须提请你注意。在豪华的湖上游来游去的鸟大都动过手术。坦率迫使我告诉你,一只翅膀的尖端通常由管理部门剪去——一个毫无痛苦的手术,全世界的动物园都是这样做的。通用的说法叫做'剪去飞羽',我相信是这样。这样使水鸟留下来,防止它离开这公园的狭小范围,飞到天上

129

去。如果一只翅膀比另一只翅膀短,鸟就失去平衡,它想飞走也飞不走。一句话,它不能飞。预感到你对你一只有力的翅膀被剪掉尖端会觉得强烈憎恶,于是我找到鸟类负责人,向他提出建议。他已经同意不剪你的翅膀。这已经讲定了。他是一个讲话算数的人。你的自由行动已经有了保证。你将不被剪掉飞羽。不过为了答谢费城动物园管理部门这么大的优待,希望你每星期日下午在这里湖上开一个免费音乐会招待费城市民,以及来这里休息的农民。可以吗?"

"可以,"路易斯说。"我将开星期日音乐会。"

"好极了!"路卡斯先生说。"暂时再见!记住晚上九点钟在北门! 10月15日。一辆出租汽车将等着你。好好吹奏吧,甜蜜的天鹅! 你将是1787年美国制宪会议[②]以来费城发生的最美好的事件。"

路易斯根本不明白这句话的意思,但是它向路卡斯先生点头告别,向湖中心的小岛游去。它在那里上岸,摆正它的东西,理好它的羽毛,蹲下来休息。它还断不定自己是不是会喜欢新工作。它还断不定自己是不是喜欢路卡斯先生。不过它急需钱,当一个人需要钱的时候,他就情愿置困难和断不定的事情于不顾了。整个交易当中有一样好东西,那就是动物园本身。它看上去是一个极其好的地方,只除了它听说的要剪掉一个翅膀尖端。路易斯可不打算让一个翅膀的尖端给剪掉。

"谁想要这样对我，我就狠狠揍他！"它对自己说。

它很高兴看见有那么多水鸟。这里有许多种类的鸭子和鹅。远远的它还看到了三只吹号天鹅。它们是这湖的老居民了。它们的名字是：好奇、幸福和冷漠。路易斯决定等一两天再去结识它们。

鸟湖周围有一道栅栏。到了去工作的那一天晚上，路易斯擦亮它的小号，挂上它所有的东西，飞过栅栏，停在北门。它在快到九点时到达那里。出租汽车像路卡斯先生答应过的那样，已经在那里等着。路易斯上了车，被送到它的新工作岗位去了。

---

① 这是美国作曲家福斯特（1826—1864）的著名歌曲。
② 美国历史上重大的制宪会议1787年在费城举行。

131

17. 塞蕾娜

接下来的十个星期，路易斯发财了。除了星期日，它每天晚上到夜总会去给顾客们吹它的小号。它根本不喜欢这个工作。夜总会又大，又拥挤，又吵闹。所有的人看上去说话都那么哇啦哇啦，吃得那么多，喝得那么厉害。鸟大都喜欢太阳下山就睡觉。它们不想待到半夜三更给人们开心。但路易斯是一个乐师，乐师是不能选择自己的工作时间的——他们的雇主要他们什么时候演奏，他们就必须在什么时候演奏。

每星期六晚上路易斯收到它的工钱——五百美元。路卡斯先生总是当场向路易斯收取他的百分之十佣金。付了路卡斯先生的佣金以后，路易斯仍旧拿到四百五十美元，它把这笔钱放进它的钱袋，跳进出租汽车回鸟湖去，到那里大约是凌晨三点。钱袋里钱胀得那么满，路易斯开始担心了。

星期日下午，如果天气好，许多人都聚到鸟湖岸边来，路易斯站在湖中心的小岛上举行一个音乐会。这成了费城家喻户晓的大事，那里星期日是没有什么活动的。路易斯

133

对待音乐会这件事十分认真。为大家演奏,它就挣到免费留在那里并且不用剪翅膀的权利。

星期日它总是吹奏最好的曲子。它不是吹爵士乐、摇滚乐、民间音乐和西部乡村音乐,而是选奏伟大作曲家如贝多芬、莫扎特、巴赫的作品,这些作品它是在库库斯库斯夏令营听唱片学来的。路易斯也喜欢乔治·格什温和斯蒂芬·福斯特的音乐作品。当它演奏格什温的歌剧《波吉和贝丝》中那首《夏日》时,费城人觉得这是他们听到过的最激动人心的音乐。路易斯被一致公认小号吹得如此之好,它受到了邀请作为客席小号手和费城交响乐团一起演出。

在圣诞节前大约一星期,有一天来了强烈的风暴。天空黑了下来。狂风怒吼,响起呼呼的声音。窗子震动着。百叶窗脱开了铰链。旧报纸和糖果纸被风吹得像狂欢节撒的五彩纸屑那样到处飞舞。动物园里许多动物惊慌不安。那边象馆里大象吓得呜呜号叫。狮子咆哮着来回走个不停。硕大的黑色凤头鹦鹉尖叫。管理员们冲到这里冲到那里去关门关窗,让一切在可怕的暴风中安然无恙。鸟湖被猛烈的风吹得波浪翻腾,一时间,这个湖看上去活像一个小型的海洋。许多水鸟到小岛上去寻找藏身之所。

路易斯在湖上迎风游向小岛躲避。它面对着风不断划着脚,眼睛闪亮,奇怪暴风的力量居然这么厉害。它忽然看见天空中有一样东西。它正冲出云层下来。起先路易斯弄不清那是什么东西。

"也许是只飞碟，"它想。

接着它明白了，这是一只白色大鸟，正拼命地顶住风下来。它的翅膀拍动得很快。转眼间，它降落在水面上，费力地上岸，在岸上趴倒下来，几乎像是死了一样。路易斯盯住它看了又看，看了又看。

"它看上去像是一只天鹅，"它想。

它是一只天鹅。

"它看上去像是一只吹号天鹅，"它又想。

它是一只吹号天鹅。

"天啊，"路易斯心里说，"它看上去像塞蕾娜。它是塞蕾娜。它终于到这里来了。我的祈祷应验了！"

路易斯没错。它日夜想念的天鹅小姐塞蕾娜逃不脱凶猛的暴风，被它一路吹过美国。当它低头看到了鸟湖的时候，它飞不动了，精疲力竭，几乎要死了。

路易斯忍不住要冲上前去。但这时候它想："不对，这样做会是个错误。这会儿它无法知道我对它的爱有多深多广。它太疲倦了。我必须等待。我必须等候我的时机。我必须给它机会恢复过来。到那时候我将和它重新会见，让我向它自我介绍。"

那天晚上路易斯没有去上班，天气太坏了。它整夜不睡，在离它心爱的天鹅小姐不远处守卫着。到了早晨，风停了。天空晴朗起来。湖上变得平静。暴风过去了。塞蕾娜动了一动，醒了过来。它还是精疲力竭，十分脏，路易斯离开了它。

"我要等着，"它想。"恋爱就得冒险。但是它疲倦得头脑不清，我可不愿冒任何险。我不急，我不担心。从前在老家上红石湖我没有嗓子。它不注意我只因为我不能向它表达我的爱情。现在谢谢我勇敢的爸爸，我有了小号。通过音乐的力量，我将能向它表达我强烈的爱和激情。它将听到我说'咯—嗬'。我要用任何人都明白的语言，音乐的语言，告诉它我爱它。它将听到天鹅号声，它将是我的。至少我**希望**它将是我的。"

通常，碰到一只陌生的鸟出现在鸟湖，管理员会向办公室就在鸟馆的鸟类负责人报告来了一只鸟。这负责人就会下令剪这只新来的鸟的一只翅膀。可是今天，那一向照料水鸟的管理员害了流行性感冒没有来上班。没有人注意到来了一只新的吹号天鹅。塞蕾娜又是生性安静——它没有引起任何人的注意。现在湖上有五只吹号天鹅了。原来是三只囚禁在这里的天鹅——好奇、幸福和冷漠。后来自然又多了路易斯。现在再新来了一只塞蕾娜。它精疲力竭,但体力已经在渐渐开始恢复了。

到傍晚时分,塞蕾娜蜷缩着身子看四周环境,它吃了点东西,洗了个澡,然后从水里出来,站了好长时间整理它的羽毛。它显然觉得好多了。等到羽毛整理得光光滑滑,它便呈现出一种极其美丽的样子来——庄重、宁静、优雅,非常娇滴滴的。

路易斯看到塞蕾娜真有那样可爱,简直都发抖了。它再次忍不住要游过去说声"咯—嗬",看它是不是还记得自己。但是它有个更好的主意。

"不着急,"它想。"今天晚上它不会离开费城。我要去上班,等我下班回来,我要整夜等候在它附近。天一亮,我就用情歌叫醒它。它那时正迷迷糊糊,我小号的声音将进入它睡意朦胧的脑子,让它动情。我的小号将是它听见的第一声。我将是它无法抗拒的。我将是它张开眼睛看到的第一个,它会从那一瞬间起爱上我的。"

路易斯对自己这个计划十分满意,开始进行准备。它游上岸,拿下它所有的东西,把它们藏在一丛矮树底下,再回到水里吃东西和洗澡。接着它仔细整理自己的羽毛。它要让自己在将要见面的第二天早晨显得最漂亮。它游了一会儿,把所有它喜欢的曲子想了一遍,要决定吹奏哪一支来叫醒塞蕾娜。它最后决定吹奏《入梦的美人,给我醒来吧》。它一直爱这支曲子。曲子忧伤而甜蜜。

"它将是一位入梦的美人，"路易斯想，"它将会给我醒来。这支曲子完全对路。"

它决定把这支曲子吹得比以前任何一次都好。这是它最好的节目之一。它的确知道怎样把它吹得非常之好。有一次它在星期日音乐会上吹了这支曲子，费城报纸一位音乐评论家听到了，第二天在报上说："小号手的有些音就像举起来对着亮光照的宝石。小号手表达的情感清莹，纯洁无瑕。"路易斯记住了那个句子。它为此感到自豪。

现在它急着等早晨来临，但它还是要到夜总会去工作。它知道这一夜很漫长，它将不能入睡。

路易斯游上岸去捡起它的东西。当它朝矮树底下一看的时候，它大大吃了一惊：它的奖章在那里，它的石板和石笔在那里，它的钱袋在那里，可小号上哪儿去了? 它的小号不见了。可怜的路易斯! 它的心几乎停止跳动了。"噢，不! "它对自己说。"噢，不! "没有了小号，它的整个生活完了，它对未来的全部计划完了。

它又气，又害怕，又不知所措，都要发疯了。它跳回水中，朝湖的这边那边看。远远它看到一只小林鸳鸯，它的嘴里像是有样什么发亮的东西。没错，是小号! 林鸳鸯想吹它。路易斯气坏了。它顺着湖飞快游过去，比那天救溺水的平果游得还要快。它一直游到林鸳鸯那里，一挥翅膀拍打在它的头上，把那宝贵的小号抢了回来。那林鸳鸯头都昏了。路易斯擦干净小号，把它里面的口水吹掉，让它挂在脖子上，它应该挂在那里。

现在它准备好了。"让夜降临吧！让时间过去吧！让早晨到来吧，到那时候，我那入梦的美人就要给我醒来！"

夜终于降临了。九点钟。路易斯坐上出租汽车去上班。动物园静下来。参观的人都回家了。许多动物都睡了或者在打呼噜。只有一些——狮虎等大野兽，浣熊，犰狳，还有过夜生活的动物——在潜行，变得坐立不安。鸟湖被黑暗笼罩着。大多数水鸟把头钻到翅膀底下在睡觉。在湖的一头，三只被囚禁的天鹅——好奇、幸福和冷漠——已经睡了。靠近小岛，塞蕾娜，美丽的塞蕾娜，已经熟睡，正在做梦。它白色的长脖子很好看地弯过来靠在背上；它的头靠在松软的羽毛上。

路易斯凌晨两点下班回家。它从矮栅栏上飞进来，在塞蕾娜附近降落，尽量不发出溅水声。它不想睡。这一夜和通常圣诞节就要降临的那些夜一样，美好清新。云朵不断地飘过天空，部分遮住点星星。路易斯眺望星星，凝视睡着的塞蕾娜，等着天亮——一个钟头又一个钟头，一个钟头又一个钟头。

最后，东方露出深深的亮光。很快动物就要动起来，早晨就要到来了。

"这是我的时刻，"路易斯想。"叫醒我真正的恋人的时刻已经到了。"

它站到塞蕾娜面前。它把小号举到它的嘴上。它歪着头：小号微微对着天空，那儿已经开始发亮。

它开始吹奏它的曲子。

"入梦的美人，"它吹道，"给我醒来……"

开头的三四个音吹得很轻柔。随着曲子吹下去，声音加强了；天空越来越亮。

每一个音像是举起来对着亮光照的宝石。动物园里从来没有在这么早的黎明时分听到过路易斯的小号吹奏声，这声音简直像充满了建筑物、动物、树木、矮树丛、小径、兽穴和笼子的整个世界。在洞里睡觉的瞌睡蒙眬的狗熊竖起了它们的耳朵。躲在洞里的狐狸倾听着在天亮时分吹起来的梦幻般的小号声。在狮子馆里，那些大狮子听着。在猴子馆里，那些老狒狒惊奇地听着这支曲子。

入梦的……美人，给……我……醒来……

140

河马听着，海豹在它的池子里也听着。灰狼听着，牦牛在它的笼子里也听着。獾、浣熊、蓬尾浣熊、臭鼬、海狸、水獭、美洲驼、单峰驼、弗吉尼亚白尾鹿——全都竖起了耳朵谛听着这支曲子。非洲大羚听着，兔子听着。海狸听着，没有耳朵的蛇也听着。沙袋鼠、负鼠、食蚁兽、犰狳、孔雀、鸽子、造园鸟、凤头鹦鹉、红鹳——全都听着，全都注意到一件不同寻常的事情正在发生。

在窗子开着的卧室里的费城人醒过来，听到了小号声。听到这支曲子的人没有一个明白，这是一只有发声缺陷而战胜了它的年轻天鹅的胜利时刻。

路易斯并不在想动物和人这些它看不见的广大听众。它的心并不在狗熊、野牛、鹤驼、蜥蜴、老鹰、猫头鹰和卧室里的人们身上。它的心全部在塞蕾娜，它看中的天鹅，入梦的美人身上。它在为它吹奏，只为它一个吹奏。

它的小号刚吹出第一个音，塞蕾娜就醒了。它抬起它的头，把它的脖子伸直，直到头抬得高高的。它所看到的使它满心惊讶。它直愣愣看着路易斯。起先，它简直记不起自己正在什么地方。就在它面前，它看到一只英俊的年轻雄天鹅，一只身材匀称的天鹅小伙子。这天鹅小伙子正举着一样奇怪的东西放在嘴上——这样的东西它自己从来没有看见过。从这东西发出声音来使它感到快活，感到一种

141

爱情,从而浑身颤抖。当这支曲子吹下去,当光线越来越亮的时候,它不由得爱上了把它从梦中惊醒过来的这个大胆号手。黑夜的梦消失了。白天的新的梦正降临到它头上。它知道自己充满了从未有过的感情——一种快乐、销魂和惊奇的感情。

它从来没有看见过更好看的天鹅小伙子。它肯定从来没有看见过一只天鹅有那么多东西挂在脖子上。在它的一生中,以前还从来没有被一种声音这样震动过。

"噢,"它想,"噢,噢,噢,噢!"

曲子结束了。路易斯放低它的小号,认真地向塞蕾娜鞠躬。接着它又举起它的小号。

"咯—嗬!"它说。

"咯—嗬!"塞蕾娜回答。

"咯—嗬,咯—嗬!"路易斯通过它的小号说。

"咯—嗬,咯—嗬!"塞蕾娜回答它。

它俩各自感到被一根神秘的爱的纽带拉向对方。

路易斯绕着塞蕾娜很快地游了一圈。

接下来塞蕾娜绕着路易斯也很快地游了一圈。这样做似乎让它们觉得很好玩。

路易斯把脖子浸到水里,把它前后晃动。

塞蕾娜把脖子浸到水里,把它前后晃动。

路易斯把一点水溅到空中，塞蕾娜把一点水溅到空中。就像做游戏。这是路易斯深怀已久的爱情；这是塞蕾娜一见倾心的爱情。

　　接着路易斯决定露一手。"我要把我自己作的曲子吹给它听，"它想。"夏天在夏令营里为它写的那支曲子。"它又举起了它的小号。

　　　　噢，到了发绿的春天，

　　　　在岸边树旁歇着，

　　　　我将为爱情而悲伤，

　　　　为我想念的天鹅。

　　一个个音清晰真纯。它们使动物园充满了美。如果塞蕾娜原先还有什么怀疑，那么它现在不再有了。它完全无法抗拒这迷人的天鹅小伙子，这英俊的小号手，这富有和才华横溢的雄天鹅。

　　路易斯知道它的计划成功了。它入梦的美人已经醒了，已经为它醒过来了。它们将永远不会再分开。它们将终生在一起。路易斯满心想着森林中那些安静小湖，那里芦苇生长，乌鸫歌唱。还想着春天、造窝和小天鹅。噢，到了发绿的春天！

路易斯的爸爸有一次告诉它，深海潜水员下到大洋深处会发生什么事情。在极深的地方，水压很大，水的世界古怪神秘，潜水员有时会碰上他们所谓的"深水销魂"。他们感觉到那么平静入迷，永远不想回到水面上去了。路易斯的爸爸警告它这一点。"当你潜到了深水的时候，"爸爸说，"要永远记住这种销魂的感觉会把你引向死亡。在水底下不管你觉得多么了不起，绝对不要忘记回到水面上，在水面上你能够重新呼吸！"

　　看着塞蕾娜，路易斯心里说："依我想，爱情就像这种'深水销魂'。我觉得那么舒服，我只想一直就待在我正待着的地方，一点也不想动了。尽管我是在水面上，我却正在体验着这种'深水销魂'。我从来没有感到过这么好，这么宁静，这么兴奋，这么快活，这么有强烈欲望，这么充满渴望。如果爱情在费城动物园一个12月的冷天是这样，那么想像一下，在遥远加拿大的湖上，在春天里会是怎么样呢！"

　　这些是路易斯暗中的想法。它是活着的最快乐的鸟。它到底是一只真正的吹号天鹅。它没有嗓子的缺陷终于克服了。它非常感谢它的爸爸。

　　它小心地把它的头搭在塞蕾娜美丽的雪白长脖子上。这似乎是非常大胆的举动，可是塞蕾娜喜欢。接着路易斯退走。塞蕾娜向它游过去。塞蕾娜小心地把它的头搭在路易斯的脖子上。它的头在那里靠了一会儿,接着塞蕾娜游走了。

"多么大胆的举动啊!"塞蕾娜想。"不过它似乎喜欢。知道我找到了一个如意郎君,这有多么高兴啊——一只我能够爱和敬重的天鹅小伙子,一只看来不仅懂音乐而且十分富有的天鹅小伙子。瞧所有那些东西,"塞蕾娜对自己说。它的眼睛盯住了那小号、那石板、那石笔、那钱袋、那"救生奖章"。

"多么快活的一只天鹅啊!"它想。"多么漂亮的一个小伙子啊!"

它们一起向着湖的另一头游去,在那里它们可以单独待着。接着睡眠不足的路易斯睡过去了,这时候塞蕾娜吃它的早餐,并且打扮起来。

18. 自由

塞蕾娜来到鸟湖的消息终于传到了鸟类负责人的耳朵里。他去看它，觉得很高兴。于是他给手下一个管理员下命令。

"你负责今天早晨给它剪翅膀——赶紧干，以免它离开我们飞走了。那天鹅是只贵重的鸟。一定不能让它飞走!"

路易斯醒来，正好看到两个管理员向塞蕾娜走去，塞蕾娜正站在岸上，靠近花纹栅栏。一个管理员拿着一个长柄大网。另一个管理员拿着手术工具。他们在塞蕾娜身后悄悄地过去，走得很慢很轻。

路易斯马上知道他们要干什么。它怒火冲天。如果这两个人做成功，捉住了塞蕾娜，把它一只翅膀尖端的羽毛剪掉，它的整个计划将玩儿完了——塞蕾娜将永远不能远走高飞，和它一起到静谧的湖上去；这样，塞蕾娜就只好留在费城度过余生，这真是可怕的命运。

"这是我的重要时刻，"路易斯想。"只要我在这里，没有人能剪我爱人的翅膀!"

147

它急忙上小岛拿下身上的东西准备行动。它把它的小号和所有其他东西藏在一棵柳树底下。然后它回到水边，等着进攻的最好时机。

拿着网的管理员从后面悄悄地向塞蕾娜爬过去。塞蕾娜没有注意到他——它就站在那里想着路易斯。那管理员慢慢地、慢慢地把他那个网举起来。当他这样做的时候，路易斯行动了。它把它那条有力的长脖子低下来，直到它像把长矛一样一直伸到前面，然后笔直冲着那管理员在水上飞冲过去，双翅拍打着空气，两脚击水。它像一道闪电那样来到现场，把它有力的尖嘴一直戳到管理员的裤子屁股上。瞄得准极了。那管理员痛得蜷曲起了身体，丢掉了网。另一个管理员打算抓住塞蕾娜的喉咙。路易斯用翅膀打他的头，两个翅膀噼噼啪啪地狠打，把那可怜家伙打倒在地。手术工具飞到空中。网落到水里。一个管理员哼哼叫着，一只手捂住给狠狠戳了一下的屁股。另一个管理员躺在地上，几乎给打昏了。

塞蕾娜马上下水，轻快地游走。路易斯跟在它后面。它做了个动作让塞蕾娜待在湖上。然后它很快地回到岸上，挂上它的小号、它的石板、它的石笔、它的奖章、它的钱袋，飞过栏杆，大踏步走进鸟馆。他还在气头上。他一直走到鸟类负责人的办公室。它叩叩门。

"进来!"里面一个声音说。

路易斯进去了。那负责人坐在他的写字台后面。

"你好,路易斯!"他说。

"咯—嗬!"路易斯用小号回答了一声。

"你有什么事吗?"那人问。

路易斯把它的小号放在地板上,从脖子上拿下石板和石笔。它写道:"我恋爱了。"

那负责人向后靠在他的椅子上,双手放在头后面。他那张脸有一种恍恍惚惚的表情。他默默地向窗外看了一会儿。

"这个嘛,"他说,"你恋爱是很自然的。你年轻。你有才能。过两个月春天就到了。春天里所有的鸟都要谈恋爱。我想你是爱上我这里一只年轻的雌天鹅吧?"

"塞蕾娜,"路易斯写道。"它是前天来的。我在蒙大拿就跟它有点认识。它也爱我。"

"这一点我不奇怪,"那负责人说。"你是一只非常不同寻常的年轻雄天鹅。哪一只年轻雌天鹅都会爱上你。你是一位伟大的小号手——最好的小号手之一。我很高兴听到这个爱情故事,路易斯。你和你的新娘可以留在这个鸟湖,在美国这个最古老的动物园舒服安全地组织小家庭,生儿育女。"

路易斯摇摇头。

"我有别的打算，"它写道。接着它放下石板，举起小号。《他们说恋爱真美妙……》这是欧文·柏林写的一支老曲子。房间充满了爱的歌声。负责人眼睛里有一种梦幻的神情。

路易斯放下它的小号，又拿起它的石板。"在一两天内我要把塞蕾娜带走，"它写道。

"噢，不，你不能把它带走！"负责人坚决地说。"塞蕾娜现在属于动物园。它是费城民众的财产。它到这里来是上帝的安排。"

"这不是上帝的安排，"路易斯写道。"这是由于风暴。"

"不管怎么样，"负责人说，"它是我的天鹅。"

"不，它是我的，"路易斯写道。"它是我的，这是由于爱情的力量——世界上最伟大的力量。"

负责人沉思起来。"你不能把塞蕾娜从动物园带走。它永远不能再飞了。我的管理员们几分钟前已经把它的一只翅膀剪去了羽毛。"

"他们想要剪，"路易斯写道，"但是我把他们狠揍了一顿。"

负责人一副惊讶的样子。"这场架打得狠吗？"

"这场架打得公平，"路易斯回答。"他们从后面偷偷向

150

塞蕾娜走去，因此我从后面偷偷地向他们走去。他们简直不知道是谁揍了他们。"

负责人格格笑。"我真希望我能看到这场打斗，"他说。"不过你听我说，路易斯，你必须明白我的处境。我对费城市民负有责任。在最近两个月内，我意外地得到了两只稀有的鸟——你和塞蕾娜。两只吹号天鹅！一只被狂风吹来，另一只和夜总会有约。这整个事件对动物园来说是再难得不过了。我对民众负有责任。作为鸟类负责人，让塞蕾娜留下是我的职责。至于你自己，当然，你什么时候要离开就可以离开，因为路卡斯先生坚持说，我们举办了你的星期日音乐会，你是自由的。不过说到塞蕾娜嘛……好了，路易斯，它的左翅膀尖端羽毛必须剪掉。动物园不能容忍只因为你碰巧恋爱了，就失去一只年轻、美丽、贵重的吹号天鹅。再说我认为你正在犯一个严重错误。如果你和塞蕾娜留在这里，你们将会安全。你们将没有敌人。你们将不用为孩子们担心。没有狐狸，没有水獭，没有狼会袭击你们，打算把你们咬死。你们永远不会挨饿。你们永远不会遭到射击。你们永远不会由于吃了天然的湖或者池塘底下总是有的猎枪枪弹而死于铅毒。你们的孩子将在每年春天孵养出来，一辈子享福，生活舒服。一只年轻的雄天鹅还要怎么样呢？"

151

"自由，"路易斯在它的石板上回答。"安全很好。但我更要自由。"写完这话，它举起小号吹奏："当风刮起来的时候，扣上你的大衣……"

负责人微笑。他明白路易斯的意思。他们两个沉默了一会儿。路易斯把它的小号放在一边。接着它写道："我请求你能答应两件事情。第一，过了圣诞节再给塞蕾娜动手术——我保证它不会逃走。第二，让我发一份电报。"

"行，路易斯，"负责人回答。他递给路易斯一张纸和一支钢笔。路易斯给萨姆·比弗写了一份电报。电报说：

> 我在费城动物园。事情紧急。请马上来。机票钱由我付。我现在有钱了。
>
> 路易斯（签名）

它把电报交给负责人，同时从钱袋里拿出四块钱给他。负责人很吃惊。他在动物园里这么久，这还是第一次有只鸟请他发电报。当然，他不知道萨姆·比弗是什么人。不过他把电报发了，同时吩咐他的管理员几天内不要去动塞蕾娜——他们也巴不得如此。

路易斯谢过他以后走了。它回到塞蕾娜那里，它们快快活活地一起过了这一天，洗澡，游泳，吃，喝，并且相互通

152

过成千个小动作表示它们多么相爱。

圣诞节第二天，萨姆赶到了动物园。他的装束就像是进森林。他一个胳肢窝里夹着一个卷得很整齐的睡袋。他的背上是一个旅行袋，里面有他的牙刷、梳子、一件干净衬衫、一把手斧、一个袖珍指南针、他的记事本、一支铅笔和一些食物。他的腰带上插着一把猎刀。萨姆现在十四岁，对他那个岁数来说，他长得又高又大。他从来没有见过一个大动物园。他和路易斯又能相互见面，真是喜出望外。

路易斯把萨姆介绍给塞蕾娜。接着它打开钱袋让萨姆看它挣来的钱：好多百元钞票，五十元钞票，二十元钞票，十元钞票，五元钞票，一元钞票，还有银币—— 一大把。

"天啊！"萨姆想。"我希望它嫁给它不是为了它的钱。"

路易斯拿出它的石板，告诉萨姆它和管理员打的那场架，又告诉他鸟类负责人怎样要剪掉塞蕾娜一只翅膀尖端的羽毛，把塞蕾娜囚禁在这里。它告诉萨姆，如果塞蕾娜丧失飞的能力，它路易斯的生活就毁了。它解释说，只等它爸爸的欠债一还清，小号名正言顺地属于它，它和塞蕾娜就打算离开文明世界，回到大自然生活中去。"天空，"它在石板上写道，"是我的起居室。森林是我的客厅。寂静的湖是我的浴缸。我不能一辈子留在栅栏里面。塞蕾娜也不能——

它不是生来就那样生活的。我们无论如何要说服负责人把塞蕾娜放走。"

萨姆在鸟湖的岸上伸直身体躺着,头枕在双手上。他抬头看广阔的天空。它纯蓝,白色的小云朵慢慢地飘过。萨姆明白路易斯有关自由的感觉。他这样躺了很久,想了很久。鸭子和鹅缓缓地游过,游过来又游过去,被囚禁在这里的鸟类没完没了地经过。它们看上去挺快乐,过得很好。好奇、幸福、冷漠——三只吹号天鹅——游过去,看看躺在地上的这个陌生男孩。最后萨姆坐起来。

"听我说,路易斯,"他说。"这个主意怎么样?你和塞蕾娜打算每年生儿育女,对吗?"

"当然,"路易斯在石板上回答。

"那好,"萨姆说。"在每一窝小天鹅中,总有一只需要特殊照顾和保护。对于这样一只需要格外保护的小天鹅,鸟湖会是一个完美的地方。这是一个美丽的湖,路易斯。这是一个大动物园。如果我能说服负责人把塞蕾娜放走,你会愿意在动物园什么时候需要一只天鹅在湖上的时候,把你们的一只小天鹅奉送给这里吗?如果你同意,我这就去跟负责人谈这件事。"

现在轮到路易斯想了又想。过了五分钟,它拿起它的石板。

"很好，"它写道。"讲定了。"

接着它举起小号。"噢，到了发绿的春天，"它吹奏，"在岸边树旁歇着……"

水鸟都停止游水，谛听着。管理员们都停止了工作，谛听着。萨姆谛听着。负责人在他鸟馆里的办公室放下铅笔，向后靠在他的椅子上，谛听着。路易斯的小号声响在空气中，整个世界好像变得更好，更明亮，更充满活力，更自由，更快活，更美得像梦一样。

"那是支好曲子，"萨姆说。"是什么曲子?"

"噢，只是自己作的小玩意儿，"路易斯在它的石板上写道。

19. 关于钱的谈话

在几乎每个人的生活中,都会有一件事改变他存在的整个进程。萨姆·比弗来到费城动物园的一天是他生活的转折点。直到这一天之前,他还决定不了自己长大以后做什么工作。可是从他一看到动物园起,他的所有犹豫都烟消云散了。他明白他要到动物园工作。萨姆喜欢所有的生物,动物园正是生物的大本营——它正好有各种各样的动物,爬的,跳的,跑的,飞的,躲着的。

萨姆急于要把它们全看到。但是他首先要解决路易斯的问题。他必须把塞蕾娜从终身囚禁中解救出来。于是他拿起他的旅行包和睡袋,走进鸟馆,走进办公室。他挺直身体走路,就像走在森林小路上。那负责人喜欢萨姆的外表,注意到他有点像印第安人。

"那么你就是萨姆·比弗了,"负责人在萨姆向他走上来的时候说。

"你为什么到这里来?"负责人问他。

"为了维护自由,"萨姆回答。"我听说你要剪一只天鹅的翅膀。我到这里来是请你不要这样做。"

萨姆坐下来，他们谈了整整一个小时。萨姆告诉那负责人，路易斯是他的老朋友。他讲到差不多三年以前他在加拿大发现了天鹅的窝，讲到路易斯怎样来到世界上少了一条嗓子，讲到路易斯在蒙大拿进学校学会了读和写，讲到路易斯的爸爸，老天鹅，偷来了那个小号，讲到库库斯库斯夏令营和波士顿的天鹅游船。

负责人全神贯注地听着，但不知道是不是该相信这个奇怪的故事。

接着萨姆提出他的那个建议，让塞蕾娜自由飞走，而不要使它成为一只被囚禁在这里的鸟。他说他认为这是动物园一个好安排，因为他们什么时候需要一只小吹号天鹅，路易斯就会给他们一只它的小天鹅。负责人听得入了迷。

"你是说，你老远到费城来是为了帮助一只鸟?"

"是的您呐，"萨姆回答说。"为了救一只鸟，我会上任何地方去。再说路易斯不同。它是我的老朋友。我们上同一个学校。你得承认它是只了不起的鸟。"

"它当然是，"那负责人说。"它的星期日下午音乐会是动物园空前轰动的事件。我们曾经有一只猩猩，名字叫做竹子——它现在死了。竹子也很了不起，但是路易斯比竹子招来更多的游客。我们由海狮招来很多游客，但是什

158

么也比不上路易斯星期日下午演奏它的小号。人们都乐疯了。音乐对于动物也有好处，——它安慰它们，让它们忘记了白天的担心害怕。路易斯走了我会想它的。整个动物园会想死它的。我希望它待在这里，把它的新娘也留在这里——那就再好也没有了。"

"那样路易斯会在囚禁生活中憔悴。它会死的，"萨姆回答。"它需要大自然——小池塘、夜里青蛙的叫声、狮子的咆哮声。路易斯正在追逐一个梦。我们全都必须追逐一个梦。请放塞蕾娜走吧您呐!请不要剪它的翅膀!"

负责人闭上眼睛。他正在想着森林深处的小湖泊，想着香蒲的色彩，想着夜间的声响和青蛙的呱呱叫声。他正在想着天鹅的窝、蛋和孵蛋的情形，以及小天鹅排成单行跟着它们爸爸飞的样子。他在想着自己小时候做的梦。

"好吧，"他忽然说。"塞蕾娜可以走。我们不剪它的翅膀。不过我怎么能够相信，当我需要的时候，路易斯会给我送来一只小吹号天鹅呢?我怎么知道它是老实的呢?"

"它是一只老实的鸟，"萨姆说。"如果它不老实，不讲信用，它就犯不着出来挣一大笔钱，为它爸爸拿走的小号去还钱给店老板了。"

"路易斯到底挣了多少钱?"那负责人问道。

"它挣到了四千六百九十一元六角五分，"萨姆说。"几分钟前我们刚数过。它给库库斯库斯夏令营吹号挣来了一百块钱，只花了六毛钱买邮票。然后它带着九十九元四角到波士顿。在那里，天鹅游船老板付给他一星期一百块钱，他在饭店住了一夜，花了三块钱小费。它又带着这一百九十六元四角来到费城。夜总会付给它五百块钱一星期，总共十星期，就是五千块钱，但是它得付五千块钱的百分之十的佣金，又花了七角五分买新石笔，四块钱打电报给我。因此共有四千六百九十一元六角五分。对于一只鸟来说，这是一大笔钱了。"

"的确是这样，"负责人说。"的确是这样。"

"不过它还要支付我从蒙大拿到这里的来回机票。这就要使总数减为四千四百二十元七角八分。"

负责人看来被这数目弄糊涂了。

"对于一只鸟来说，这依然是一大笔钱，"他说。"这么大一笔钱它怎么花呢？"

"它要把它交给它的老天鹅爸爸。"

"那么它又把这么大一笔钱怎么用呢？"

"它要飞回比林斯那家音乐商店，把钱交给店老板，付清偷掉的小号的钱。"

"全部给他？"

"是的。"

"不过一把小号不值四千四百二十元七角八分啊。"

"这我知道，"萨姆说。"可是商店本身遭到了损坏。老天鹅像魔鬼那样冲过玻璃橱窗，打破了它。它把里面的东西也捣毁得很厉害。"

"对，"负责人说。"但是把事情料理好仍旧不要那么多钱啊。"

"我想也不要，"萨姆说。"不过路易斯拿钱再没有用处了，因此它打算把它们全交托给那音乐商店的老板。"

那负责人对钱这个话题似乎很感兴趣。他想到，钱都不再有什么用处了会是多么快活。他向后靠在椅子上。他觉得很难相信他的一只天鹅能积下四千多块钱，而这一大笔钱又正好在它脖子上挂着的钱袋里。

"说到钱，"他说，"鸟比人好办得多。鸟挣到点钱，几乎是纯利润。鸟不用上超级市场去买一打鸡蛋或者两磅牛油、两卷纸巾、一盒电视便餐、一罐番茄汁、一磅半牛肉饼、一罐切片桃子、两夸脱脱脂牛奶、一瓶塞馅橄榄。鸟用不着付房租，或者抵押借款利息。鸟不用向保险公司买人寿保险，然后按规定付保险费。鸟不用买汽车，买汽油和石油，付汽车修理费，把汽车送去洗付洗车费。鸟兽真幸运。它们不像人那样需要这个需要那个。你可以教一只猴子开摩托车，但我从来没听说过一只猴子出去买一辆摩托车。"

161

"这话不假，"萨姆回答。"不过有些野兽的确想要这个那个，尽管它们不为此付任何钱。"

"比方说呢?"负责人问。

"老鼠，"萨姆说，"老鼠给自己置个家，接着往它的家里拖来各种各样乱七八糟的小东西——它碰到的任何东西。"

"你说得对，"负责人说。"你说得绝对正确，萨姆。你对动物似乎懂得很多。"

"我喜欢动物，"萨姆说。"我爱观察它们。"

"那么跟我来吧，我们参观一下这个动物园，"负责人从他的椅子上站起来。"今天我不想再做什么工作了。我带你去看看这个动物园。"

他们出去了，两个人。

那天晚上，萨姆得到特别允许，睡在这位负责人的办公室里。他在地板上把睡袋打开，爬了进去。带他回家的飞机早晨开。萨姆的脑袋里充满了他在动物园看到的所有东西。在他关灯以前，他从背包里拿出他的记事本，写了一首诗。这就是他写的诗:

萨姆·比弗的诗

在陆地和大海上的所有处所，
费城动物园最最适合我。

162

那里吃的东西、工作多得不得了，

那里有小鸊鷉和军舰鸟；

那里有白足鼠和两趾树懒，

应该说这两样我都喜欢。

那里有北极熊和黑额黑雁，

以及鸟兽来自八方四面。

那里有许多东西你见所未见，

例如蜜熊以及狼獾。

你实在该上动物园去，

看看刚出生的岩大袋鼠，

或者白尾牛羚，或者扁角鹿。

在美丽的湖上有些鸟令人惊奇咋舌，

那里有狼和猪鼻蛇。

那里吸引人的动物不少，

例如蜂鸟和斑海豹。

那里有供人骑的马驹，有食肉猛禽，

每天会有好玩的事情。

那里有狼和狐狸，老鹰和猫头鹰，

有狮子爬来爬去的大坑。

那里池塘平静，笼子悦目，

里面躺着爬行动物，咆哮着老虎。

房舍整洁，管理员亲善对待动物，

一只狒狒有个粉红色的屁股。

一个办得好的动物园，

唯一目的是把动物世界在你面前展现。

萨姆·比弗(签名)

萨姆把这首诗留在那位负责人的写字台上。

第二天一大早，人们到动物园来上班还有好大一会儿，而此时萨姆已经乘飞机离开了费城。路易斯和塞蕾娜送他到机场。它们要向他挥动翅膀告别。它们而且计划好同时同地离开费城回蒙大拿去。当机场工作人员看见两只大白鸟走到外面飞机跑道时，他们一下子可怕地骚乱起来。指挥塔上的工作人员向刚到达机场的飞机驾驶员发出警告。地勤人员赶快纷纷走出建筑物，向路易斯和塞蕾娜跑过去要把它们赶走。萨姆正坐在他那班飞机的窗口准备起飞，看到了整个场面。

路易斯抓起它那把小号。

"我们出发了，"它吹奏道，"飞到上面无边无际的蓝天中去了！"小号声传过机场，使每个人为之吃惊。"咯—嗬！咯—嗬！"路易斯大叫。它把它的小号放下，开始飞快地顺着飞机跑道飞跑，塞蕾娜跑在它的后面。就在这时候，萨姆的飞机迎风起飞了。两只天鹅也并排飞起来。可是飞机还没有飞起来，它们已经到了空中，飞得很快。萨姆从窗口向它们挥手。路易斯的"救生奖章"在早晨的太阳光中闪烁。飞机升了起来，开始向上攀升。路易斯和塞蕾娜也很快地向上攀升。

"再见，费城！"路易斯想。"再见，鸟湖！再见，夜总会！"

飞机速度更快，赶过了两只天鹅。它们开始落后了。它们跟着飞机朝西飞了好一会儿。接着路易斯向塞蕾娜示意，它要改变航向了。它向左侧身，转过来朝南。

"我们朝南飞回家，飞得从从容容的，"它对自己说。

它们就这样做。它们朝南飞过马里兰州和弗吉尼亚州。它们朝南飞过北卡罗来纳州和南卡罗来纳。它们在耶马西过了一夜，看到巨大的橡树，苔藓从它们的树枝上挂下来。它们参观了佐治亚州的大沼泽，看到了鳄鱼，听到了嘲鸫[①]的叫声。它们飞过佛罗里达州，在长沼过了几天，那地方鸽子在柏树间咕咕叫，小蜥蜴在太阳下爬。它们转向西飞到路易斯安那州。接着它们转向北朝着它们处在红石湖上游的家飞去。

这是怎样的凯旋啊！离开蒙大拿的时候路易斯身无分文。现在它有了钱。离开的时候它是个无名小卒。现在它有名了。离开的时候它在这个世界上孤孤单单。现在它身

165

边有了新娘——它心爱的天鹅。它的奖章挂在脖子上,它宝贵的小号在微风中晃荡,它苦苦挣来的钱在它的钱袋里。它完成了它动身时要去做的事。都在短短的几个月里!

自由给人的感觉那么了不起!爱情给人的感觉那么好!

---

① 嘲鸫善于模仿其他鸟的叫声。

20.比林斯

1月里一个明朗的日子,路易斯和塞蕾娜回家来到红石湖。在几千只水鸟中,它们很快就找到了它们自己家的成员——它们的爸爸妈妈和兄弟姐妹。这是热闹的归家场面。个个想马上说声你们好。咯—嗬,咯—嗬,咯—嗬!流浪者终于回家了。

路易斯的老爸作了一番美妙的讲话——相当长,不过是真心话。

路易斯举起它的小号,吹起了"没有地方能比得上家。家,家,甜蜜的家!"关于路易斯终于使塞蕾娜成为它的妻子,在水鸟之间有许多传闻。个个祝贺这快乐的一对。路易斯和塞蕾娜的所有兄弟姐妹围在一起看路易斯的东西。它们非常喜欢它所有的那些东西。它们喜欢那"救生奖章",它们爱那小号的声音,它们急于要看钱袋里的钱。但是路易斯没有打开钱袋,而是把它的爸爸和妈妈带到一边。它们三个上了岸。到了岸上,路易斯把钱袋从脖子上拿下来,鞠着躬把它交给老爸。四千四百二十元七角八分。

接着路易斯拿起石板,给比林斯那家音乐商店的老板写了一些话,让它爸爸到了那里给他看。写的话是这样的:

比林斯的店老板:

请查收带上的4 420.78元。这笔钱是偿还你的小号和商店损失的。很抱歉这件事给你带来的麻烦。

天鹅老爸不会数钱,也不会读,但是它拿起钱袋和石板,把它们挂在脖子上,它明白地感觉到,它现在能偿还偷来小号所欠的债了。

"我这就去,"它对它的妻子说。"我要恢复我的名誉。我要回到我犯了罪的比林斯去——一个生机勃勃的大城市……"

"这话我们先前听到过了,"它的妻子说。"你就带着钱和石板尽快上比林斯去吧。到了那里,看在老天爷分上,你要十分小心!那音乐商店老板有支枪。他会记起他上次看到一只天鹅上他那儿把他抢了。因此要当心自己!你这是个危险的使命。"

"危险!"天鹅老爸说,"危险!我欢迎危险和冒险。冒险是我突出的个性。为了恢复我的名誉和重新获得我高尚的感觉,我甘愿冒我生命的危险。我要还清债款,洗刷掉玷污我好名声的污点。我要永远摆脱掉偷盗和做不法事情的耻辱。我要……"

"你再不住口,"它的妻子说,"你就不能在商店打烊前赶到比林斯了。"

"又是你说得对,"天鹅老爸回答。它把钱袋和石板挂挂正准备飞行。接着它飞上空中,又快又高地朝北飞去。它的妻子和儿子看着它,直到它消失不见为止。

"多好的一只天鹅啊,"它的妻子说。"你有一个好爸爸,路易斯。我希望它平安无事。跟你说实在话,我很担心。"

老天鹅飞得很快,飞了很远。当它看到比林斯的教堂、工厂、店铺和住家的时候,打了一个圈,然后开始向下滑翔——一直对准那家音乐商店。

"我的时候到了,"它对自己说。"证明我诚实的时刻就在眼前。我很快就不再欠债,我很快就不再呆在羞耻和不光彩的乌云底下,许多个月来,它一直在我的生活中投下阴影。"

老天鹅已经被下面的人看见。音乐商店的一个伙计站在前面橱窗旁边,朝着外面看。当他看到那只白色巨鸟飞下来的时候,他大声对老板说:"大鸟来了。准备你的枪!"

店老板抓住他的猎枪，跑到店外人行道上。天鹅在天上很低了，一直向商店飞下来。

店老板举起枪。他连续迅速地双管齐放。老天鹅感到左肩一阵刺痛。它回过头，看到胸前有一滴鲜红的血。但它还是对着店老板一直飞下来。

"末日快到了，"天鹅对自己说。"我将死于尽我职责的时候。我只有几分钟可以活了。这个人干了蠢事，使我受了致命的伤。鲜红的血从我的血管里汩汩流出来。我的力气用完了。不过即使在临死的最后时刻，我也要还清小号的钱。再见了，生命！再见了，美丽的世界！再见了，北方的小湖！永别了，充满激情的我所熟悉的春天！永别了，忠诚的妻子和我心爱的子女！我，马上就要死的我，向你们问好！我必须死得潇洒，就像惟有天鹅能够做到的那样。"

说着，它就落到了人行道上。它把钱袋和石板递给了目瞪口呆的店老板以后，看到自己身上的血，昏过去了。它软弱无力地躺在人行道上，像是死了。

人们很快围了上来。

"这是什么？"店老板在天鹅身上弯下腰来说。"这到底怎么回事？"

他很快地读了石板上的话。接着他打开钱袋，拿出那些百元大钞和五十元大钞。

170

一位警察赶到现场，开始把群众往后推。

"退后!"他叫道。"这天鹅受伤了。让它透透空气!"

"它死了，"一个小男孩说。"这鸟死了。"

"它没有死，"店伙计说。"它是吓昏了。"

"叫救护车!"人群中一位太太尖叫。

老天鹅脖子下面淌了一小摊血。它看上去活不成了。就在这时候，一位渔猎法执行官出现了。

"谁开枪打这只鸟的?"他问。

"是我，"店老板说。

"那么你被捕了，"那执行官说。

"为什么?"店老板问。

"为了你开枪射击一只吹号天鹅。这种鸟是受法律保护的。你不可以向野天鹅开枪。"

"不过，"店老板回答说，"你也不能逮捕我啊。我正好认识这只鸟。它是个贼。你应该逮捕的是它。它曾经来过这里，从我的店里偷走了一把小号。"

"叫救护车!"那位太太大叫。

"你手里拿着什么?"警察问。店老板赶紧把钱放回钱袋，把钱袋和石板藏到身后。

"来，把它给我看!"警察说。

"我也要看，"执行官说。

"我们全都要看!"人群里一个人叫。"那口袋里是什么东西?"

店老板很窘地把钱袋和石板递给那执行官。执行官把身体站直,戴上眼镜,大声念出石板上的话。"比林斯的店老板:请查收带上的4 420.78元。这笔钱是偿还你的小号和商店损失的。很抱歉这件事给你带来的麻烦。"

提到钱数,人群一下子倒抽一口冷气。人人都马上开口说起话来。

"叫救护车!"那位太太尖叫。

"我必须把这笔钱送到警察局,"警察说。"这是一个复杂的案子。任何事情一牵涉到钱都是复杂的。我要把钱送去安全保管起来,直到事情解决。"

"不,你不能拿走,"那位执行官说。"这钱归我。"

"为什么?"警察问。

"因为,"执行官回答。

"因为什么?"警察问。

"因为法律规定,鸟类在我管辖范围之内。钱在鸟身上。因此,钱归我管,直到这事了结。"

"噢,不,你不能这么办,"店老板生气地说。"钱归我。这块石板上就是这么说的。这四千四百二十元七角八分归我。没有人能把它从我这里拿走。"

"没那回事!"警察说。"我拿才对。"

"不,该我拿,"渔猎法执行官说。

"你们当中有律师吗?"店老板问道。"这件事我们就现在当场解决。"

一个高高的人走上前来。

"我是里基茨法官,"他说。"我来判决这个案子。现在听我说,谁看见这鸟飞来的?"

"是我,"店伙计说。

"叫救护车!"那位太太尖叫。

"我也看见了那鸟,"一个叫艾尔弗雷德·戈尔的小男孩说。

"好,"法官说。"完全按照你们看到的情形,把经过讲一遍。"

店伙计先说。"是这样的,"他说,"我正好朝橱窗外面看,看到一只天鹅飞下来。于是我叫了。老板拿来他的枪,就开了,天鹅落到人行道上。有一两滴血。"

"你注意到这鸟有什么特别的东西吗?"里基茨法官问道。

"它带着钱,"店伙计回答。"鸟身上带着钱不常见,因此我注意到了。"

"好,"法官说。"现在让艾尔弗雷德·戈尔说说他所见到的。把你看到的讲出来吧，艾尔弗雷德。"

"好，"那小男孩说，"我当时很渴，因此要到糖果店去弄点什么喝喝。"

"请就说你看到的，艾尔弗雷德，"法官说。"别管你有多渴。"

"我正在街上一路走，"艾尔弗雷德说下去，"因为当时我非常渴。因此我沿着街道一路走，要到糖果店去弄点什么喝喝，就在那里，在天上，忽然之间有一只大白鸟在天上，就在我头顶上，它正这样从天上滑降下来，"艾尔弗雷德张开双臂学鸟飞。"就这样，我一看见那大鸟就不再去想我有多渴。转眼间，这大鸟——它实在大——就在人行道上，死了，到处是血，这就是我看到的。"

"你注意到这鸟有什么特别的东西吗?"里基茨法官问。

"血，"艾尔弗雷德说。

"还有别的吗?"

"没有，就是血。"

"你听到开枪吗?"

"没有，就是血，"艾尔弗雷德说。

"谢谢你!"法官说。"就说到这里吧。"

正在这时候报警器呜呜地响——呜啊，呜啊，呜啊。

救护车呜呜尖叫着一路开来了。它停在人群前面。两个人从车上跳下来。他们抬着个担架，放在躺着的天鹅旁边。老天鹅抬起头朝四周看。"我已经到了死亡之门，"它想，"可现在我想，我又回到生活中来了。我复活了。我会活下去的!我将展开强壮的翅膀回到广阔的天空。我将重又在世界上那些池塘上空滑翔，听青蛙叫，欣赏黑夜的声音和白天的降临。"

它正在想着这些愉快的念头，只觉自己被抬起来。救护车护理员把它的石板挂在它的脖子上，抬起它，把它轻轻放在担架上，抬到顶上有盏红灯转来转去的救护车里。其中一个人把一个氧气罩罩在老天鹅的头上，给它接点氧气。他们响起很大的呜呜声，把车开到医院去。到了医院，它被放在病床上，给注射了一针盘尼西林。一位年轻医生进来检查了猎枪枪弹打的伤口。那医生说这伤是表面的。老天鹅不明白"表面的"什么意思，但它听了觉得很严重。

护士们围拢来。其中一个给老天鹅量血压，在一张表格上写了几个字。老天鹅又开始感到非常好了。它觉得躺在床上有护士照料非常好——其中一位护士十分漂亮。医生洗干净伤口，在上面贴上护创膏。

现在回过头去讲音乐商店前面的人行道，法官正在宣布他的判决。

"根据证词，"他严肃地说，"我把钱判给店老板，偿还小号和店铺受破坏的损失，我又把天鹅判给渔猎法执行官照管。"

"阁下，"执行官说，"请别忘了店老板由于射击野天鹅应被逮捕。"

"那就是非法逮捕，"法官聪明地说。"店老板对天鹅开枪是由于他害怕天鹅又要来抢他的店。他不知道天鹅是带着钱来付小号的账。开枪属于自卫。每一个都是无罪的，天鹅是诚实的，债还清了，店老板有钱了，案子也就结了。"

群众欢呼。执行官看上去绷着脸。警察看上去不高兴。可是店老板红光满面。他是个快活的人。他觉得裁决得很公正。

"我要宣布，"他说，"我只收下被偷掉的小号和店铺修理的钱。多下来的钱将用于只要我能想出来的良好用途。诸位有什么人能想出一个要花钱的有价值用途吗?"

"救世军，"一个妇人建议。

"不，"店老板说。

"童子军?"一个男孩建议。

"不，"店老板说。

"美国公民自由联盟呢?"一个男人建议。

176

"不，"店老板说。"还没有人想出我该把钱送去的合适地方。"

"奥松邦协会①怎么样?"有个鸟嘴鼻的小家伙问道。

"好极了!你想出来了!"店老板叫道。"一只鸟对我非常好，现在我要为鸟类做点事。奥松邦协会对鸟类很好。我要这笔钱用于帮助鸟类。有些鸟真正遇到麻烦。它们濒临灭绝。"

"什么叫灭绝?"艾尔弗雷德·戈尔问道。

店老板说:"灭绝就是一种东西消灭了，不再存在了，这种东西没有了。例如旅鸽和东方的琴鸡、渡渡鸟以及恐龙。"

"吹号天鹅也几乎灭绝了，"渔猎法执行官说。"人们射击它们，就像这位发神经的店老板。不过现在它们正在恢复回来。"

店老板看看执行官。

"我要说它们是回来了，"他说。"刚才就在这里的那只天鹅回到了比林斯来，带着四千四百二十元七角八分，把它们全给了我。我说这是非常好的回来。我想像不出它从哪里弄来这么大一笔钱。这是极其有趣的事。"

店老板回到他的音乐商店，警察回到警察局，法官回到法院，渔猎法执法官一路步行到医院，还感到口渴的艾尔

177

弗雷德·戈尔继续去找糖果店。其他人也都散开走了。

在医院里，老天鹅平静地躺在病床上想它美丽的念头。它觉得能活着真是谢天谢地，也为还清了债感到轻松愉快。

天快黑了。医院里许多病人早已睡觉。一位护士走进天鹅的房间来打开窗子。

等到她几分钟后回来，要给天鹅量体温和擦背，病床是空的——房间里什么也没有。天鹅已经跳出窗子，展开它宽阔的双翅，穿过寒冷的夜空，一直朝家飞去了。它飞了一整夜，飞过高山，天亮后不久就到家，它妻子正在等着它。

"事情怎么样？"妻子问道。

"很好，"它说。"是个不同寻常的冒险。正像你预言的，我给击中了。店老板用枪对准我就开。我当时觉得左肩膀痛得厉害——我一向认为在两个肩膀里这边肩膀更加漂亮。血从我的伤口涌出来，我优雅地落到人行道上，在那里，我交出了钱，从而重新恢复了我的名誉和我的高贵品质。我已经到了死亡之门。许多人围上来。到处是血。我晕过去了，在所有人面前庄严地晕倒。警察来了——好几十个。许多渔猎法执法官拥到现场，关于钱还发生了很大的争论。"

"你都失去知觉了，这一切你是怎么知道的？"它的妻

178

子问道。

"我亲爱的，"天鹅老爸说，"在我讲我旅行的故事时，我希望你不要打断我的话。看到我情况严重，人群里有人叫来救护车，我给送进了医院，给放到病床上。我躺在那里样子十分好看，雪白的被单衬托着我的黑嘴。在我受苦挨痛的时候，医生和护士来看我，安慰我。我只要告诉你，有一位医生检查我的伤时说它是表面的，你就可以知道我的伤有多么厉害了。"

"我倒看不出它怎么糟糕，"它的妻子说。"我想你只是擦伤了一点。如果糟糕，你不可能这么快就飞回来。反正不管表面不表面，我很高兴看到你太平无事地回了家。你走了我总是想念你。我不知道为什么，但我就是想念你。"

它说着把头靠在它丈夫的脖子上，轻轻地揉它的丈夫。接着它们吃早饭，到冰冻的湖上一块没冻住的地方游泳。天鹅老爸把护创膏拉下来扔掉。

---

① 奥松邦协会是美国一个保护野生动物等的团体，以美国鸟类学家，美术家约翰·奥松邦（1785—1851）的姓命名。他编有七卷本《美洲鸟类图谱》。

21. 发绿的春天

　　路易斯和塞蕾娜更加相爱了。春天到来，它们飞往北方，路易斯挂着它的小号、它的石板、它的石笔和它的奖章，塞蕾娜却什么东西也没有挂。现在路易斯不再干活挣钱，它觉得有一种极大的解脱感。它再也用不着在脖子上挂上一个钱袋。

　　两只天鹅飞得很高，离地足有一千英尺，它们飞得也快。它们最后来到路易斯自己给孵出来的那个丛林中的小池塘。和心爱的天鹅一起回到加拿大它最初看到日光的地方——这是它的梦。它带着塞蕾娜从池塘的这一头游到那一头，又重新游回来。它指给塞蕾娜看曾经有过它妈妈的窝的那个小岛。它指给塞蕾娜看萨姆·比弗曾经坐过的那根大木头，当时它不会毕毕叫，就拉他的鞋带。塞蕾娜着了迷。它们相爱。这是春天。青蛙从它们的长睡中醒来。乌龟在小睡之后又苏醒了。金花鼠感觉到轻柔的温暖空气吹过树木，就像在那个春天一样，当时路易斯的爸爸和妈妈到这池塘来造窝和生儿育女。

太阳照下来,一直强烈地照着。冰在融化,池塘上出现了一道道水。路易斯和塞蕾娜感觉到了这变化着的世界,新生活、狂喜、希望激动着它们的心。空气中有一股气味,土地在漫长冬季后醒来的气味。树木爆出很小的绿芽,这些绿芽在长大。更好的日子,更容易过的日子就要来了。一对绿头鸭飞来。一只白喉咙的麻雀飞来就唱:"噢,美丽的加拿大,加拿大,加拿大!"

塞蕾娜挑了一个麝鼠窠,在那上面造它的窝。这窠离水的高度正合适,麝鼠是用烂泥和树枝搭建的。路易斯本来希望它妻子能决定在它妈妈的原来地方造窝,但雌天鹅都满有主意,要照自己的办法办,还挺固执,塞蕾娜知道自己在干什么。路易斯看到塞蕾娜开始营造它的窝了,感到很高兴,其实它也不真正在乎窝造在哪里。它把小号举到嘴上,吹起一支老曲子的开头,这支曲子叫做:《结婚好,结结结结结结结婚……》。接着它帮忙叼来几根粗草。

不管下雨出太阳,不管天冷天热,对于这两只天鹅来说,天天是快活的日子。到时候,蛋下了,小天鹅孵出来了—— 一共四只。这些天鹅小宝宝听到的第一个声音是它们爸爸那个小号清纯、雄壮的声音。

"噢,到了发绿的春天,"它吹奏道,"在岸边树旁歇着……"

在北方森林中寂静的小池塘里，生活是愉快、忙碌和甜蜜的。萨姆·比弗不时来访，他们在一起真是快活极了。

路易斯从来不忘记它做过的工作，不忘记它的老朋友或者它答应过费城鸟类负责人的话。一年年过去，每年春天它和塞蕾娜回到池塘上来造窝，产下它们的小天鹅。每年夏末，当换羽过程结束，飞羽又长出来，小天鹅也要试试它们翅膀的时候，路易斯带它的一家作快活的长途旅行，横跨美国。它带它们先到库库斯库斯夏令营，在那里它曾救过平果·斯金纳的命，并且获得了它的奖章。这时候夏令营因为夏天已过，不开放了，但路易斯还是喜欢旧地重游，在那里走来走去，回忆那些男孩，回忆它怎样当夏令营号手，挣来它的第一次一百块钱。

接着这群天鹅会飞到波士顿，天鹅游船的那位老板每次都对它们热烈欢迎。路易斯会擦亮它的小号，吹掉小号里的口水，重新游在那些游船前面，吹起"摇摇摇你的船"，波士顿人听到天鹅小号那熟悉的歌声，都成群结队到公园来。然后天鹅游船老板会请路易斯和塞蕾娜到里茨饭店去过一夜，而那些小天鹅自顾自在湖上过夜，由那船老板保护着。塞蕾娜极其喜欢里茨饭店。它吃好几打水田芥叶三明治，在镜子里左顾右盼，在浴缸里游泳。当路易斯站在窗口看下面的公园时，塞蕾娜会走来走去，为了好玩，把灯开了又关，关了又开。最后它们双双进浴缸睡觉。

路易斯把一家又从波士顿带到费城动物园，让大家看鸟湖。在这里，它受到鸟类负责人的热烈欢迎。万一动物园需要一只吹号天鹅来补充水鸟数目时，路易斯会信守诺言，把它的一只小天鹅送给动物园。最近这些年，费城也是它们可以见到萨姆·比弗的地方。萨姆一到工作年龄，就在这动物园找到了一份差使。当萨姆和路易斯在一起的时候，他们总是很快活。路易斯会拿出它的石板，一起长谈他们过去的时光。

访问完费城，路易斯就带着它的妻子儿女向南飞，这样它们就能看到佛罗里达州的无树草原，那里鳄鱼在沼泽里睡觉，红头美洲鹫在天空中翱翔。然后它们回家去蒙大拿的红石湖，在可爱平静的百年谷过冬，在那里，所有的吹号天鹅都感到安全，不用担惊受怕。

天鹅的生活一定非常快活有趣。自然，路易斯的生活特别快活有趣，因为它是一位音乐家。路易斯把它的小号保护得非常好。它让小号保持清洁，花上好几个钟头用它翅膀羽毛的尖尖擦它。它活一天就感谢它爸爸一天，这位勇敢的天鹅老爸甘冒生命危险，给它弄来了它那么需要的小号。每次路易斯看着塞蕾娜，它就想起，正是这小号的声

184

音使塞蕾娜愿意成为它的伴侣。

天鹅寿命非常长。一年又一年，路易斯和塞蕾娜在春天回到加拿大那同一个小池塘生儿育女。这些日子非常平静。在天就快黑的时候，小天鹅要想睡了，路易斯总是举起它的小号吹起了熄灯号，正像它许多年前在夏令营一直做的那样。这些音忧郁而又美丽，飘过平静的水，飘进夜空。

一年夏天，这时萨姆·比弗已将二十，他和他父亲坐在他们在加拿大的帐篷里。这是晚饭以后，比弗先生钓了一天鱼累了，坐在椅子上摇来摇去休息，萨姆在看书。

"爸，"萨姆说，"'黄昏出没的'是什么意思？"

"我怎么知道？"比弗先生回答。"这词儿我从来没有碰到过。"

"这是跟兔子有关的，"萨姆说。"这里说，兔子是这样的动物。"

"意思可能是胆小吧，"比弗先生说。"或者是能够跑得和魔鬼一样快。或者是愚蠢。兔子夜里就会这样坐在路当中，盯住你的车头灯看，从不让路，因此有许多兔子给轧死了。它们愚蠢。"

"那么我想，"萨姆说，"要知道这是什么意思，只有查字典了。"

"我们这里没带着字典，"比弗先生说。"只好等回到牧

185

场以后了。"

正好这时候,在天鹅们待着的池塘那边,路易斯举起它的小号在吹熄灯号,让它的孩子们知道,一天已经结束了。顺风正好把号声吹过了沼泽地。

比弗先生停止摇动。

"奇怪,"他说。"我想我刚才听到了小号声。"

"我不明白你怎么会听到,"萨姆回答说。"在这森林里只有我们。"

"我知道只有我们,"比弗先生说。"不过我还是认为我听到了小号声。或者是号角声。"

萨姆格格笑。他从来没有告诉过他爸爸附近池塘里有天鹅。他保守着它们的秘密。他到池塘总是独自一个人去的。他喜欢这样。天鹅它们也喜欢这样。

"你的朋友路易斯怎么样了?"比弗先生问。"路易斯是个小号手。你不认为它在这儿什么地方吗?"

"有可能,"萨姆说。

"最近你听到过它的消息没有?"比弗先生问。

"没有,"萨姆回答。"它再没写过信来。它邮票用光了,又没有钱买。"

"噢,"比弗先生说。"说真格的,那鸟的整个事情十分奇怪——我从来没有彻底弄明白过。"

186

萨姆望过去看他爸爸,看到他的眼睛闭上了。比弗先生已经睡着。简直没有一点声音打扰这森林中的寂静。

萨姆也疲倦了,昏昏欲睡。他拿出他的记事本,在桌旁火油灯的灯光下坐下来。这是他写的话:

今天晚上我听到了路易斯的小号声。我的爸爸也听到了。顺风,天一黑下来,我就听到熄灯号的号声。整个世界上,再没有东西比得上这天鹅的小号更让我喜欢的。**"黄昏出没的"**是什么意思呢?

萨姆放下他的记事本。他脱掉衣服钻进被窝。他躺在那里想"黄昏出没的"是什么意思。不到三分钟,他已经睡着了。

在天鹅所在的池塘上,路易斯放下它的小号。小天鹅们爬到它们妈妈的翅膀底下。黑暗笼罩着森林、田野和沼泽地。一只潜鸟叫出它夜间那种狂野的叫声。当路易斯放松下来准备睡觉的时候,它的全部念头是:它生活在这样一个美丽世界是多么幸运,它的问题由音乐解决了是多么幸运,而且又是多么快活啊;接下来是又一个安眠之夜和又一个明天,又一个清新的早晨和随着一天到来而回来的亮光。

187

E.B.White

The Trumpet of The Swan

Contents

Chapter 1

Sam

WALKING BACK to camp through the swamp, Sam wondered whether to tell his father what he had seen.

"I know *one* thing," he said to himself. "I'm going back to that little pond again tomorrow. And I'd like to go alone. If I tell my father what I saw today, he will want to go with me. I'm not sure that's a very good idea."

Sam was eleven. His last name was Beaver. He was strong for his age and had black hair and dark eyes like an Indian. Sam walked like an Indian, too, putting one foot straight in front of the other and making very little noise. The swamp through which he was travelling was a wild place—there was no trail, and it was boggy underfoot, which made walking difficult. Every four or five minutes Sam took his compass out of his pocket and checked his course to make sure he was headed in a westerly direction. Canada is a big place. Much of it is wilderness. To get lost in the woods and swamps of western Canada would be a serious matter.

As he trudged on, the boy's mind was full of the wonder of what he had seen. Not many people in the world have seen the nest of a Trumpeter Swan. Sam had found one on the lonely pond on this day in spring. He had seen the two great white birds with their long white necks and black bills. Nothing he had ever seen before in all his life had made him feel quite the way he felt, on that wild little pond, in the presence of those two enormous swans. They were so much bigger than any bird he had ever seen before. The nest was big, too—a mound of sticks and grasses. The female was sitting on eggs; the male glided slowly back and forth, guarding her.

When Sam reached camp, tired and hungry, he found his father frying a couple of fish for lunch.

"Where have *you* been?" asked Mr. Beaver.

"Exploring," replied Sam. "I walked over to a pond about a mile and a half from here. It's the one we see from the air as we're coming in. It isn't much of a place —nowhere near as big as this lake we're on."

"Did you see anything over there?" asked his father.

"Well," said Sam, "it's a swampy pond with a lot of reeds and cattails. I don't think it would be any good for fishing. And it's hard to get to—you have to cross a swamp."

"See anything?" repeated Mr. Beaver.

"I saw a muskrat," said Sam, "and a few Red-winged Blackbirds."

Mr. Beaver looked up from the wood stove, where the fish were sizzling in a pan.

"Sam," he said, "I know you like to go exploring. But don't forget—these woods and marshes are not like the country around home in Montana. If you ever go over to that pond again, be careful you don't get lost. I don't like you crossing swamps. They're treacherous. You could step into a soggy place and get bogged down, and there wouldn't be anybody to pull you out."

"I'll be careful," said Sam. He knew perfectly well he would be going back to the pond where the swans were. And he had no intention of getting lost in the woods. He felt relieved that he had not told his father about seeing the swans, but he felt queer about it, too. Sam was not a sly boy, but he was odd in one respect: he liked to keep things to himself. And he liked being alone, particularly when he was in the woods. He enjoyed the life on his father's cattle ranch in the Sweet Grass country in Montana. He loved his mother. He loved Duke, his cow pony. He loved riding the range. He loved watching the guests who came to board at the Beaver's ranch every summer.

But the thing he enjoyed most in life was these camping trips in Canada with his father. Mrs. Beaver didn't care for the woods, so she seldom went along—it was usually just Sam and Mr. Beaver. They would motor to the border and cross into Canada. There Mr. Beaver would hire a bush pilot to fly them to the lake where his camp was, for a few days of fishing and loafing and exploring. Mr. Beaver did most of the fishing and loafing. Sam did the exploring. And then the pilot would return to take them out. His name was Shorty. They would hear the sound of his motor and run out and wave and watch him glide down on to the lake and taxi his plane in to the dock. These were the pleasantest days of Sam's life, these days in the woods, far, far from everywhere—no automobiles, no roads, no people, no noise, no school, no homework, no problems, except the problem of getting lost. And, of course, the problem of what to be when he grew up. Every boy has *that* problem.

After supper that evening, Sam and his father sat for a while on the porch. Sam was reading a bird book.

"Pop," said Sam, "do you think we'll be coming back to camp again about a month from now—I mean, in about thirty-five days or something like that?"

"I guess so," replied Mr. Beaver. "I certainly hope so. But why thirty-five days? What's so special about thirty-five days?"

"Oh, nothing," said Sam. "I just thought it might be very nice around here in thirty-five days."

"That's the craziest thing I ever heard of," said Mr.

Beaver. "It's nice here *all* the time."

Sam went indoors. He knew a lot about birds, and he knew it would take a swan about thirty-five days to hatch her eggs. He hoped he could be at the pond to see the young ones when they came out of the eggs.

Sam kept a diary—a daybook about his life. It was just a cheap notebook that was always by his bed. Every night, before he turned in, he would write in the book. He wrote about things he had done, things he had seen, and thoughts he had had. Sometimes he drew a picture. He always ended by asking himself a question so he would have something to think about while falling asleep. On the day he found the swan's nest, this is what Sam wrote in his diary:

I saw a pair of trumpeter swans today on a small pond east of camp. The female has a nest with eggs in it. I saw three, but I'm going to put four in the picture—I think she was laying another one. This

is the greatest discovery I ever made in my entire life. I did not tell Pop. My bird book says baby swans are called cygnets. I am going back tomorrow to visit the great swans again. I heard a fox bark today. Why does a fox bark? Is it because he is mad, or worried, or hungry, or because he is sending a message to another fox? *Why does a fox bark?*

Sam closed his notebook, undressed, crawled into his bunk, and lay there with his eyes closed, wondering why a fox barks. In a few minutes he was asleep.

Chapter 2
The Pond

THE POND Sam had discovered on that spring morning was seldom visited by any human being. All winter, snow had covered the ice; the pond lay cold and still under its white blanket. Most of the time there wasn't a sound to be heard. The frog was asleep. The chipmunk was asleep. Occasionally a jay would cry out. And sometimes at night the fox would bark—a high, rasping bark. Winter seemed to last forever.

But one day a change came over the woods and the pond. Warm air, soft and kind, blew through the trees. The ice, which had softened during the night, began to melt. Patches of open water appeared. All the creatures that lived in the pond and in the woods were glad to feel the warmth. They heard and felt the breath of spring, and they stirred with new life and hope. There was a good, new smell in the air, a smell of earth waking after its long sleep. The frog, buried in the mud at the bottom of the pond, knew that spring was here. The chickadee knew and was delighted (almost everything delights a chickadee). The vixen, dozing in her den, knew she would soon have cubs. Every creature knew that a better, easier time was at hand—warmer days, pleasanter nights. Trees were putting out green buds; the buds were swelling. Birds began arriving from the south. A pair of ducks flew in. The Red-winged Blackbird arrived and scouted the pond for nesting sites. A small sparrow with a white throat arrived and sang, "Oh, sweet Canada, Canada, Canada!"

And if you had been sitting by the pond on that first warm day of spring, suddenly, toward the end of the afternoon, you would have heard a stirring sound high above you in the air—a sound like the sound of trumpets.

"Ko-hoh, ko-hoh!"

And if you had looked up, you would have seen, high overhead, two great white birds. They flew swiftly, their legs stretched out straight behind, their long white necks stretched out ahead, their powerful wings beating steady and strong. "Ko-hoh, ko-hoh, ko-hoh!" A thrilling noise in the sky, the trumpeting of swans.

When the birds spotted the pond, they began circling, looking the place over from the air. Then they glided down and came to rest in the water, folding their long wings neatly along their sides and turning their heads this way and that to study their new surroundings. They were Trumpeter Swans, pure white birds

with black bills. They had liked the looks of the swampy pond and had decided to make it their home for a while and raise a family.

The two swans were tired from the long flight. They were glad to be down out of the sky. They paddled slowly about and then began feeding, thrusting their necks into the shallow water and pulling roots and plants from the bottom. Everything about the swans was white except their bills and their feet; these were black. They carried their heads high. The pond seemed a different place because of their arrival.

For the next few days, the swans rested. When they were hungry, they ate. When they were thirsty— which was a great deal of the time—they drank. On the tenth day, the female began looking around to find a place to build her nest.

In the spring of the year, nest-building is uppermost in a bird's mind: it is the most important thing there is. If she picks a good place, she stands a good chance of hatching her eggs and rearing her young. If she picks a poor place, she may fail to raise a family. The female swan knew this; she knew the decision she was making was extremely important.

The two swans first investigated the upper end of the pond, where a stream flowed slowly in. It was pleasant there, with reeds and bulrushes. Red-winged

Blackbirds were busy nesting in this part of the pond, and a pair of Mallard Ducks were courting. Then the swans swam to the lower end of the pond, a marsh with woods on one side and a deer meadow on the other. It was lonely here. From one shore, a point of land extended out into the pond. It was a sandy strip, like a little peninsula. And at the tip of it, a few feet out into the water, was a tiny island, hardly bigger than a dining table. One small tree grew on the island, and there were rocks and ferns and grasses.

"Take a look at this!" exclaimed the female, as she swam round and around.

"Ko-hoh!" replied her husband, who liked to have someone ask his advice.

The swan stepped cautiously out on to the island. The spot seemed made to order—just right for a nesting place. While the male swan floated close by, watching, she snooped about until she found a pleasant spot on the ground. She sat down, to see how it felt to be sitting there. She decided it was the right size for her body. It was nicely located, a couple of feet from the water's edge. Very convenient. She turned to her husband.

"What do you think?" she said.

"An ideal location!" he replied. "A perfect place! And I will tell you *why* it's a perfect place," he continued, majestically. "If an enemy—a fox or a coon or a coyote or a skunk—wanted to reach this spot with murder in his heart, he'd have to enter the water and get wet. And before he could enter the water, he'd have to walk the whole length of that point of land. And by that time we'd see him or hear him, and I would give him a hard time."

The male stretched out his great wings, eight feet from tip to tip, and gave the water a mighty clout to show his strength. This made him feel better right away. When a Trumpeter Swan hits an enemy with his wing, it is like being hit by a baseball bat. A male swan, by the way, is called a "cob." No one knows why, but that's what he's called. A good many animals have special names: a male goose is called a gander, a male cow is called a bull, a male sheep is called a ram, a male chicken is called a rooster, and so on. Anyway, the thing to remember is that a male swan is called a cob.

The cob's wife pretended not to notice that her husband was showing off, but she saw it, all right, and she was proud of his strength and his courage. As husbands go, he was a good one.

The cob watched his beautiful wife sitting there on the tiny island. To his great joy, he saw her begin to turn slowly round and around, keeping always in the same spot, treading the mud and grass. She was making the first motions of nesting. First she squatted down in the place she had chosen. Then she twisted round and around, tamping the earth with her broad webbed feet, hollowing it out to make it like a saucer. Then she reached out and pulled twigs and grasses toward her and dropped them at her sides and under her tail, shaping the nest to her body.

The cob floated close to his mate. He studied every move she made.

"Now another medium-sized stick, my love," he said. And she poked her splendid long white graceful neck as far as it would go, picked up a stick, and placed it at her side.

"Now another bit of coarse grass," said the cob, with great dignity.

The female reached for grasses, for moss, for twigs—anything that was handy. Slowly, carefully, she built up the nest until she was sitting on a big grassy mound. She worked at the task for a couple of hours, then knocked off for the day and slid into the pond again, to take a drink and have lunch.

"A fine start!" said the cob, as he gazed back at the nest. "A perfect beginning! I don't know how you manage it so cleverly."

"It comes naturally," replied his wife. "There's a lot of work to it, but on the whole it is pleasant work."

"Yes," said the cob. "And when you're done, you

have something to show for your trouble—you have a swan's nest, six feet across. What other bird can say that?"

"Well," said his wife, "maybe an eagle can say it."

"Yes, but in that case it wouldn't be a swan's nest, it would be an eagle's nest, and it would be high up in some old dead tree somewhere, instead of right down near the water, with all the conveniences that go with water."

They both laughed at this. Then they began trumpeting and splashing and scooping up water and throwing it on their backs, darting about as though they had suddenly gone crazy with delight.

"Ko-hoh! Ko-hoh! Ko-hoh!" they cried.

Every wild creature within a mile and a half of the pond heard the trumpeting of the swans. The fox heard, the raccoon heard, the skunk heard. One pair of ears heard that did not belong to a wild creature. But the swans did not know that.

Chapter 3

A Visitor

ONE DAY, almost a week later, the swan slipped quietly into her nest and laid an egg. Each day she tried to deposit one egg in the nest. Sometimes she succeeded, sometimes she didn't. There were now three eggs, and she was ready to lay a fourth.

As she sat there, with her husband, the cob, floating gracefully nearby, she had a strange feeling that she was being watched. It made her uneasy. Birds don't like to be stared at. They particularly dislike being stared at when they are on a nest. So the swan twisted and turned and peered everywhere. She gazed intently at the point of land that jutted out into the pond near the nest. With her sharp eyes, she searched the nearby shore for signs of an intruder. What she finally saw gave her the surprise of her life. There, seated on a log on the point of land, was a small boy. He was being very quiet, and he had no gun.

"Do you see what I see?" the swan whispered to her husband.

"No. What?"

"Over there. On that log. It's a boy! *Now* what are we going to do?"

"How did a boy get here?" whispered the cob. "We are deep in the wilds of Canada. There are no human beings for miles around."

"That's what I thought too," she replied. "But if that isn't a boy over there on that log, my name isn't Cygnus Buccinator."

The cob was furious. "I didn't fly all the way north into Canada to get involved with a *boy*," he said. "We came here to this idyllic spot, this remote little hideaway, so we could enjoy some well-deserved privacy."

"Well," said his wife, "I'm sorry to see the boy, too, but I must say he's behaving himself. He sees us, but he's not throwing stones. He's not throwing sticks. He's not messing around. He's simply observing."

"I do not *wish* to be observed," complained the cob. "I did not travel all this immense distance into the heart of Canada to be observed. Furthermore, I don't want *you* to be observed—except by me. You're laying an egg—that is, I *hope* you are—and you are entitled to privacy. It has been my experience that all boys throw stones and sticks—it is their nature. I'm going over and strike that boy with my powerful wing, and he'll think he has been hit with a billy club. I'll knock him cold!"

"Now, just wait a minute!" said the swan. "There's no use starting a fight. This boy is not bothering me at the moment. He's not bothering you either."

"But how did he *get* here?" said the cob, who was no longer talking in a whisper but was beginning to shout. "How did he get here? Boys can't fly, and there are no roads in this part of Canada. We're fifty miles from the nearest highway."

"Maybe he's lost," said the swan. "Maybe he's starving to death. Maybe he wants to rob the nest and eat the eggs, but I doubt it. He doesn't look hungry. Anyway, I've started this nest, and I have three beautiful eggs, and the boy's behaving himself at the moment, and I intend to go right ahead and try for a fourth egg."

"Good luck, my love!" said the cob. "I shall be here at your side to defend you if anything happens. Lay the egg!"

For the next hour, the cob paddled slowly round and around the tiny island, keeping watch. His wife remained quietly on the nest. Sam sat on his log, hardly moving a muscle. He was spellbound at the sight of the swans. They were the biggest water birds he had ever seen. He had heard their trumpeting and had searched the woods and swamps until he had found the pond and located the nest. Sam knew enough about birds to know that these were Trumpeters. Sam always felt happy when he was in a wild place among wild creatures.

Sitting on his log, watching the swans, he had the same good feeling some people get when they are sitting in church.

After he had watched for an hour, Sam got up. He walked slowly and quietly away, putting one foot straight ahead of the other, Indian-fashion, hardly making a sound. The swans watched him go. When the female left the nest, she turned and looked back. There, lying safely in the soft feathers at the bottom of the nest, was the fourth egg. The cob waddled out on to the island and looked in the nest.

"A masterpiece!" he said. "An egg of supreme beauty and perfect proportions. I would say that that egg is almost five inches in length."

His wife was pleased.

When the swan had laid five eggs, she felt satisfied. She gazed at them proudly. Then she settled herself on the nest to keep her eggs warm. Carefully, she reached down with her bill and poked each egg until it was in just the right spot to receive the heat from her body. The cob cruised around close by, to keep her company and protect her from enemies. He knew that a fox prowled somewhere in the woods; he had heard him barking on nights when the hunting was good.

Days passed, and still the swan sat quietly on the five eggs. Nights passed. She sat and sat, giving her warmth to the eggs. No one disturbed her. The boy was gone—perhaps he would never come back. Inside of each egg, something was happening that she couldn't see: a little swan was taking shape. As the weeks went by, the days grew longer, the nights grew shorter. When a rainy day came, the swan just sat still and let it rain.

"My dear," said her husband, the cob, one afternoon, "do you never find your duties onerous or irksome? Do you never tire of sitting in one place and in one position, covering the eggs, with no diversions, no pleasures, no escapades, or capers? Do you never suffer from boredom?"

"No," replied his wife. "Not really."

"Isn't it uncomfortable to sit on eggs?"

"Yes, it is," replied the wife. "But I can put up with a certain amount of discomfort for the sake of bringing young swans into the world."

"Do you know how many more days you must sit?" he asked.

"Haven't any idea," she said. "But I notice that the ducks at the other end of the pond have hatched their young ones; I notice that the Red-winged Blackbirds have hatched theirs, and the other evening I saw a Striped Skunk hunting along the shore, and she had four little skunks with her. So I think I must be getting near the end of my time. With any luck, we will soon be able to see our children—our beautiful little cygnets."

"Don't you ever feel the pangs of hunger or suffer the tortures of thirst?" asked the cob.

"Yes, I do," said his mate. "As a matter of fact, I could use a drink right now."

The afternoon was warm; the sun was bright. The swan decided she could safely leave her eggs for a few minutes. She stood up. First she pushed some loose feathers around the eggs, hiding them from view and giving them a warm covering in her absence. Then she

stepped off the nest and entered the water. She took several quick drinks. Then she glided over to a shallow place, thrust her head underwater, and pulled up tender greens from the bottom. She next took a bath by tossing water over herself. Then she waddled out on to a grassy bank and stood there, preening her feathers.

The swan felt good. She had no idea that an enemy was near. She failed to notice the Red Fox as he watched her from his hiding place behind a clump of bushes.

The fox had been attracted to the pond by the sound of splashing water. He hoped he would find a goose. Now he sniffed the air and smelled the swan. Her back was turned, so he began creeping slowly toward her. She would be too big for him to carry, but he decided he would kill her anyway and get a taste of blood. The cob, her husband, was still floating on the pond. He spied the fox first.

"Look out!" he trumpeted. "Look out for the fox, who is creeping toward you even as I speak, his eyes bright, his bushy tail out straight, his mind lusting for blood, his belly almost touching the ground! You are in grave danger, and we must act immediately."

While the cob was making this elegant speech of warning, something happened that surprised everybody. Just as the fox was about to spring and sink his teeth in the swan's neck, a stick came hurtling through the air. It struck the fox full on the nose, and he turned and ran away. The two swans couldn't imagine what had happened. Then they noticed a movement in the bushes. Out stepped Sam Beaver, the boy who had visited them a month ago. Sam was grinning. In his hand he held another stick, in case the fox should return. But the fox was in no mood to return. He had a very sore nose, and he had lost his appetite for fresh swan.

"Hello," said Sam in a low voice.

"Ko-hoh, ko-hoh!" replied the cob.

"Ko-hoh!" said his wife. The pond rang with the trumpet sounds—sounds of triumph over the fox, sounds of victory and gladness.

Sam was thrilled at the noise of swans, which some people say is like the sound of a French horn. He walked slowly around the shore to the little point of land near the island and sat down on his log. The swans now realized, beyond any doubt, that the boy was their friend. He had saved the swan's life. He had been in the right place at the right time and with the right ammunition. The swans felt grateful. The cob swam over toward Sam, climbed out of the pond, and stood close to the boy, looking at him in a friendly way and arching his neck gracefully. Once, he ran his neck far out, cautiously, and almost touched the boy. Sam never moved a muscle. His heart thumped from excitement and joy.

The female paddled back to her nest and returned to the job of warming the eggs. She felt lucky to be alive.

That night before Sam crawled into his bunk at camp, he got out his notebook and found a pencil. This is what he wrote:

I don't know of anything in the entire world more wonderful to look at than a nest with eggs in it. An egg, because it contains life, is the most perfect thing there is. It is beautiful and mysterious. An egg is a far finer thing than a tennis ball or a cake of soap. A tennis ball will always be just a tennis ball. A cake of soap will always be just a cake of soap—until it gets so small nobody wants it and they throw it away. But an egg will someday be a living creature. A swan's egg will open and out will come a little swan. A nest is almost as wonderful and mysterious as an egg. How does a bird know how to make a nest? Nobody ever taught her. How does a bird know how to build a nest?

Sam closed his notebook, said good night to his father, blew out his lamp, and climbed into his bunk. He lay there wondering how a bird knows how to build a nest. Pretty soon his eyes closed, and he was asleep.

Chapter 4
The Cygnets

DURING THE night, the swan thought she heard a pipping sound from the eggs. And in the hour just before dawn, she was sure she felt a slight movement under her breast, as though a tiny body were wiggling there. Perhaps the eggs at last were hatching. Eggs, of course, can't wiggle, so the swan decided she must have something under her that wasn't an egg. She sat perfectly still, listening and waiting. The cob floated nearby, keeping watch.

A little swan enclosed in an egg has a hard time getting out. It never *would* get out if Nature had not provided it with two important things: a powerful neck-muscle and a small dagger-tooth on the tip of its bill. This tooth is sharp, and the baby swan uses it to pick a hole in the tough shell of the egg. Once the hole is made, the rest is easy. The cygnet can breathe now; it just keeps wiggling until it wiggles free.

The cob was expecting to become a father any

minute now. The idea of fatherhood made him feel poetical and proud. He began to talk to his wife.

"Here I glide, swanlike," he said, "while earth is bathed in wonder and beauty. Now, slowly, the light of day comes into our sky. A mist hangs low over the pond. The mist rises slowly, like steam from a kettle, while I glide, swanlike, while eggs hatch, while young swans come into existence. I glide and glide. The light strengthens. The air becomes warmer. Gradually the mist disappears. I glide, I glide, swanlike. Birds sing their early song. Frogs that have croaked in the night stop croaking and are silent. Still I glide, ceaselessly, like a swan."

"Of course you glide like a swan," said his wife. "How else could you glide? You couldn't glide like a moose, could you?"

"Well, no. That is quite true. Thank you, my dear, for correcting me." The cob felt taken aback by his mate's commonsense remark. He enjoyed speaking in fancy phrases and graceful language, and he liked to think of himself as gliding swanlike. He decided he'd better do more gliding and less talking.

All morning long, the swan heard the pipping of the shells. And every once in a while, she felt something wriggle beneath her in the nest. It was an odd sensation. The eggs had been quiet for so many, many days—thirty-five days in all—and now at last they were stirring with life. She knew that the proper thing to do was to sit still.

Late in the afternoon, the swan was rewarded for her patience. She gazed down, and there, pushing her feathers aside, came a tiny head—the first baby, the first cygnet. It was soft and downy. Unlike its parents, it was grey. Its feet and legs were the colour of mustard. Its eyes were bright. On unsteady legs, it pushed its way up until it stood beside its mother, looking around at the world it was seeing for the first time. Its mother spoke softly to it, and it was glad to hear her voice. It was glad to breathe the air, after being cooped up so long inside an egg.

The cob, who had been watching intently all day, saw the little head appear. His heart leapt up with joy. "A cygnet!" he cried. "A cygnet at last! I am a father, with all the pleasant duties and awesome responsibilities of fatherhood. O blessed little son of mine, how good it is to see your face peering through the protecting feathers of your mother's breast, under these fair skies, with the pond so quiet and peaceful in the long light of afternoon!"

"What makes you think it's a son?" inquired his wife. "For all you know, it's a daughter. Anyway, it's a cygnet, and it's alive and healthy. I can feel others under me, too. Perhaps we'll get a good hatch. We may even get all five. We'll know by tomorrow."

"I have every confidence that we will," said the cob.

Next morning very early, Sam Beaver crawled out of his bunk while his father was still asleep. Sam dressed and lit a fire in the stove. He fried a few strips of bacon, toasted two slices of bread, poured a glass of milk, and sat down and ate breakfast. When he was through, he found a pencil and paper and wrote a note.

I have gone for a walk. Will be back for lunch.

Sam left the note where his father would find it; then he took his field glasses and his compass, fastened his hunting knife to his belt, and set out through the woods and over the swamp to the pond where the swans lived.

He approached the pond cautiously, his field glasses slung over his shoulder. It was still only a little after seven o'clock; the sun was pale, the air was chill. The morning smelled delicious. When he reached his log, Sam sat down and adjusted his glasses. Seen through the glasses, the nesting swan appeared to be only a few feet away. She was sitting very close, not moving. The cob was nearby. Both birds were listening and waiting. Both birds saw Sam, but they didn't mind his being there—in fact, they rather liked it. They *were* surprised at the field glasses, though.

"The boy seems to have very big eyes today," whispered the cob. "His eyes are enormous."

"I think those big eyes are actually a pair of field glasses," replied the swan. "I'm not sure, but I think that when a person looks through field glasses, everything appears closer and bigger."

"Will the boy's glasses make me appear even larger than I am?" asked the cob, hopefully.

"I think so," said the swan.

"Oh, well, I *like* that," said the cob. "I like that very much. Perhaps the boy's glasses will make me appear not only larger than I am but even more graceful than I am. Do you think so?"

"It's possible," said his wife, "but it's not likely. You'd better not get *too* graceful—it might go to your head. You're quite a vain bird."

"All swans are vain," said the cob. "It is right for swans to feel proud, graceful—that's what swans are for."

Sam could not make out what the swans were saying; he merely knew they were having a conversation, and just hearing them talk stirred his blood. It satisfied him to be keeping company with these two great birds in the wilderness. He was perfectly happy.

In midmorning, when the sun had gained the sky, Sam lifted his glasses again and focused them on the nest. At last he saw what he had come to see: a tiny head, thrusting through the mother's feathers, the head of a baby Trumpeter. The youngster scrambled up on to the edge of the nest. Sam could see its grey head and neck, its body covered with soft down, its yellow legs and feet with their webs for swimming. Soon another cygnet appeared. Then another. Then the first one worked his way down into his mother's feathers again, for warmth. Then one tried to climb up his mother's back, but her feathers were slippery, and he slid off and settled himself neatly at her side. The swan just sat and sat, enjoying her babies, watching them gain the use of their legs.

An hour went by. One of the cygnets, more daring than the others, left the nest and teetered around on the shore of the little island. When this happened, the mother swan stood up. She decided the time had come to lead her children into the water.

"Come on!" she said. "And stay together! Note carefully what I do. Then you do the same. Swimming is easy."

"One, two, three, four, five," Sam counted. "One, two, three, four, five. Five cygnets, just as sure as I'm alive!"

The cob, as he saw his children approach the water, felt that he should act like a father. He began by making a speech.

"Welcome to the pond and the swamp adjacent!" he said. "Welcome to the world that contains this lonely pond, this splendid marsh, unspoiled and wild! Welcome to sunlight and shadow, wind and weather; welcome to water! The water is a swan's particular element, as you will soon discover. Swimming is no problem for a swan. Welcome to danger, which you must guard against—the vile fox with his stealthy tread and sharp teeth, the offensive otter who swims up under you and tries to grab you by the leg, the stinking skunk who hunts by night and blends with the shadows, the coyote who hunts and howls and is bigger than a fox. Beware of lead pellets that lie on the bottom of all ponds, left there by the guns of hunters. Don't eat them—they'll poison you! Be vigilant, be strong, be brave, be graceful, and *always* follow me! I will go first, then you will come along in single file, and your devoted mother will bring up the rear. Enter the water quietly and confidently!"

The mother swan, glad the speech was over, stepped into the water and called her little ones. The cygnets gazed for a second at the water, then tottered forward, gave a jump, and were afloat. The water felt good. Swimming was simple—nothing to it. The water was good to drink. Each baby dipped up a mouthful. Their happy father arched his long graceful neck over and around them, protectively. Then he set off very slowly, with the cygnets following along in single file. Their mother brought up the rear.

"What a sight!" Sam said to himself. "What a terrific sight! Seven Trumpeters all in line, five of them just out of the egg. This is my lucky day." He hardly noticed how stiff he had become from sitting so long on the log.

Like all fathers, the cob wanted to show off his children to somebody. So he led the cygnets to where Sam was. They all stepped out of the water and stood in front of the boy—all but the mother swan. She stayed behind.

"Ko-hoh!" said the cob.

"Hello!" said Sam, who hadn't expected anything like this and hardly dared breathe.

The first cygnet looked at Sam and said, "Beep." The second cygnet looked at Sam and said, "Beep." The third cygnet greeted Sam the same way. So did the fourth. The fifth cygnet was different. He opened his mouth but didn't say a thing. He made an effort to say beep, but no sound came. So instead, he stuck his little neck out, took hold of one of Sam's shoelaces, and gave it a pull. He tugged at the lace for a moment. It came untied. Then he let it go. It was like a greeting. Sam grinned.

The cob now looked worried. He ran his long white neck between the cygnets and the boy and guided the babies back to the water and to their mother.

"Follow me!" said the cob. And he led them off, full of grace and bursting with pride.

When the mother thought her young ones had had enough swimming and might be chilly, she stepped out on to a sandy shore and squatted down and called them. They quickly followed her out of the pond and burrowed down under her feathers to get warm. In a moment there wasn't a cygnet in sight.

At noon, Sam got up and walked back to camp, his mind full of what he had seen. Next day, he and his father heard Shorty's motor in the sky and saw the plane approaching. They grabbed their duffel bags. "Good-bye, camp! See you in the fall!" said Mr. Beaver, as he shut the door and gave it a pat. He and Sam climbed into the plane and were soon aloft, on their way home to Montana. Mr. Beaver did not know that his son had seen a Trumpeter Swan bring off her young ones. Sam kept the matter to himself.

"If I live to be a hundred years old," thought Sam, "I'll never forget what it feels like to have my shoelace pulled by a baby swan."

Sam and his father were late arriving home at the ranch, but late as it was, Sam got out his diary before he turned in for the night. He wrote:

> There are five cygnets. They are sort of a dirty brownish-grey colour, but very cute. Their legs are yellow, like mustard. The old cob led them right up to me. I wasn't expecting this, but I kept very still. Four of the babies said beep. The fifth one tried to, but he couldn't. He took hold of my shoelace as though it was a worm and gave it a tug and untied it. I wonder what I'm going to be when I grow up?

He switched off the light, pulled the sheet up over his head, and fell asleep wondering what he was going to be when he grew up.

Chapter 5

Louis

ONE EVENING a few weeks later, when the cygnets were asleep, the swan said to the cob, "Have you noticed anything different about one of our children, the one we call Louis?"

"Different?" replied the cob. "In what way is Louis different from his brothers and sisters? Louis looks all right to me. He is growing well; he swims and dives beautifully. He eats well. He will soon have his flight feathers."

"Oh, he *looks* all right," said the swan. "And heaven knows he eats enough. He's healthy and bright and a great swimmer. But have you ever heard Louis make any sound, as the others do? Have you ever heard him use his voice or say anything? Have you ever heard him utter a single beep or a single burble?"

"Come to think of it, I never have," replied the cob, who was beginning to look worried.

"Have you ever heard Louis say good night to us, as the others do? Have you ever heard him say good morning, as the others do in their charming little way, burbling and beeping?"

"Now that you mention it, I never have," said the cob. "Goodness! What are you getting at? Do you wish me to believe that I have a son who is *defective* in any way? Such a revelation would distress me greatly. I want everything to go smoothly in my family life so that I can glide gracefully and serenely, now in the prime of my life, without being haunted by worry or disappointment. Fatherhood is quite a burden, at best. I do not want the added strain of having a defective child, a child that has something the matter with him."

"Well," said the wife, "I've been watching Louis lately. It is my opinion the little fellow can't talk. I've never heard him make one sound. I think he came into the world lacking a voice. If he had a voice, he'd use it, same as the others do."

"Why, this is terrible!" said the cob. "This is distressing beyond words. This is a very serious matter."

His wife looked at him in amusement. "It's not too serious now," she said. "But it *will* be serious two or three years from now when Louis falls in love, as he will surely do. A young male swan will be greatly handicapped in finding a mate if he is unable to say ko-hoh, ko-hoh, or if he can't utter the usual endearments to the young female of his choice."

"Are you sure?" asked the cob.

"Certainly I'm sure," she replied. "I can remember perfectly well the springtime, years ago, when you fell in love with me and began chasing after me. What a sight you were, and what a lot of noise you made! It was in Montana, remember?"

"Of course I remember," said the cob.

"Well, the thing that attracted me most to you was your voice—your wonderful voice."

"It *was*?" said the cob.

"Yes. You had the finest, most powerful, most resonant voice of any of the young male swans in the Red Rock Lakes National Wildlife Refuge in Montana."

"I *did*?" said the cob.

"Yes, indeed. Every time I heard you say something in that deep voice of yours, I was ready to go anywhere with you."

"You *were*?" said the cob. He was obviously delighted with his wife's praise. It tickled his vanity and made him feel great. He had always fancied himself as having a fine voice, and now to hear it from his wife's own lips was a real thrill. In the pleasure of the moment, he forgot all about Louis and thought entirely of himself. And, of course, he did remember that enchanted springtime on the lake in Montana when he had fallen in love. He remembered how pretty the swan had been, how young and innocent she seemed, how attractive, how desirable. Now he realized fully that he would

229

never have been able to woo her and win her if he had been unable to *say* anything.

"We'll not worry about Louis for the time being," said the swan. "He's still very young. But we must watch him next winter when we are in Montana for the season. We must stay together as a family until we see how Louis makes out."

She walked over to where her sleeping cygnets were and settled down next to them. The night was chill. Carefully, she lifted one wing and covered the cygnets with it. They stirred in their sleep and drew close to her.

The cob stood quietly, thinking about what his wife had just told him. He was a brave, noble bird, and already he was beginning to work out a plan for his little son Louis.

"If it's really true that Louis has no voice," said the cob to himself, "then I shall provide him with a device of some sort, to enable him to make a lot of noise. There must be *some* way out of this difficulty. After all, my son is a Trumpeter Swan; he should have a voice like a trumpet. But first I will test him to make certain that what his mother says is true."

The cob was unable to sleep that night. He stood on one leg, quietly, but sleep never came. Next morning, after everyone had enjoyed a good breakfast, he led Louis apart from the others.

"Louis," he said, "I wish to speak to you alone. Let's just you and I take a swim by ourselves to the other end of the pond, where we can talk privately without being interrupted."

Louis was surprised by this. But he nodded his head and followed his father, swimming strongly in his wake. He did not understand why his father wanted to speak to him alone, without his brothers and sisters.

"Now!" said the cob, when they reached the upper end of the pond. "Here we are, gracefully floating, supremely buoyant, at some distance from the others, in perfect surroundings—a fine morning, with the pond quiet except for the song of the blackbirds, making the air sweet."

"I wish my father would get to the point," thought Louis.

"This is an ideal place for our conference," continued the cob. "There is something I feel I should discuss with you very candidly and openly—something that concerns your future. We need not range over the whole spectrum of bird life but just confine our talk to the one essential thing that is before us on this unusual occasion."

"Oh, I *wish* my father would get to the point," thought Louis, who by this time was getting very nervous.

"It has come to my attention, Louis," continued the

cob, "that you rarely *say* anything. In fact, I can't recall ever hearing you utter a sound. I have never heard you speak, or say ko-hoh, or cry out, either in fear or in joy. This is most unusual for a young Trumpeter. It is serious. Louis, let me hear you say beep. Go ahead, say it! Say beep!"

Poor Louis! While his father watched, he took a deep breath, opened his mouth, and let the air out, hoping it would say beep. But there wasn't a sound.

"Try again, Louis!" said his father. "Perhaps you're not making enough of an effort."

Louis tried again. It was no use. No sound came from his throat. He shook his head, sadly.

"Watch me!" said the cob. He raised his neck to its full height and cried ko-hoh so loud it was heard by every creature for miles around.

"Now let me hear you go beep!" he commanded. "Say beep, Louis—loud and clear!"

Louis tried. He couldn't beep.

"Let me hear you burble! Go ahead and burble! Like this: burble, burble, burble."

Louis tried to burble. He couldn't do it. No sound came.

"Well," said the cob, "I guess it's no use. I guess you are dumb."

When he heard the word "dumb," Louis felt like crying. The cob saw that he had hurt Louis's feelings.

"You misunderstand me, my son," he said in a comforting voice. "You failed to understand my use of the word 'dumb,' which has two meanings. If I had called you a dumb cluck or a dumb bunny, that would have meant that I had a poor opinion of your intelligence. Actually, I think you are perhaps the brightest, smartest, most intelligent of all my cygnets. Words sometimes have two meanings; the word 'dumb' is such a word. A person who can't see is called blind. A person who can't hear is called deaf. A person who can't speak is called dumb. That simply means he can't say anything. Do you understand?"

Louis nodded his head. He felt better, and he was grateful to his father for explaining that the word had two meanings. He still felt awfully unhappy, though.

"Do not let an unnatural sadness settle over you, Louis," said the cob. "Swans must be cheerful, not sad; graceful, not awkward; brave, not cowardly. Remember that the world is full of youngsters who have some sort of handicap that they must overcome. *You* apparently have a speech defect. I am sure you will overcome it, in time. There may even be some slight advantage, at your age, in not being able to say anything. It compels you to be a good listener. The world is full of talkers, but it is rare to find anyone who listens. And I assure you that you can pick up more information when you are listening than when you are talking."

"My father does quite a lot of talking himself," thought Louis.

"Some people," continued the cob, "go through life chattering and making a lot of noise with their mouth; they never really *listen* to anything—they are too busy expressing their opinions, which are often unsound or based on bad information. Therefore, my son, be of good cheer! Enjoy life; learn to fly! Eat well; drink well! Use your ears; use your eyes! And I promise that someday I will make it possible for you to use your voice. There are mechanical devices that convert air into beautiful sounds. One such device is called a trumpet. I saw a trumpet once, in my travels. I think you may need a trumpet in order to live a full life. I've never *known* a Trumpeter Swan to need a trumpet, but your case is different. I intend to get you what you need. I don't know how I will manage this, but in the fullness of time it shall be accomplished. And now that our talk has come to a close, let us return gracefully to the other end of the pond, where your mother and your brothers and sisters await us!"

The cob turned and swam off. Louis followed. It had been an unhappy morning for him. He felt frightened at being different from his brothers and sisters. It scared him to be different. He couldn't understand why he had come into the world without a voice. Everyone else seemed to have a voice. Why didn't he? "Fate is cruel," he thought. "Fate is cruel to me." Then he remembered that his father had promised to help, and he felt better. Soon they joined the others, and everyone started water games, and Louis joined in, dipping and splashing and diving and twisting. Louis could splash water farther than any of the others, but he couldn't shout while he was doing it. To be able to shout while you are splashing water is half the fun.

Chapter 6

Off to Montana

A T THF end of the summer, the cob gathered his family around him and made an announcement.

"Children," he began, "I have news for you. Summer is drawing to a close. Leaves are turning red, pink, and pale yellow. Soon the leaves will fall. The time has come for us to leave this pond. The time has come for us to go."

"Go?" cried all the cygnets except Louis.

"Certainly," replied their father. "You children are old enough to learn the facts of life, and the principal fact of our life right now is this: we can't stay in this marvellous location much longer."

"Why not?" cried all the cygnets except Louis.

"Because summer is over," said the cob, "and it is the way of swans to leave their nesting site at summer's end and travel south to a milder place where the food supply is good. I know that you are all fond of this pretty pond, this marvellous marsh, these reedy shores and restful retreats. You have found life pleasant and amusing here.

You have learned to dive and swim underwater. You have enjoyed our daily recreational trips when we formed in line, myself in front swimming gracefully, like a locomotive, and your charming mother bringing up the rear, like a caboose. Daylong, you have listened and learned. You have avoided the odious otter and the cruel coyote. You have listened to the little owl that says co-co-co-co. You have heard the partridge say kwit-kwit. At night you have dropped off to sleep to the sound of frogs—the voices of the night. But these pleasures and pastimes, these adventures, these games and frolics, these beloved sights and sounds must come to an end. All things come to an end. It is time for us to go."

"Where will we go?" cried all the cygnets except Louis. "Where will we go, ko-hoh, ko-hoh? Where will we go, ko-hoh, ko-hoh?"

"We will fly south to Montana," replied the cob.

"What is Montana?" asked all the cygnets except Louis. "What is Montana—banana, banana? What is Montana—banana, banana?"

"Montana," said their father, "is a state of the Union. And there, in a lovely valley surrounded by high mountains, are the Red Rock Lakes, which nature has designed especially for swans. In these lakes you will enjoy warm water, arising from hidden springs. Here, ice never forms, no matter how cold the nights. In the Red Rock Lakes, you will find other Trumpeter Swans, as well as the lesser waterfowl—the geese and the ducks. There are few enemies. No gunners. Plenty of muskrat houses. Free grain. Games every day. What more can a swan ask, in the long, long cold of winter?"

Louis listened to all this in amazement. He wanted to ask his father how they would learn to fly and how they would find Montana even after they learned to fly. He began to worry about getting lost. But he wasn't able to ask any questions. He just had to listen.

One of his brothers spoke up.

"Father," he said, "you said we would *fly* south. I don't know *how* to fly. I've never been up in the air."

"True," replied the cob. "But flying is largely a matter of having the right attitude—plus, of course, good wing feathers. Flying consists of three parts. First, the takeoff, during which there is a lot of fuss and commotion, a lot of splashing and rapid beating of the wings. Second, the ascent, or gaining of altitude—this requires hard work and fast wing action. Third, the levelling-off, the steady elevated flight, high in air, wings beating slower now, beating strongly and regularly, carrying us swiftly and surely from zone to zone as we cry ko-hoh, ko-hoh, with all the earth stretched out far below."

"It sounds very nice," said the cygnet, "but I'm not

sure I can do it. I might get dizzy way up there—if I look down."

"Don't *look* down!" said his father. "Look straight ahead. And don't lose your nerve. Besides, swans do not get dizzy—they feel wonderful in the air. They feel exalted."

"What does 'exalted' mean?" asked the cygnet.

"It means you will feel strong, glad, firm, high, proud, successful, satisfied, powerful, and elevated—as though you had conquered life and had a high purpose."

Louis listened to all this with great attention. The idea of flying frightened him. "I won't be able to say ko-hoh," he thought. "I wonder whether a swan can fly if he has no voice and can't say ko-hoh."

"I think," said the cob, "the best plan is for me to demonstrate flying to you. I will make a short exhibition flight while you watch. Observe everything I do! Watch me pump my neck up and down before the takeoff! Watch me test the wind by turning my head this way and that! The takeoff must be *into* the wind— it's much easier that way. Listen to the noise I make trumpeting! Watch how I raise my great wings! See how I beat them furiously as I rush through the water with my feet going like mad! This frenzy will last for a couple of hundred feet, at which point I will suddenly be airborne, my wings still chopping the air with terrific force but my feet no longer touching the water!

Then watch what I do! Watch how I stretch my long white elegant neck out ahead of me until it has reached its full length! Watch how I retract my feet and allow them to stream out behind, full-length, until they extend beyond my tail! Hear my cries as I gain the upper air and start trumpeting! See how strong and steady my wingbeat has become! Then watch me bank and turn, set my wings, and glide down! And just as I reach the pond again, watch how I shoot my feet out in front of me and use them for the splashdown, as though they were a pair of water skis! Having watched all this, then you can join me, and your mother, too, and we will all make a practice flight together, until you get the hang of it. Then tomorrow we will do it again, and instead of returning to the pond, we will head south to Montana. Are you ready for my exhibition flight?"

"Ready!" cried all the cygnets except Louis.

"Very well, here I go!" cried the cob.

As the others watched, he swam downwind to the end of the pond, turned, tested the wind, pumped his neck up and down, trumpeted, and after a rush of two hundred feet, got into the air and began gaining altitude. His long white neck stretched out ahead. His big black feet stretched out behind. His wings had great power. The beat slowed as he settled into sustained flight. All eyes watched. Louis was more excited than he had ever been. "I wonder if I can really do it?" he thought. "Suppose I fail! Then the others will fly away, and I will be left here all alone on this deserted pond, with winter approaching, with no father, no mother, no sisters, no brothers, and no food to eat when the pond freezes over. I will die of starvation. I'm scared."

In a few minutes, the cob glided down out of the sky and skidded to a stop on the pond. They all cheered. "Ko-hoh, ko-hoh, beep beep, beep beep!" All but Louis. He had to express his approval simply by beating his wings and splashing water in his father's face.

"All right," said the cob. "You've seen how it's done. Follow me, and we'll give it a try. Extend yourselves to the utmost, do everything in the proper order, never forget for a minute that you are swans and therefore excellent fliers, and I'm sure all will be well."

They all swam downwind to the end of the pond. They pumped their necks up and down. Louis pumped his harder than any of the others. They tested the wind by turning their heads this way and that. Suddenly the cob signalled for the start. There was a tremendous commotion—wings beating, feet racing, water churned to a froth. And presently, wonder of wonders, there were seven swans in the air—two pure white ones and five dirty grey ones. The takeoff was accomplished, and they started gaining altitude.

Louis was the first of the young cygnets to become airborne, ahead of all his brothers and sisters. The minute his feet lifted clear of the water, he knew he could fly. It was a tremendous relief—as well as a splendid sensation.

"Boy!" he said to himself. "I never knew flying could be such fun. This is great. This is sensational. This is superb. I feel exalted, and I'm not dizzy. I'll be able

to get to Montana with the rest of the family. I may be defective, but at least I can fly."

The seven great birds stayed aloft about half an hour, then returned to the pond, the cob still in the lead. They all had a drink to celebrate the successful flight. Next day they were up early. It was a beautiful fall morning, with mist rising from the pond and the trees shining in all colours. Toward the end of the afternoon, as the sun sank low in the sky, the swans took off from the pond and began their journey to Montana. "This way!" cried the cob. He swung to his left and straightened out on a southerly course. The others followed, trumpeting as they went. As they passed over the camp where Sam

Beaver was, Sam heard them and ran out. He stood watching as they grew smaller and smaller in the distance and finally disappeared.

"What was it?" asked his father, when Sam returned indoors.

"Swans," replied Sam. "They're headed south."

"We'd better do the same," said Mr. Beaver. "I think Shorty will be here tomorrow to take us out."

Mr. Beaver lay down on his bunk. "What kind of swans were they?" he asked.

"Trumpeters," said Sam.

"That's funny," said Mr. Beaver. "I thought Trumpeter Swans had quit migrating. I thought they spent the whole year on the Red Rock Lakes, where they are protected."

"Most of 'em do," replied Sam. "But not all of 'em."

It was bedtime. Sam got out his diary. This is what he wrote:

I heard the swans tonight. They are headed south. It must be wonderful to fly at night. I wonder whether I'll ever see one of them again. How does a bird know how to get from where he is to where he wants to be?

Chapter 7

School Days

A FEW DAYS after the swans arrived at their winter home on the Red Rock Lakes, Louis had an idea. He decided that since he was unable to use his voice, he should learn to read and write. "If I'm defective in one respect," he said to himself, "I should try and develop myself along other lines. I will learn to read and write. Then I will hang a small slate around my neck and carry a chalk pencil. In that way I will be able to communicate with anybody who can read."

Louis liked company, and he already had many friends on the lakes. The place was a refuge for water birds—swans, geese, ducks, and other waterfowl. They lived there because it was a safe place and because the water stayed warm even in the coldest winter weather. Louis was greatly admired for his ability as a swimmer. He liked to compete with other cygnets to see who could swim underwater the greatest distance and stay down the longest.

When Louis had fully made up his mind about

learning to read and write, he decided to visit Sam Beaver and get help from him. "Perhaps," thought Louis, "Sam will let me go to school with him, and the teacher will show me how to write." The idea excited him. He wondered whether a young swan would be accepted in a classroom of children. He wondered whether it was hard to learn to read. Most of all, he wondered whether he could find Sam. Montana is a big state, and he wasn't even sure Sam lived in Montana, but he hoped he did.

Next morning, when his parents were not looking, Louis took off into the air. He flew northeast. When he came to the Yellowstone River, he followed it to the Sweet Grass country. When he saw a town beneath him, he landed next to the schoolhouse and waited for the boys and girls to be let out. Louis looked at every boy, hoping to see Sam. But Sam wasn't there.

"Wrong town, wrong school," thought Louis. "I'll try again." He flew off, found another town, and located the school, but all the boys and girls had gone home for the day.

"I'll just have a look around anyway," thought Louis. He didn't dare walk down the main street, for fear somebody would shoot him. Instead, he took to the air and circled around, flying low and looking carefully at every boy in sight. After about ten minutes, he saw a ranch house where a boy was splitting wood near the kitchen door. The boy had black hair. Louis glided down.

"I'm lucky," he thought. "It's Sam."

When Sam saw the swan, he laid down his axe and stood perfectly still. Louis walked up timidly, then reached down and untied Sam's shoelace.

"Hello!" said Sam in a friendly voice.

Louis tried to say ko-hoh, but not a sound came from his throat.

"I know *you*," said Sam. "You're the one that never said anything and used to pull my shoelaces."

Louis nodded.

"I'm glad to see you," said Sam. "What can I do for you?"

Louis just stared straight ahead.

"Are you hungry?" asked Sam.

Louis shook his head.

"Thirsty?"

Louis shook his head.

"Do you want to stay overnight with us, here at the ranch?" asked Sam.

Louis nodded his head and jumped up and down.

"O.K.," said Sam. "We have plenty of room. It's just a question of getting my father's permission."

Sam picked up his axe, laid a stick of wood on the chopping block, and split the stick neatly down the middle. He looked at Louis.

"There's something wrong with your voice, isn't there?" he asked.

Louis nodded, pumping his neck up and down hard. He knew Sam was his friend, although he didn't know that Sam had once saved his mother's life.

In a few minutes Mr. Beaver rode into the yard on a cow pony. He got off and tied his pony to a rail. "What have you got there?" he asked Sam.

"It's a young Trumpeter Swan," said Sam. "He's only a few months old. Will you let me keep him awhile?"

"Well," said Mr. Beaver, "I think it's against the law to hold one of these wild birds in captivity. But I'll phone the game warden and see what he says. If he says yes, you can keep him."

"Tell the warden the swan has something the matter with him," called Sam as his father started toward the house.

"What's wrong with him?" asked his father.

"He has a speech problem," replied Sam. "Something's wrong with his throat."

"What are you talking about? Who ever heard of a swan with a speech problem?"

"Well," said Sam, "this is a Trumpeter Swan that can't trumpet. He's defective. He can't make a sound."

Mr. Beaver looked at his son as though he didn't know whether to believe him or not. But he went into the house. In a few minutes he came back. "The warden says you can keep the young swan here for a while if you can help him. But sooner or later the bird will have to go back to the Red Rock Lakes, where he belongs. The warden said he wouldn't let just *anybody* have a young swan, but he'd let *you* have one because you understand about birds, and he trusts you. That's quite a compliment, son."

Mr. Beaver looked pleased. Sam looked happy. Louis was greatly relieved. After a while everyone went in to supper in the kitchen of the ranch house. Mrs. Beaver allowed Louis to stand beside Sam's chair. They fed him some corn and some oats, which tasted good. When Sam was ready for bed, he wanted Louis to sleep in his room with him, but Mrs. Beaver said no. "He'll mess up the room. He's no canary; he's enormous. Put the bird out in the barn. He can sleep in one of the empty stalls; the horses won't mind."

Next morning, Sam took Louis to school with him. Sam rode his pony, and Louis flew along. At the schoolhouse, the other children were amazed to see this great bird, with his long neck, bright eyes, and big feet. Sam introduced him to the teacher of the first grade, Mrs. Hammerbotham, who was short and fat. Sam explained that Louis wanted to read and write because he was unable to make any sound with his throat.

Mrs. Hammerbotham stared at Louis. Then she shook her head. "No birds!" she said. "I've got enough trouble."

Sam looked disappointed.

"Please, Mrs. Hammerbotham," he said. "Please let him stand in your class and learn to read and write."

"Why does a bird need to read and write?" replied the teacher. "Only *people* need to communicate with one another."

"That's not quite true, Mrs. Hammerbotham," said Sam, "if you'll excuse me for saying so. I have watched birds and animals a great deal. All birds and animals talk to one another—they really have to, in order to get along. Mothers have to talk to their young. Males have to talk to females, particularly in the spring of the year when they are in love."

"In *love*?" said Mrs. Hammerbotham, who seemed to perk up at this suggestion. "What do *you* know about love?"

Sam blushed.

"What kind of a bird *is* he?" she asked.

"He's a young Trumpeter Swan," said Sam. "Right now he's sort of a dirty grey colour, but in another year he'll be the most beautiful thing you ever saw—pure white, with black bill and black feet. He was hatched last spring in Canada and now lives in the Red Rock Lakes, but he can't say ko-hoh the way the other swans can, and this puts him at a terrible disadvantage."

"Why?" asked the teacher.

"Because it does," said Sam. "If *you* wanted to say ko-hoh and couldn't make a single solitary sound, wouldn't *you* feel worried?"

"I don't *want* to say ko-hoh," replied the teacher. "I don't even know what it means. Anyway, this is all just foolishness, Sam. What makes you think a bird can learn to read and write? It's impossible."

"Give him a chance!" pleaded Sam. "He is well behaved, and he's bright, and he's got this very serious speech defect."

"What's his name?"

"I don't know," replied Sam.

"Well," said Mrs. Hammerbotham, "if he's coming into my class, he's got to have a name. Maybe we can find out what it is." She looked at the bird. "Is your name Joe?"

Louis shook his head.

"Jonathan?"

Louis shook his head.

"Donald?"

Louis shook his head again.

"Is your name Louis?" asked Mrs. Hammerbotham.

Louis nodded his head very hard and jumped up and down and flapped his wings.

"Great Caesar's ghost!" cried the teacher. "Look at

those wings! Well, his name is Louis—that's for sure. All right, Louis, you may join the class. Stand right here by the blackboard. And don't mess up the room, either! If you need to go outdoors for any reason, raise one wing."

Louis nodded. The first-graders cheered. They liked the look of the new pupil and were eager to see what he could do.

"Quiet, children!" said Mrs. Hammerbotham sternly. "We'll start with the letter *A*."

She picked up a piece of chalk and made a big **A** on the blackboard. "Now *you* try it, Louis!"

Louis grabbed a piece of chalk in his bill and drew a perfect **A** right under the one the teacher had drawn.

"You see?" said Sam. "He's an unusual bird."

"Well," said Mrs. Hammerbotham, "*A* is easy. I'll give him something harder." She wrote **CAT** on the board. "Let's see you write *cat*, Louis!"

Louis wrote *cat*.

"Well *cat* is easy, too," muttered the teacher. "*Cat* is easy because it is short. Can anyone think of a word that is longer than *cat*?"

"*Catastrophe*," said Charlie Nelson, who sat in the first row.

"Good!" said Mrs. Hammerbotham. "That's a good hard word. But does anyone know what it means? What *is* a catastrophe?"

252

"An earthquake," said one of the girls.

"Correct!" replied the teacher. "What else?"

"War is a catastrophe," said Charlie Nelson.

"Correct!" replied Mrs. Hammerbotham. "What else is?"

A very small, redheaded girl named Jennie raised her hand.

"Yes, Jennie? What is a catastrophe?"

In a very small, high voice, Jennie said, "When you get ready to go on a picnic with your father and mother and you make peanut-butter sandwiches and jelly rolls and put them in a thermos box with bananas and an apple and some raisin cookies and paper napkins and some bottles of pop and a few hard-boiled eggs and then you put the thermos box in your car and just as you are starting out it starts to *rain* and your parents say there is no point in having a picnic in the rain, that's a catastrophe."

"Very good, Jennie," said Mrs. Hammerbotham. "It isn't as bad as an earthquake, and it isn't as bad as war. But when a picnic gets called off on account of rain, it *is* a catastrophe for a child, I guess. Anyway, *catastrophe* is a good word. No bird can write *that* word, I'll bet. If I can teach a bird to write *catastrophe*, it'll be big news all over the Sweet Grass country. I'll get my picture in *Life* magazine. I'll be famous."

Thinking of all these things, she stepped to the

blackboard and wrote **CATASTROPHE**.

"O.K., Louis, let's see you write *that*!"

Louis picked up a fresh piece of chalk in his bill. He was scared. He took a good look at the word. "A long word," he thought, "is really no harder than a short one. I'll just copy one letter at a time, and pretty soon it will be finished. Besides, my life is a catastrophe. It's a catastrophe to be without a voice." Then he began writing. **CATASTROPHE**, he wrote, making

each letter very neatly. When he got to the last letter, the pupils clapped and stamped their feet and banged on their desks, and one boy quickly made a paper aeroplane and zoomed it into the air. Mrs. Hammerbotham rapped for order.

"Very good, Louis," she said. "Sam, it's time you went to your own classroom—you shouldn't be in my room. Go and join the fifth grade. I'll take care of your friend the swan."

Back in his own room, Sam sat down at his desk, feeling very happy about the way things had turned out. The fifth-graders were having a lesson in arithmetic, and their teacher, Miss Annie Snug, greeted Sam with a question. Miss Snug was young and pretty.

"Sam, if a man can walk three miles in one hour, how many miles can he walk in four hours?"

"It would depend on how tired he got after the first hour," replied Sam.

The other pupils roared. Miss Snug rapped for order.

"Sam is quite right," she said. "I never looked at the problem that way before. I always supposed that man could walk twelve miles in four hours, but Sam may be right: that man may not feel so spunky after the first hour. He may drag his feet. He may slow up."

Albert Bigelow raised his hand. "My father knew a man who tried to walk twelve miles, and he died of heart failure," said Albert.

"Goodness!" said the teacher. "I suppose *that* could happen, too."

"Anything can happen in four hours," said Sam. "A man might develop a blister on his heel. Or he might find some berries growing along the road and stop to pick them. That would slow him up even if he wasn't tired or didn't have a blister."

"It would indeed," agreed the teacher. "Well, children, I think we have all learned a great deal about arithmetic this morning, thanks to Sam Beaver. And now, here is a problem for one of the girls in the room. If you are feeding a baby from a bottle, and you give the baby eight ounces of milk in one feeding, how many ounces of milk would the baby drink in *two* feedings?"

Linda Staples raised her hand.

"About fifteen ounces," she said.

"Why is that?" asked Miss Snug. "Why wouldn't the baby drink sixteen ounces?"

"Because he spills a little each time," said Linda. "It runs out of the corners of his mouth and gets on his mother's apron."

By this time the class was howling so loudly the arithmetic lesson had to be abandoned. But everyone had learned how careful you have to be when dealing with figures.

Chapter 8

Love

WHEN LOUIS's father and mother discovered that Louis was missing, they felt awful. No other young swan had disappeared from the lakes—only Louis.

"The question now arises," said the cob to his wife, "whether or not I should go and look for our son. I am disinclined to leave these attractive lakes now, in the fall of the year, with winter coming on. I have, in fact, been looking forward to this time of serenity and peace and the society of other waterfowl. I like the life here."

"There's another little matter to consider besides your personal comfort," said his wife. "Has it occurred to you that we have no idea which direction Louis went when he left? You don't know where he went any more than I do. If you were to start out looking for him, which way would you fly?"

"Well," replied the cob, "in the last analysis, I believe I would go south."

"What do you mean, 'in the last analysis'?" said the swan impatiently. "You haven't analyzed anything. Why do you say 'in the last analysis'? And why do you pick south as the way to go looking for Louis? There are other directions. There's north, and east, and west. There's northeast, southeast, southwest, northwest."

"True," replied the cob. "And there are all those in-between directions: north-northeast, east-southeast, west-southwest. There's north by east, and east by north. There's south-southeast a half east, and there's west by north a half north. The directions a young swan could start off in are almost too numerous to think about."

So it was decided that no search would be made. "We'll just wait here and see what happens," said the cob. "I feel sure Louis will return in the fullness of time."

Months went by. Winter came to the Red Rock Lakes. The nights were long and dark and cold. The days were short and bright and cold. Sometimes the wind blew. But the swans and geese and ducks were safe and happy. The warm springs that fed the lakes kept the ice from covering them—there were always open places. There was plenty of food. Sometimes a man would arrive with a bag of grain and spread the grain where the birds could get it.

Spring followed winter; summer followed spring. A year went by, and it was springtime again. Still no sign of Louis. Then one morning when Louis's grown-up brothers were playing a game of water polo, one of them looked up and saw a swan approaching in the sky.

"Ko-hoh!" cried the cygnet. He rushed to his father and mother. "Look! Look! Look!"

All the waterfowl on the lake turned and gazed up at the approaching swan. The swan circled in the sky.

"It's Louis!" said the cob. "But what is that peculiar little object hanging around his neck by a string? What is that?"

"Wait and see," said his wife. "Maybe it's a gift."

Louis looked down from the sky and spotted what looked like his family. When he was sure, he glided down and skidded to a stop. His mother rushed up and embraced him. His father arched his neck gracefully and raised his wings in greeting. Everyone shouted "Ko-hoh!" and "Welcome back, Louis!" His family was overjoyed. He had been gone for a year and a half— almost eighteen months. He looked older and handsomer. His feathers were pure white now, instead of a dirty grey. Hanging by a cord around his neck was a small slate. Attached to the slate by a piece of string was a white chalk pencil.

When the family greetings were over, Louis seized the chalk in his bill and wrote "Hi, there!" on the slate. He held the slate out eagerly for all to see.

The cob stared at it. The mother swan stared at it. The cygnets stared at it. They just stared and stared. Words on a slate meant nothing to them. They couldn't read. None of the members of his family had ever seen a slate before, or a piece of chalk. Louis's attempt to greet his family was a failure. He felt as though he had wasted a year and a half by going to school and learning to write. He felt keenly disappointed. And, of course, he was unable to speak. The words on the slate were all he could offer by way of greeting.

Finally his father, the cob, spoke up.

"Louis, my son," he began in his deep, resonant voice, "this is the day we have long awaited—the day of your return to our sanctuary in the Red Rock Lakes. No one can imagine the extent of our joy or the depth of our emotion at seeing you again, you who have been absent from our midst for so long, in lands we know not of, in pursuits we can only guess at. How good it is to see your countenance again! We hope you have enjoyed good health during your long absence, in lands we know not of, in pursuits we can only guess at—"

"You've said that once already," said his wife. "You're repeating yourself. Louis must be tired after his trip, no matter where he's been or what he's been up to."

"Very true," said the cob. "But I must prolong my welcoming remarks a bit longer, for my curiosity is aroused by that odd little object Louis is wearing around his neck and by the strange symbols he has placed upon it by rubbing that white thing up and down and leaving those strange white tracings."

"Well," said Louis's mother, "we're *all* interested in it, naturally. But Louis can't explain it because he is defective and can't talk. So we'll just have to forget our curiosity for the moment and let Louis take a bath and have dinner."

Everyone agreed this was a good idea.

Louis swam to the shore, placed his slate and his chalk pencil under a bush, and took a bath. When he was through, he dipped the end of one wing in the water and sorrowfully rubbed out the words "Hi, there!" Then he hung the slate around his neck again. It felt good to be home with his family. And his family had increased during the months he had spent with Sam Beaver at school. There were now six new cygnets. Louis's father and mother had spent the summer on a trip to Canada, and while there, they had nested and hatched six little cygnets, and in the fall they had all joined up again at the Red Rock Lakes in Montana.

One day, soon after Louis's return, the grain man stopped by with a sack of grain. Louis saw him and swam over. When the man spread the grain on the ground to feed the birds, Louis took off his slate and wrote, "Thank you very much!" He held the slate up to the man, who appeared surprised.

"Say!" said the man. "You're quite a bird! Where did *you* learn to write?"

Louis erased the slate and wrote, "At school."

"School?" said the grain man. "What school?"

"Public school," wrote Louis. "Mrs. Hammerbotham taught me."

"Never heard of her," said the grain man. "But she must be a darned good teacher."

"She is," wrote Louis. He was overjoyed to be carrying on a conversation with a stranger. He realized that even though the slate was no help with other birds, it *was* going to be a help with people, because people could read. This made him feel a whole lot better. Sam Beaver had given Louis the slate as a good-bye present when he left the ranch. Sam had bought the slate and the chalk pencil with money he had saved. Louis decided he would always carry them with him, no matter where he went in the world.

The grain man wondered whether he had been dreaming or whether he had really seen a swan write words on a slate. He decided to say nothing about it to anyone, for fear people might think he was crazy in the head.

For birds, spring is the time to find a mate. The warm sweet airs of spring stir strange feelings in young swans. The males begin to notice the females. They show off in front of them. The females begin to notice the males, too, but they pretend they are not noticing anything at all. They act very coy.

Louis felt so queer one day, he knew he must be in love. And he knew which bird he was in love with. Whenever he swam past her, he could feel his heart beat faster, and his mind was full of thoughts of love and desire. He thought he had never seen such a beautiful young female swan. She was a trifle smaller than the others, and she seemed to have a more graceful neck and more attractive ways than any of his other friends on the lake. Her name was Serena. He wished he could do something to attract her attention. He wanted her for his mate but was unable to tell her so because he couldn't make a sound. He swam in circles around her and pumped his neck up and down and made a great show of diving and staying down to prove he could hold his breath longer than any other bird. But the little female paid no attention to Louis's antics. She pretended he didn't exist.

When Louis's mother found out that Louis was

courting a young female, she hid behind some bulrushes and watched what was going on. She could tell
that he was in love by the way he acted, and she saw
that he was having no success.

Once, in desperation, Louis swam up to Serena, his
beloved, and made a bow. His slate, as usual, was
around his neck. Taking the chalk pencil in his mouth,
he wrote "I love you" on the slate and showed it to her.

She stared at it for a moment, then swam away. She
didn't know how to read, and although she rather liked
the look of a young cob who had something hanging

around his neck, she couldn't really get interested in a bird that was unable to *say* anything. A Trumpeter Swan that couldn't trumpet was a bust as far as she was concerned.

When Louis's mother saw this, she went to her husband, the cob.

"I have news for you," she said. "Your son Louis is in love, and the swan of his choice, the female of his desiring, pays no attention to him. It's just as I predicted: Louis won't be able to get a mate because he has no voice. That snippety little female he's chasing

265

after gives me a pain in the neck, the way she acts. But just the same, I'm sorry for Louis. He thinks she's the greatest thing on the lake, and he can't say, 'Ko-hoh, I love you,' and that's what she's waiting to hear."

"Why, this is terrible news," said the cob, "news of the most serious import. I know what it is like to be in love. Well do I remember how painful love can be, how exciting, and, in the event of unsuccess, how disappointing and doleful the days and nights. But I am Louis's father, and I'm not going to take this situation lying down. I shall act. Louis is a Trumpeter Swan, noblest of all the waterfowl. He is gay, cheerful, strong, powerful, lusty, good, brave, handsome, reliable, trustworthy, a great flier, a tremendous swimmer, fearless, patient, loyal, true, ambitious, desirous—"

"Just a minute," said his wife. "You don't need to tell me all these things. The point is, what are you going to do to help Louis get himself a mate?"

"I'm leading up to that in my own graceful way," replied the cob. "You say that what this young female wants is to hear Louis say, 'Ko-hoh, I love you'?"

"That's right."

"Then she shall hear it!" exclaimed the cob. "There are devices made by men—horns, trumpets, musical instruments of all sorts. These devices are capable of producing sounds similar to the wild sound of our trumpeting. I shall begin a search for such a device, and if I have to go to the ends of the earth to find a trumpet for our young son, I shall find it at last and bring it home to Louis."

"Well, if I may make a suggestion," said his wife, "don't go to the ends of the earth, go to Billings, Montana. It's nearer."

"Very well, I will try Billings. I shall look for a trumpet in Billings. And now, without further ado, I go. There is no time to lose. Springtime doesn't last forever. Love is fleeting. Every minute counts. I'm leaving this instant for Billings, Montana, a great city teeming with life and with objects made by man. Goodbye, my love! I shall return!"

"What are you going to use for money?" asked his practical wife. "Trumpets cost money."

"Leave that to me," replied the cob. And with that, he took off into the air. He climbed steeply, like a jet plane, then levelled off, flying high and fast toward the northeast. His wife watched him until he was out of sight. "What a swan!" she murmured. "I just hope he knows what he's doing."

Chapter 9

The Trumpet

AS THE cob flew toward Billings on his powerful white wings, all sorts of troublesome thoughts whirled in his head. The cob had never gone looking for a trumpet before. He had no money to pay for a trumpet. He feared he might arrive after the shops had closed for the day. He realized that in the whole continent of North America he was undoubtedly the only Trumpeter Swan who was on his way to a city to get a trumpet.

"This is a queer adventure," he said to himself. "Yet it is a noble quest. I will do anything to help my son Louis—even if I run into real trouble."

Toward the end of the afternoon, the cob looked ahead and in the distance saw the churches and factories and shops and homes of Billings. He decided to act quickly and boldly. He circled the city once, looking for a music store. Suddenly he spied one. It had a very big, wide window, solid glass.

The cob flew lower and circled so he could get a better look. He gazed into the store. He saw a drum painted gold. He saw a fancy guitar with an electric cord. He saw a small piano. He saw banjos, horns, violins, mandolins, cymbals, saxophones, marimbaphones, cellos, and many other instruments. Then he saw what he wanted: he saw a brass trumpet hanging by a red cord.

"Now is my time to act!" he said to himself. "Now is my moment for risking everything on one bold move, however shocking it may be to my sensibilities, however offensive it may be to the laws that govern the lives of men. Here I go! May good luck go with me!"

With that, the old cob set his wings for a dive. He aimed straight at the big window. He held his neck straight and stiff, waiting for the crash. He dove swiftly and hit the window going full speed. The glass broke. The noise was terrific. The whole store shook. Musical instruments fell to the floor. Glass flew everywhere. A salesgirl fainted. The cob felt a twinge of pain as a jagged piece of broken glass cut into his shoulder, but he grabbed the trumpet in his beak, turned sharply in the air, flew back through the hole in the window, and began climbing fast over the roofs of Billings. A few drops of blood fell to the ground below. His shoulder hurt. But he had succeeded in getting what he had come for. Held firmly in his bill, its red cord dangling, was a beautiful brass trumpet.

You can imagine the noise in the music store when the cob crashed through the window. At the moment the glass broke, one of the clerks was showing a bass drum to a customer, and the clerk was so startled at seeing a big white bird come flying through the window, he hit the drum a tremendous wallop.

"Bom!" went the drum.

"Crash!" went the splinters of flying glass.

When the salesgirl fainted, she fell against the keys of the piano.

"Rrrongee-rrrongee-rrrongee! " went the piano.

The owner of the store grabbed his shotgun, which went off by mistake, blasting a hole in the ceiling and sending down a shower of plaster. Everything was flying around and falling and making a noise.

"Bom!" went the drum.

"Plunk!" went the banjo.

"Rrrongee-rrrongee-rrrongee!" went the piano.

"Ump!" went the bull fiddle.

"Help!" screamed a clerk. "We've been robbed."

"Make way!" shouted the owner. He ran for the door, stepped outside, and fired another shot—*bang!*—at the disappearing bird. His shot was too late. The cob was safe in the sky, beyond the range of gunfire. He was headed home, toward the southwest, high above the roofs and spires of Billings. In his beak was the trumpet. In his heart was the pain of having committed a crime.

"I have robbed a store," he said to himself. "I have become a thief. What a miserable fate for a bird of my excellent character and high ideals! Why did I do this? What led me to commit this awful crime? My past life has been blameless—a model of good behavior and correct conduct. I am by nature law-abiding. Why, oh, why did I do this?"

Then the answer came to him, as he flew steadily on through the evening sky. "I did it to help my son. I did it for love of my son Louis."

Back in Billings, the news spread rapidly. This was the first time a swan had broken into a music store and made off with a trumpet. A lot of people refused to believe it had happened. The editor of the newspaper sent a reporter to the store to look around. The reporter interviewed the owner and wrote an article about the event for the paper. The article was headed:

LARGE BIRD BREAKS
INTO MUSIC STORE

White Swan Crashes Through Window
and Makes Off With Valuable Trumpet

Everybody in Billings bought a copy of the paper and read all about the extraordinary event. It was talked about all over town. Some people believed it; others said it never could have happened. They said the store owner had just invented it to get some publicity for his store. But the clerks in the store agreed that it had really happened. They pointed to the drops of blood on the floor.

The police came to look over the damage, which was estimated at nine hundred dollars. The police promised they would try to find the thief and arrest him, but the police were sorry to hear that the thief was a bird. "Birds are a special problem," they said. "Birds are hard to deal with."

Back at the Red Rock Lakes, Louis's mother waited anxiously for her husband to return. When he showed up in the night sky, she saw that he had a trumpet with him. It was slung around his neck by its cord.

"Well," she said, as he glided to a stop in the water, "I see you made it."

"I did, my dear," said the cob. "I travelled fast and far, sacrificed my honour, and I have returned. Where is Louis? I want to give him his trumpet right away."

"He's over there sitting on a muskrat house, dreaming about that empty-headed young female he's so crazy about."

The cob swam over to his son and made a presentation speech.

"Louis," he said, "I have been on a journey to the haunts of men. I visited a great city teeming with life and commerce. Whilst there, I picked up a gift for you, which I now bestow upon you with my love and my blessing. Here, Louis, is a trumpet. It will be your voice—a substitute for the voice God failed to give you. Learn to blow it, Louis, and life will be smoother and richer and gayer for you! With the help of this horn, you will be able at last to say ko-hoh, like every other swan. The sound of music will be in our ears. You will be able to attract the attention of desirable young females. Master this trumpet, and you will be able to play love songs for them, filling them with ardour and surprise and longing. I hope it will bring you happiness, Louis, and a new and better life. I procured it at some personal sacrifice to myself and my pride, but we won't go into that now. The long and short of it is, I had no money; I took the trumpet without paying for it. This was deplorable. But the important thing is that you learn to play the instrument."

So saying, the cob removed the trumpet from around his neck and hung it on Louis, alongside the slate and the white chalk pencil.

"Wear it in health!" he said. "Blow it in happiness! Make the woods and the hills and the marshes echo with the sounds of your youthful desire!"

Louis wanted to thank his father, but he was unable to say a word. And he knew it would do no good to write "Thank you" on the slate, because his father wouldn't be able to read it, never having had an education. So Louis just bobbed his head and waggled his tail and fluttered his wings. The cob knew by these signs that he had found favour in the sight of his son and that the gift of a trumpet was acceptable.

Chapter 10

Money Trouble

LOUIS WAS the best-liked young male swan on Upper Red Rock Lake. He was also the best equipped. He not only had a slate and a chalk pencil around his neck, he had a brass trumpet on a red cord. The young females were beginning to notice him because he looked entirely different from the other cygnets. He stood out in a crowd. None of the others carried anything with them.

Louis was delighted with the new trumpet. All day, the first day he had it, he tried to get it to make a noise. Holding the trumpet was not easy. He tried several different positions, bending his neck and blowing. At first, no sound came out. He blew harder and harder, puffing out his cheeks and getting red in the face.

"This is going to be tough," he thought.

But then he discovered that, by holding his tongue in a certain way, he could get the trumpet to emit a small gasping sound. It wasn't a very pretty noise, but at

least it was a noise. It sounded a little like hot air escaping from a radiator.

"Puwoowf, puwoowf," went the trumpet.

Louis kept at it. Finally, on the second day of trying, he got it to play a note—a clear note.

"Ko!" went the trumpet.

Louis's heart skipped a beat when he heard it. A duck, swimming nearby, stopped to listen.

"Ko! Ko ee oo oooph," went the trumpet.

"It will take time," thought Louis. "I'm not going to become a trumpeter in a day, that's for sure. But Rome wasn't built in a day, and I'm going to learn to blow this horn if it takes me all summer."

Louis had other problems besides learning the trumpet. For one thing, he knew that his trumpet wasn't paid for—it had been stolen. He didn't like that at all. For another thing, Serena, the swan he was in love with, had gone away. She had left the lakes with several other young swans and had flown north to the Snake River. Louis was afraid he might never see her again. So he found himself with a broken heart, a stolen trumpet, and no one to give him any lessons.

Whenever Louis was in trouble, his thoughts turned to Sam Beaver. Sam had helped him before; perhaps he could help him again. Besides, springtime was making him restless: he felt an urge to leave the lakes and fly somewhere. So he took off one morning and headed straight for the Bar Nothing Ranch, in the Sweet Grass country, where Sam lived.

Flying was not as easy as it once had been. If you've ever tried to fly with a trumpet dangling from your neck and a slate flapping in the wind and a chalk pencil bouncing around at the end of its string, you know how hard it can be. Louis realized that there were advantages in travelling light and not having too many possessions clinging to you. Nevertheless, he was a strong flier, and the slate and the chalk pencil and the trumpet were important to him.

When he reached the ranch where Sam lived, he circled once, then glided down and walked into the barn. He found Sam grooming his pony.

"Well, look who's here!" exclaimed Sam. "You look like a travelling salesman with all that stuff around your neck. I'm glad to see you."

Louis propped the slate up against the pony's stall. "I'm in trouble," he wrote.

"What's the matter?" asked Sam. "And where did you get the trumpet?"

"That's the trouble," wrote Louis. "My father stole it. He gave it to me because I have no voice. The trumpet hasn't been paid for."

Sam whistled through his teeth. Then he led the pony into his stall, tied him, came out, and sat down on a bale of hay. For a while he just stared at the bird.

Finally he said, "You've got a money problem. But that's not unusual. Almost everybody has a money problem. What you need is a job. Then you can save your earnings, and when you get enough money saved up, your father can pay back the man he stole the trumpet from. Can you actually *play* that thing?"

Louis nodded. He raised the trumpet to his beak.

"Ko!" said the trumpet. The pony jumped.

"Hey!" said Sam. "That's pretty good. Do you know any other notes?"

Louis shook his head.

"I've got an idea," said Sam. "I have a job this summer as a junior counselor at a boys' camp in Ontario. That's in Canada. I'll bet I can get you a job as camp bugler if you can learn a few more notes. The camp wants somebody that can blow a horn. The idea is, you blow a lot of loud fast notes in the early morning to wake the boys up. That's called reveille. Then you blow some other notes to call the campers to their meals. That's called the mess call. Then at night when everybody is in bed and the light has faded from the sky and the lake is calm and the mosquitoes are busy in the tents, biting the boys, and the boys are getting sleepy in their beds, you blow some other notes, very soft and sweet and sad. That's called taps. Do you want to go to camp with me and try it?"

"I'll try anything," wrote Louis. "I am desperate for money."

Sam chuckled. "O.K.," he said. "Camp opens in about three weeks. That'll give you time to learn the bugle calls. I'll buy you a music book that tells what the notes are."

And Sam did. He found a book of trumpet calls, such as they use in the Army. He read the instructions to Louis. "Stand erect. Always hold the trumpet straight from the body. Do not point it down toward the ground as this position cramps the lungs and gives the performer a very poor appearance. The instrument should be cleaned once a week to remove the spit."

Every afternoon, when the guests on Mr. Beaver's ranch had gone off on pack trips in the hills, Louis practiced the calls. Pretty soon he could play reveille, mess call, and taps. He particularly liked the sound of taps. Louis was musically inclined and was eager to become a really good trumpeter. "A Trumpeter Swan," he thought, "should blow a good trumpet." He liked the idea of getting a job, too, and earning money. He was just the right age for going to work. He was almost two years old.

On the night before they were to leave for camp, Sam packed all his camping things in a duffel bag. He packed sneakers and moccasins. He packed jerseys that said "Camp Kookooskoos" on the front. He rolled his camera in a towel and packed that. He packed his fishing rod, his toothbrush, his comb and brush, his sweater, his poncho, and his tennis racquet. He packed a pad and pencils and postage stamps and a first-aid kit and a book that told how to identify birds. Before he went to bed, he opened his diary and wrote:

Tomorrow is the last day of June. Pop is going to drive Louis and me to Camp Kookooskoos. I bet it will be the only boys' camp in the world that has a trumpeter swan for the camp bugler. I like having a job. I wish I knew what I was going to be when I am a man. Why does a dog always stretch when he wakes up?

Sam closed his diary, shoved it into the duffel bag with the rest of his stuff, got into bed, turned out the light, and lay there wondering why a dog always stretches when it wakes up. In two minutes he was asleep. Louis, out in the barn, had gone to sleep long ago.

Bright and early next morning, Louis arranged his slate and his chalk pencil and his trumpet neatly around his neck and climbed into the back seat of Mr. Beaver's car. The car was a convertible, so Mr. Beaver put the top down. Sam got in front with his father. Louis stood tall and white and handsome in the back seat. Mrs. Beaver kissed Sam good-bye. She told him to be a good boy and to take care of himself and not to drown in the lake and not to get into fights with other boys and not to go out in the rain and get sopping wet and then sit around in the chilly air without putting a sweater on, not to get lost in the woods, not to eat too much candy and drink too much pop, not to forget to write letters home every few days, and not to go out in a canoe when it was windy on the lake.

Sam promised.

"O.K.!" cried Mr. Beaver. "Off we go to Ontario, beneath the open sky!" He started the car and tooted the horn.

"Good-bye, Mom!" called Sam.

"Good-bye, son!" called his mother.

The car sped away toward the big main gate of the ranch. Just as it was disappearing from view, Louis turned around in his seat and put his trumpet to his mouth.

"Ko-hoh!" he blew. "Ko-hoh, ko-hoh!"

The sound carried—a wild, clear, stirring call. Everybody back at the ranch heard it and was thrilled by the sound of the trumpet. It was like no other sound they had ever heard. It reminded them of all the wild and wonderful things and places they had ever known: sunsets and moonrises and mountain peaks and valleys and lonely streams and deep woods.

"Ko-hoh! Ko-hoh! Ko-hoh!" called Louis.

The sound of the trumpet died away. The ranchers returned to their breakfast. Louis, on his way to his first job, felt as excited as he had felt on the day he learned to fly.

Chapter 11
Camp Kookooskoos

CAMP KOOKOOSKOOS was on a small lake, deep in the woods of Ontario. There were no summer cottages on the lake, no outboard motors, no roads with cars rushing by. It was a wilderness lake, just right for boys. Mr. Beaver left Sam and Louis at the end of a dirt road, and they finished their journey to camp by canoe. Sam sat in the stern and paddled, Louis stood in the bow and looked straight ahead.

The camp consisted of a big log cabin where everybody ate, seven tents where the boys and the counselors slept, a dock out front, and a privy out back. The woods closed in all around, but there was a bare spot that had been made into a tennis court, and there were plenty of canoes in which to take trips to other lakes. There were about forty boys.

When Sam's canoe grounded on the sandy beach next to the camp dock, Louis stepped ashore wearing his slate, his chalk pencil, and his trumpet. About twenty boys rushed down to the landing to see what was going on. They could hardly believe their eyes.

"Hey, look what's here!" one of the boys yelled.

"A bird!" cried another. "Look at the *size* of him!"

Everybody crowded around Louis, wanting to get a close look at the new camper. Sam had to push some of the boys back, to keep Louis from getting crushed.

"Take it easy, will you?" Sam implored.

That evening after supper, the director of the camp, Mr. Brickle, built a big campfire in front of the main lodge. The boys gathered around. They sang songs and toasted marshmallows and swatted mosquitoes. Sometimes you couldn't understand the words of a song because the boys sang with marshmallows in their mouths. Louis did not join the group. He stood by himself at a little distance.

After a while, Mr. Brickle rose to his feet and addressed the boys and the counselors.

"I call your attention," he said, "to a new camper in our midst—Louis the Swan. He is a Trumpeter Swan, a rare bird. We are lucky to have him. I have employed him at the same salary I pay my junior counselors: one hundred dollars for the season. He is gentle and has a speech defect. He came here from Montana with Sam Beaver. Louis is a musician. Like most musicians, he is in need of money. He will wake you at daybreak with his trumpet; he will call you to meals; and at night, when you are dropping off to sleep, he will play taps, and that will bring the day to a close. I caution you to treat him as an equal and to treat him with respect—he packs a terrific wallop with one of those wings. I now introduce, for your listening pleasure, Louis the Swan. Take a bow, Louis!"

Louis was embarrassed, but he came forward and bowed. Then he raised his trumpet to his mouth and blew a long ko. When he finished, from the opposite shore of the lake there came the echo: ko-oo.

The boys clapped. Louis bowed again. Sam Beaver, sitting with the others, his mouth full of marshmallows, was delighted that his plan had succeeded. At the end of the summer, Louis would have a hundred dollars.

A boy named Applegate Skinner stood up.

"Mr. Brickle," he said, "what about me? I don't care for birds. I've never liked birds."

"O.K., Applegate," said Mr. Brickle. "You don't have to like birds. If that's the way you feel about it, just go ahead not-liking birds. Everyone is entitled to his likes and dislikes and to his prejudices. Come to think of it, *I* don't care for pistachio ice cream. I don't know *why* I don't like it, but I don't. Do not forget, however, that Louis is one of your counselors. Whether you like him or not, he must be treated with respect."

One of the new boys who had never been to camp before stood up.

"Mr. Brickle," he said, "why is this camp called Camp Kookooskoos? What does Kookooskoos mean?"

"It's an Indian name for the Great Horned Owl," replied Mr. Brickle.

The new boy thought about this for a minute.

"Then why didn't you just call it Camp Great Horned Owl instead of Camp Kookooskoos?"

"Because," replied Mr. Brickle, "a boys' camp should have a peculiar name; otherwise it doesn't sound interesting. Kookooskoos is a terrific name. It is a long word, but it has only three letters in it. It has two *s*'s, three *k*'s, and six *o*'s. You don't find many names as kooky as that. The queerer the name, the better the camp. Anyway, welcome to Camp Kookooskoos. It rhymes with moose—that's another good thing about it.

"And now it's time for everybody to go to bed. You may take a swim before breakfast tomorrow, and you don't need to wear your swim trunks. Just jump out of bed when you hear the trumpet of the swan, strip off your pajamas, race to the dock, and dive in. I will be there ahead of you to do my celebrated backflip from the diving tower. It freshens me up for the hard day ahead. Good night, Louis! Good night, Sam!

Good night, Applegate! Good night, all!"

The light was fading. The boys straggled off to their tents in the darkness. The senior counselors sat together on the porch and smoked one last pipe.

Sam crawled in under his blankets in Tent Three. Louis walked to a high, flat rock by the shore and stood there, waiting. When the lights were all out, he faced the camp, raised his horn to his mouth, and blew taps.

Day is done, gone the sun, From the lake, from the hills, From the sky; All is well, safe-ly rest, God is nigh.

The last note seemed to linger on the still waters of the lake. From their beds, the boys heard the beautiful sound. They felt sleepy and serene and happy—all but Applegate Skinner, who didn't care for birds at bedtime. But even Applegate was soon asleep, along with

the others in his tent. He was asleep, and he was snor-
ing. People who dislike birds often snore.

A deep peace fell over Camp Kookooskoos.

Chapter 12

A Rescue

LOUIS LIKED to sleep on the lake. At night, after blowing taps, he would waddle down to the sandy beach by the dock. There he removed his slate, his chalk pencil, and his trumpet and hid them under a bush. Then he shoved off into the water. As soon as he was afloat, he would tuck his head under a wing. For a while he would doze and think about home and his parents. Then he would think about Serena—how beautiful she was and how much he loved her. Pretty soon he would be fast asleep. When daylight came, he would swim ashore and eat a light breakfast of water plants. Then he'd put on his things, climb on to the flat rock, and blow reveille. The boys, hearing the trumpet, would wake and rush to the dock to swim before breakfast.

After supper at night the campers would often play volleyball. Louis loved the game. He couldn't hop around as fast as the boys, but he could reach far out with his long neck and poke the ball into the air and

over the net. It was very hard to get a ball past Louis—
he could return almost any shot. When the boys chose
sides at the start of the game, Louis was always the
first to be chosen.

The boys loved camp life in Ontario. They learned
how to handle a canoe. They learned to swim. Sam
Beaver took them on nature walks and taught them
to sit quietly on a log and observe wild creatures and
birds. He showed them how to walk in the woods
without making a lot of noise. Sam showed them where
the kingfisher had his nest, in a hole in the bank by
a stream. He showed them the partridge and her chicks.
When the boys heard a soft *co-co-co-co*, Sam told
them they were listening to the Sawwhet Owl, smallest
of the owls, no bigger than a man's hand. Sometimes in
the middle of the night the whole camp would wake
to the scream of a wildcat. Nobody ever *saw* a wildcat
during the entire summer, but his scream was heard
at night.

One morning when Sam was playing tennis with
Applegate Skinner, Sam heard a clanking noise. He
looked behind him, and there, coming out of the woods,
was a skunk. The skunk's head was stuck in a tin can;
he couldn't see where he was going. He kept bumping
into trees and rocks, and the can went clank, clank,
clank.

"That skunk is in trouble," said Sam, laying down

his racquet. "He's been to the dump, looking for food. He poked his head into that empty can, and now he can't get it out."

The word spread quickly through camp that a skunk had arrived. The boys came running to see the fun. Mr. Brickle warned them not to get too close—the skunk might squirt them with perfume. So the boys danced around, keeping their distance and holding their noses.

The big question was how to get the can off the skunk's head without getting squirted.

"He's going to need help," said Sam. "That skunk will starve to death if we don't get that can off."

All the boys had suggestions.

One boy said they should make a bow and arrow, tie a string to the arrow, and shoot the arrow at the can. Then, when they hit the can, they could pull the string and the can would come off the skunk's head. Nobody thought much of *that* suggestion—it sounded like too much work.

Another boy suggested that two boys climb a tree, and one boy could hang by his feet from the other boy's hands, and when the skunk walked under the tree, the boy who was hanging by his feet could reach down and pull the can off, and if the skunk squirted, the perfume wouldn't hit the boy because he would be hanging in the air. Nobody thought much of *that* suggestion. Mr. Brickle didn't like it at all. He said it was extremely impractical and furthermore he wouldn't permit it.

Another boy suggested that they get a block of wood, smear it with glue, and when the skunk knocked against it, the can would stick to the block of wood. Nobody thought much of *that* suggestion. Mr. Brickle said he didn't have any glue anyway.

While everybody was making suggestions, Sam Beaver walked quietly to his tent. He returned in a few minutes with a long pole and a piece of fishline. Sam tied one end of the fishline to the pole. Then he tied a slipknot in the other end of the line and formed a noose. Then he climbed to the roof of the porch and asked the other boys not to get too close to the skunk.

The skunk all this time was blundering around, blindly bumping into things. It was a pitiful sight.

Sam, holding his pole, waited patiently on the roof. He looked like a fisherman waiting for a bite. When the skunk wandered close to the building, Sam reached over, dangled the noose in front of the skunk, slipped the noose around the can, and gave a jerk. The noose tightened, and the can came off. As it did so, the skunk turned around and squirted—right at Mr. Brickle, who jumped back, stumbled, and fell. All the boys danced around, holding their noses. The skunk ran off into the woods. Mr. Brickle got up and dusted himself off. The air smelled strong of skunk. Mr. Brickle smelled, too.

"Congratulations, Sam!" said Mr. Brickle. "You have aided a wild creature and have given Camp Kookooskoos a delicious dash of wild perfume. I'm sure we'll all remember this malodorous event for a long time to come. I don't see how we can very well forget it."

"Ko-hoh!" cried Louis, lifting his trumpet. The lake echoed with the sound. The air was heavy with the rich, musky smell of skunk. The boys danced and danced, holding their noses. Some of them held their stomachs and pretended to throw up. Then Mr. Brickle announced it was time for the morning swim.

"A swim will clear the air," he said, as he walked away toward his cottage to change his clothes.

After lunch each day, the campers went to their tents for a rest period. Some of them read books. Some wrote letters home, telling their parents how bad the food was. Some just lay on their cots and talked. One afternoon during rest period, the boys in Applegate's tent began teasing him about his name.

"Applegate Skinner," said one boy. "Where did you get such a crazy name, Applegate?"

"My parents gave it to me," replied Applegate.

"I know what his name is," said another boy. "*Sour* Applegate. Sour Applegate Skinner." The boys howled at this and began chanting, "Sour Applegate, Sour Applegate, Sour Applegate."

"Quiet!" bellowed the tent leader.

"I don't think it's funny," said Applegate.

"His name isn't Sour Applegate," whispered another boy. "His name is *Wormy* Applegate. Wormy Applegate Skinner." This suggestion was greeted with screams of laughter.

"Quiet!" bellowed the tent leader. "I want quiet in this tent. Leave Applegate alone!"

"Leave *Rotten* Applegate alone!" whispered another boy. And some of the other boys had to pull their pillows over their heads so their snickering couldn't be heard.

Applegate was sore. When the rest period was over, he wandered down to the dock. He didn't like being made fun of, and he wanted to do something to get even. Without saying anything to anybody, he slid a canoe into the water and paddled out into the lake, heading for the opposite shore a mile away. No one noticed him.

Applegate had no business taking a canoe out alone. He had not passed his swimming test. He had not passed his canoe test. He was disobeying a camp rule. When he was a quarter of a mile from shore, in deep water, the wind grew stronger. The waves got higher. The canoe was hard to manage. Applegate got scared. Suddenly, a wave caught the canoe and spun it around. Applegate leaned hard on his paddle. His hand slipped, and he lost his balance. The canoe tipped over. Applegate found himself in the water. His clothes felt terribly soggy and heavy. His shoes dragged him down, and he could barely keep his head above water. Instead of hanging on to the canoe, he started swimming toward shore—which was a crazy thing to do. One wave hit him square in the face, and he got a mouthful of water.

"Help!" he screamed. "Help me! I'm drowning. It'll give the camp a bad name if I drown. Help! Help!"

Counselors sprinted to the waterfront. They jumped into canoes and rowboats and started for the drowning boy. One counselor kicked his moccasins off, dove in, and began swimming toward Applegate. Mr. Brickle raced to the dock, climbed to the diving tower, and directed the rescue operation, shouting through a megaphone.

"Hang on to the canoe, Applegate!" he shouted. "Don't leave the canoe!"

But Applegate had already left the canoe. He was all alone, thrashing about and wasting his strength. He felt sure he would soon go to the bottom and drown. He felt weak and scared. Water had got into his lungs. He couldn't last much longer.

The first boat to get away from the dock was rowed by Sam Beaver, and Sam was pulling hard at the oars, straining every muscle. But things didn't look good for Applegate. The boats were still a long way from the boy.

When the first cry of "Help" was heard in camp, Louis was coming around the corner of the main lodge. He spied Applegate immediately and responded to the call.

"I can't *fly* out there," thought Louis, "because my flight feathers have been falling out lately. But I can certainly make better time than those boats."

Dropping his slate and his chalk pencil and his trumpet, Louis splashed into the water and struck out, beating his wings and kicking with his great webbed feet. A swan, even in summer when he can't fly, can scoot across the water at high speed. Louis's powerful wings beat the air. His feet churned the waves, as though he were running on top of the water. In a moment he had passed all the boats. When he reached Applegate, he quickly dove, pointed his long neck between Applegate's legs, then came to the surface with Applegate sitting on his back.

Cheers came from the people on the shore and in the boats. Applegate clung to Louis's neck. He had been saved in the nick of time. Another minute and

he would have gone to the bottom. Water would have filled his lungs. He would have been a goner.

"Thank God!" shouted Mr. Brickle through his megaphone. "Great work, Louis! Camp Kookooskoos will never forget this day! The reputation of the camp has been saved. Our record for safety is still untarnished."

Louis didn't pay much attention to all the shouting. He swam very carefully over to Sam's boat, and Sam pulled Applegate into the boat and helped him into the stern seat.

"You looked pretty funny, riding a swan," Sam said. "And you're lucky to be alive. You're not supposed to go out alone in a canoe."

But Applegate was too scared and wet to say anything. He just sat and stared straight ahead, spitting water out of his mouth and breathing hard.

At supper that night, Mr. Brickle placed Louis at his right, in the place of honour. When the meal was over, he rose and made a speech.

"We all saw what happened on the lake today. Applegate Skinner broke a camp rule, took a canoe out alone, and upset. He was drowning when Louis the Swan, rapidly outdistancing all other campers, reached his side, held him up, and saved his life. Let us all give Louis a standing ovation!"

The boys and the counselors stood up. They cheered and clapped and beat on tin plates with spoons. Then they sat down. Louis looked embarrassed.

"And now, Applegate," said Mr. Brickle, "I hope

the rescue has caused you to change your opinion of birds. The first day you were here in camp, you told us you didn't care for birds. How do you feel now?"

"I feel sick at my stomach," replied Applegate. "It makes you sick at your stomach to almost drown. My stomach still has a lot of lake water in it."

"Yes, but what about birds?" asked Mr. Brickle.

Applegate thought hard for a moment. "Well," he said, "I'm grateful to Louis for saving my life. But I still don't like birds."

"Really?" said Mr. Brickle. "That's quite remarkable. Even though a bird saved you from drowning, you don't care for birds? What have you got *against* birds?"

"Nothing," replied Applegate. "I have nothing against them. I just don't care for them."

"O.K.," said Mr. Brickle. "I guess we'll just have to leave it at that. But the camp is proud of Louis. He is our most distinguished counselor—a great trumpet player, a great bird, a powerful swimmer, and a fine friend. He deserves a medal. In fact, I intend to write a letter recommending that he be given the Lifesaving Medal."

Mr. Brickle did as he promised. He wrote a letter. A few days later, a man arrived from Washington with the Lifesaving Medal, and while all the campers watched, he hung the medal around Louis's neck, alongside the trumpet, the slate, and the chalk pencil. It was a beautiful medal. Engraved on it were the words:

TO LOUIS THE SWAN, WHO, WITH OUTSTANDING COURAGE AND COMPLETE DISREGARD FOR HIS OWN SAFETY, SAVED THE LIFE OF APPLEGATE SKINNER.

Louis took off his slate and wrote, "Thank you for this medal. It is a great honour."

But he thought to himself, "I'm beginning to get overloaded with stuff around my neck. I've got a trumpet, I've got a slate, I've got a chalk pencil; now I've got a medal. I'm beginning to look like a hippie. I hope I'll still be able to fly when my flight feathers grow in again."

That night when darkness came, Louis blew the most beautiful taps he had ever blown. The man who had brought the medal was listening and watching. He could hardly believe his ears and his eyes. When he returned to the city, he told people what he had seen and heard. Louis's fame was growing. His name was known. People all over were beginning to talk about the swan that could play a trumpet.

Chapter 13
End of Summer

A TRUMPET has three little valves. They are for the fingers of the player. They look like this:

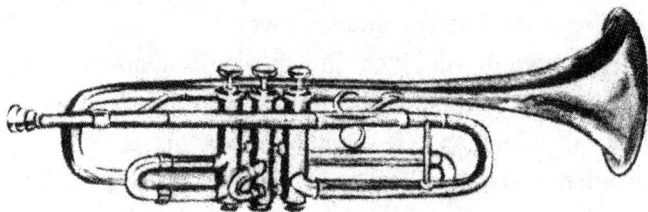

By pushing them down in the right order, the player can produce all the notes of the musical scale. Louis had often examined these three little valves on his horn, but he had never been able to use them. He had three front toes on each foot, but, being a water bird, he had webbed feet. The webbing prevented him from using his three toes independently. Luckily, the valves on a trumpet are not needed for bugle calls because bugle calls are just combinations of *do, mi,* and *sol,* and a trumpeter can play *do, mi,* and *sol* without pressing down any of the valves.

"If I could just work those three valves with my three toes," he said to himself, "I could play all sorts of music, not just bugle calls. I could play jazz. I could play country-and-western. I could play rock. I could play the great music of Bach, Beethoven, Mozart, Sibelius, Gershwin, Irving Berlin, Brahms, everybody. I could really be a trumpet player, not just a camp bugler. I might even get a job with an orchestra." The thought filled him with ambition. Louis loved music, and besides, he was already casting about for ways of making money after camp was over.

Although he enjoyed life at Camp Kookooskoos, Louis often thought of his home on Upper Red Rock Lake in Montana. He thought about his parents, his brothers and sisters, and about Serena. He was terribly in love with Serena, and he often wondered what was happening to her. At night, he would look up at the stars and think about her. In the late evening, when the big bullfrogs were calling *trooonk* across the still lake, he would think of Serena. Sometimes he felt sad, lonely, and homesick. His music, however, was a comfort to him. He loved the sound of his own trumpet.

Summer passed all too quickly. On the last day of camp, Mr. Brickle called his counselors together and paid them what he owed them. Louis received one hundred dollars—the first money he had ever earned. He had no wallet and no pockets, so Mr. Brickle placed the money in a waterproof bag that had a drawstring. He hung this moneybag around Louis's neck, along with the trumpet, the slate, the chalk pencil, and the lifesaving medal.

Louis went to Sam Beaver's tent and found Sam packing his things. Louis took off his slate and pencil.

"I need another job," he wrote. "Where should I go?"

Sam sat down on his bed and thought for a while. Then he said, "Go to Boston. Maybe you can get a job with the Swan Boat."

Louis had never been to Boston, and he had no idea what the Swan Boat was, but he nodded his head. Then on his slate he wrote: "Do me a favour?"

"Sure," said Sam.

"Take a razor blade and slit the web on my right foot, so I can wiggle my toes." He held out his foot.

"Why do you want to wiggle your toes?" asked Sam.

"You'll see," wrote Louis. "I need my toes in my business."

Sam hesitated. Then he borrowed a razor blade from one of the older counselors. He made a long, neat cut between Louis's inner toe and middle toe. Then he made another cut between Louis's middle toe and outer toe.

"Does it hurt?"

Louis shook his head. He lifted his trumpet, placed his toes on the valves, and played *do, re, mi, fa, sol, la, ti, do. Do, ti, la, sol, fa, mi, re, do.* Ko-hoh!

Sam grinned. "The Swan Boat will hire *you*, all right," he said. "You're a real trumpeter now. But with your web cut, swimming will be harder for you. You

will have a tendency to swim in circles, because your left foot will push better than your right foot."

"I can manage," wrote Louis. "Thanks very much for the surgery."

Next day, the campers left. The canoes had been hoisted on to racks in the boathouse, the float had been hauled on to the beach, the windows of the lodge had been boarded up against bears and squirrels, mattresses had been packed into zipper bags; everything was snug and ready for the long, silent winter. Of all the campers, only Louis stayed behind. His flight feathers were growing fast, but he still couldn't fly. He made up his mind he would remain at camp, all alone, until he was able to take to the air again, and then he would fly straight to Boston.

The lake was lonely without the boys, but Louis didn't mind being alone. For the next three weeks he took life easy. He grew his flight feathers, dreamed of Serena by day and by night, and practiced his trumpet. He had listened to music all summer—several of the boys had radios and record players—and now he practiced the songs on his trumpet. Every day he got better and better. One day, he composed a love song for Serena and wrote the words and music on his slate:

Oh, ev-er in the green-ing spring, By bank and bough re-tir-ing, For love shall I be sor-row-ing And swans of my de-sir-ing.

He was really thinking of Serena, but he left her name out of it and kept it impersonal.

His plumage was beautiful now, and he felt great. On the twenty-first of September, he tried his wings. To his great relief, they lifted him. Louis rose into the air. The trumpet banged against the slate, the slate knocked against the moneybag, the lifesaving medal clinked against the chalk pencil—but Louis was air-borne again. He climbed and climbed and headed for Boston. It was wonderful to be in the sky again.

"Flying is a lot harder than it was before I acquired all these possessions," thought Louis. "The best way to travel, really, is to travel light. On the other hand, I have to *have* these things. I've got to have the trumpet if I am to win Serena for my wife; I've got to carry this moneybag to hold the money to pay my father's debts; I've got to have the slate and pencil so I can communicate with people; and I ought to wear the medal because I really did save a life, and if I didn't wear it, people might think I was ungrateful."

On and on he flew, toward Boston, which is the capital of Massachusetts, and which is famous for its baked beans, its codfish, its tea parties, its Cabots, its Lowells, its Saltonstalls, and its Swan Boats.

Chapter 14

Boston

LOUIS LIKED Boston the minute he saw it from the sky. Far beneath him was a river. Near the river was a park. In the park was a lake. In the lake was an island. On the shore was a dock. Tied to the dock was a boat shaped like a swan. The place looked ideal. There was even a very fine hotel nearby.

Louis circled twice, then glided down and splashed to a stop in the lake. Several ducks swam up to look him over. The park was called the Public Garden. Everybody in Boston knows about it and goes there to sit on benches in the sun, to stroll about, to feed the pigeons and the squirrels, and to ride the Swan Boat. A ride costs twenty-five cents for grown-ups, fifteen cents for children.

After a short rest and a bite to eat, Louis swam over to the dock and climbed out on the shore. The man who was taking tickets for the Swan Boat ride seemed surprised to see an enormous white swan wearing so many things around his neck.

"Hello!" said the Boatman.

Louis lifted his trumpet. "Ko-hoh!" he replied.

At the sound, every bird in the park looked up. The Boatman jumped. Boston residents as far as a mile away looked up and said, "What's *that*?" Nobody in Boston had ever heard a Trumpeter Swan. The sound made a big impression. People eating a late breakfast in the Ritz Hotel on Arlington Street looked up from their food. Waiters and bellboys said, "What's *that*?"

The man in charge of the Swan Boat was probably the most surprised man in Boston. He examined Louis's trumpet, his moneybag, his lifesaving medal, his slate, and his chalk pencil. Then he asked Louis what he wanted. Louis wrote on his slate: "Have trumpet. Need work."

"O.K.," said the Boatman. "You've got yourself a job. A boat leaves here in five minutes for a trip around the lake. Your job will be to swim in front of the boat, leading the way and blowing your horn."

"What salary do I get?" asked Louis on his slate.

"We'll settle that later, when we see how you make out," said the Boatman. "This is just a tryout."

Louis nodded. He arranged his things neatly around his neck, entered the water quietly, took up a position a few yards in front of the boat, and waited. He wondered what would make the boat go. He couldn't see any outboard motor, and there were no oars. In the forward part of the boat were benches for the passengers. In the stern was a structure that was shaped like a swan. It was hollow. Inside of it was a seat, like a bicycle seat. And there were two pedals inside, like the pedals of a bicycle.

When the passengers were all aboard, a young man appeared. He climbed on to the stern of the boat and sat down on the seat inside the hollow swan-shaped structure and began to push the pedals with his feet, as though he were riding a bike. A paddle wheel began to turn. The Boatman cast the lines off, and as the young man pedalled, the Swan Boat slowly moved out into the lake. Louis led the way, swimming with his left foot, holding his trumpet with his right foot.

"Ko-hoh!" said Louis's trumpet. The wild sound rang loud and clear and stirred everyone's blood. Then, realizing that he should play something appropriate, Louis played a song he had heard the boys sing at camp.

> *Row, row, row your boat*
> *Gently down the stream;*
> *Merrily, merrily, merrily, merrily,*
> *Life is but a dream.*

The Swan Boat passengers were beside themselves with

joy and excitement. A real live swan, playing a trumpet! Life was a dream, all right. What a lark! What fun! What pleasure!

"This is real groovy!" cried a boy in the front seat. "That bird is as good as Louis Armstrong, the famous trumpet player. I'm going to call him Louis."

When Louis heard this, he swam alongside the boat, took his chalk pencil in his mouth, and wrote: "That's actually my name."

"Hey, how about that?" yelled the boy. "This swan can *write*, too. Louis can write. Let's give him a cheer!"

The passengers cheered loudly. Louis swam ahead again, leading the way. Slowly and gracefully, the boat circled the island, while Louis played "Gentle on My Mind" on his trumpet. It was a lovely September morning, hazy and warm. Trees were beginning to show their autumn colours. Louis played "Ol' Man River."

When the Swan Boat docked and the passengers got off, long lines of people were waiting to get aboard for the next ride. Business was booming. Another boat was being made ready, to accommodate the crowds. Everyone wanted to ride the Swan Boats behind a real live swan playing a trumpet. It was the biggest happening in Boston in a long time. People *like* strange events and queer happenings, and the Swan Boat, with Louis out front leading the way, suddenly became the most popular attraction in Boston.

"You're hired," said the Boatman, when Louis climbed out on to the bank. "With you playing the trumpet, I can double my business. I can triple it. I can quadruple it. I can quintuple it. I can . . . I can . . . I can *sextoople* it. Anyway, I'll give you a steady job."

Louis lifted his slate. "What salary?" he asked.

The Boatman gazed around at the crowds waiting to get aboard.

"A hundred dollars a week," he said. "I'll pay you a hundred dollars every Saturday if you'll swim ahead of the boats and play your horn. Is it a deal?"

Louis nodded his head. The man seemed pleased but puzzled. "If it isn't too much to ask," said the Boatman, "would you mind telling me why you're so interested in money?"

"Everybody is," replied Louis on his slate.

"Yeah, I know," said the Boatman. "Everybody likes money. It's a crazy world. But, I mean, why would a *swan* need money? You can get your meals just by dipping down and pulling up tasty plants at the bottom of the lake. What do you need money for?"

Louis erased his slate. "I'm in debt," he wrote. And he thought about his poor father who had stolen the trumpet and about the poor storekeeper in Billings who had been robbed and whose store had been damaged. Louis knew he must go on earning money until he could pay off what he owed.

"O.K.," said the Boatman, addressing the crowd, "this swan says he's in debt. All aboard for the next ride!" And he began selling tickets. The Boatman owned several boats, all of them shaped like a swan. Pretty soon every boat was full and money was flowing in.

All day long, the Swan Boats circled the lake, carrying their load of happy people, many of them children. Louis played his trumpet as he had never played it before. He liked the job. He loved to entertain people. And he loved music. The Boatman was just as pleased as he could be.

When the day was over and the boats had made their last trip, the Boatman walked over to Louis, who was standing on shore arranging his things.

"You've done great," said the Boatman. "You're a good swan. I wish I'd had you long ago. And now—where are you planning to spend the night?"

"Here on the lake," Louis wrote.

"Well, I don't know about that," said the man uneasily. "An awful lot of people are curious about you. They might make trouble for you. Bad boys might molest you. I don't trust the people who hang around this park at night. You might get kidnapped. I don't want to lose you. I think I'll take you across to the Ritz Carlton Hotel and get you a room for the night. It's clean, and the food is good. It would be safer. Then I can be sure you'll come to work in the morning."

Louis didn't think much of this idea, but he agreed to go. He thought, "Well, I've never *spent* a night in a hotel—maybe it would be an interesting experience." So he walked along with the Boatman. They left the park and crossed Arlington Street and entered the lobby of the Ritz. It had been a long, tiring day for Louis, but he felt relieved to know that he had a good job and that he could earn money in Boston as a musician.

Chapter 15
A Night at the Ritz

WHEN THE desk clerk at the Ritz Hotel saw the Boatman enter the lobby followed by an enormous snow-white swan with a black beak, the clerk didn't like it at all. The clerk was a carefully-dressed man—very neat, his hair nicely combed. The Boatman stepped boldly up to the desk.

"I'd like a single room for tonight for my friend here," said the Boatman.

The clerk shook his head.

"No birds," he said. "The Ritz doesn't take birds."

"You take celebrities, don't you?" asked the Boatman.

"Certainly," replied the clerk.

"You'd take Richard Burton and Elizabeth Taylor, wouldn't you, if they wanted to spend the night?"

"Of course," replied the clerk.

"You'd take Queen Elizabeth, wouldn't you?"

"Of course."

"O.K.," said the Boatman. "My friend here is a

celebrity. He is a famous musician. He created a sensation in the Public Garden this afternoon. You must have heard the commotion. He's a Trumpeter Swan and plays like the great Armstrong."

The clerk gazed suspiciously at Louis.

"Has he any luggage?" asked the clerk.

"*Luggage?*" cried the Boatman. "Take a *look* at him! Look at the stuff he's got with him!"

"Well, I don't know," said the clerk, staring at Louis's possessions—his trumpet, his moneybag, his slate, his chalk pencil, his lifesaving medal. "A bird is a bird. How do I know he hasn't got lice? Birds often have lice. The Ritz won't take anybody that has lice."

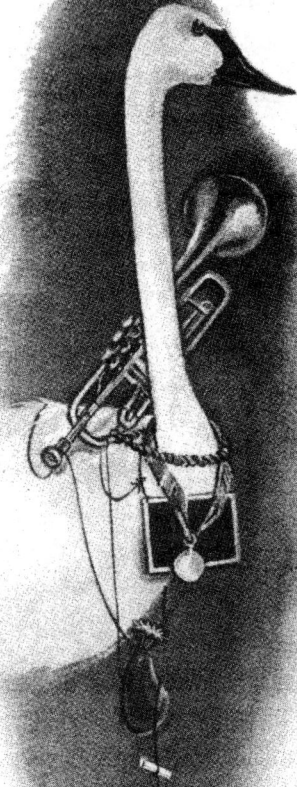

"Lice?" roared the Boatman. "Did you ever see a cleaner guest in your whole life? Look at him! He's immaculate."

At this, Louis held his slate up to the clerk. "No lice," he wrote.

The clerk stared in amazement. He was beginning to weaken.

"Well, I have to be careful," he said to the Boatman. "You say he's a celebrity. How do *I* know he's famous. You may be just kidding me about that."

Just then, three young girls entered the lobby. They were giggling and squealing. One of them pointed at Louis.

"There he is!" she screamed. "There he is! I'll get his autograph."

The girls rushed up to Louis. The first girl held out a pad and pencil.

"May I have your autograph?" she asked.

Louis took the pencil. Very gracefully, he wrote "Louis" on the pad.

More squeals, more giggles, and the girls rushed away. The clerk watched in silence.

"There!" said the Boatman. "Is he a celebrity or isn't he?"

The clerk hesitated. He was beginning to think he would have to give Louis a room.

At this point, Louis had an idea. He lifted his trumpet

and began to play an old song called "There's a Small Hotel."

There's a small ho-tel with a wish-ing well

His tone was beautiful. Guests passing through the lobby paused to listen. The clerk leaned his elbows on the desk and listened attentively. The man behind the news stand looked up and listened. People sitting upstairs in the lounge put down their cocktails and listened. The bellboys stared and listened. For a few minutes, everything stopped in the lobby while Louis played. He charmed everyone who could hear. Chambermaids in the bedrooms paused in their work to listen to the trumpet. It was a moment of sheer magic. As the song came to an end, people who knew the words sang them softly.

> *When the steeple bell*
> *Says "Good night, sleep well,"*
> *We'll thank the small hotel, together.*

"How about that?" asked the Boatman, grinning at the clerk. "Is this swan a musician or isn't he?"

"He plays a sweet trumpet," the clerk said. "But

there is one more question that I hesitate to bring up. What about his personal habits? Will he mess the room all up? Actors are bad enough. Musicians are worse. I can't allow a large bird to occupy one of our beds—it might put us out of business. Other guests might complain."

"I sleep in the bathtub," Louis wrote on his slate. "Will not disturb bed."

The clerk shifted his weight from one foot to the other. "Who's going to pay the bill?" he asked.

"I am," replied the Boatman. "I'll be here early tomorrow morning when Louis checks out."

The clerk couldn't think of any more reasons for not letting the swan have a room.

"Very well," he said. "Sign the register, please!" He handed Louis a pen and a card.

Louis wrote:

Louis the Swan
Upper Red Rock Lake
Montana

The clerk studied it. He seemed satisfied at last. He summoned a bellboy and handed him a key. "Take this gentleman to his room!" he ordered.

Louis removed his medal, his trumpet, his slate, his chalk pencil, and his moneybag and handed them to the bellboy. Together, they walked to the elevators. The Boatman said good-bye.

"Sleep well, Louis!" called the Boatman. "And be ready to come to work promptly in the morning!"

Louis nodded. The elevator door opened. "This way, sir!" said the bellboy. They entered the elevator and waited for the door to close. A rich smell of perfume filled the air. Louis stood very still. Then he felt himself rising. The elevator stopped at the seventh floor, and the bellboy led Louis to a room, unlocked the door, and ushered him in.

"Here you are, sir!" he said. "Would you like a window open?"

The bellboy put Louis's luggage down, snapped on a few lights, opened a window, and laid the room key on the dresser. Then he waited.

"I guess he wants a tip," thought Louis. So he went to his moneybag, loosened the drawstring, and took out a dollar.

"Thank you very much, sir," said the bellboy, taking the dollar. He went out and closed the door softly behind him. Louis was alone at last—alone in a room at the Ritz.

Louis had never spent a night alone in a hotel. First he walked round and around, switching lights on and off, examining everything. In the writing desk, he found a few sheets of letter paper that said:

Ritz Carlton
BOSTON

He felt mussy and dirty, so he went into the bathroom, climbed into the tub, pulled the shower curtain across, and took a shower bath. It felt good and reminded him of the water fights he used to have with his brothers and sisters. He was careful not to splash any water out of the tub. When he was finished, he stood for a while, admiring the bath mat and preening his feathers. Then he felt hungry.

On the wall of the bedroom, he found a button that said WAITER. Louis put his beak against the button and pressed hard. In a few minutes, there was a knock at the door and a waiter entered. He was nicely dressed and tried not to show surprise at finding a swan in the room.

"May I get you something?" he asked.

Louis picked up his chalk pencil. "Twelve watercress sandwiches, please," he wrote on the slate.

The waiter thought for a moment. "Are you expecting guests?" he asked.

Louis shook his head.

"And you want *twelve* watercress sandwiches?"

Louis nodded.

"Very good, sir," said the waiter. "Do you wish them with mayonnaise?"

Louis didn't know what mayonnaise tasted like, but he thought fast. He cleaned his slate and wrote: "One with. Eleven without."

The waiter bowed and left the room. Half an hour later he was back. He rolled a table into the room, placed a huge platter of watercress sandwiches on it, along with a plate, a knife, a fork, a spoon, salt and pepper, a glass of water, and a linen napkin, nicely folded. There was also a butter dish, with several pieces of butter covered with cracked ice. The waiter arranged everything carefully, then handed Louis a bill to sign. The bill said:

12 w/c sandwiches: $18.00

"Goodness!" thought Louis. "This is an expensive place. I hope the Boatman won't be mad when he sees this supper charge on the bill tomorrow morning."

He borrowed a pencil from the waiter and signed the bill: "Louis the Swan."

The waiter took the bill and stood there, waiting.

"I guess he wants a tip," thought Louis. So he opened his moneybag again, drew out two dollars, and handed it to the waiter, who thanked him, bowed again, and went away.

Because a swan has such a long neck, the table was

just the right height for Louis. He didn't need a chair; he ate his supper standing up. He tried the sandwich that had mayonnaise on it and decided he didn't like mayonnaise. Then he carefully pulled each sandwich apart. All he really wanted was the watercress. He piled the slices of bread in two neat piles, scooped the watercress on to his plate, and had a nice supper. He did not touch the butter. When he was thirsty, instead of drinking from the glass of water, he walked into the bathroom, drew a basinful of cold water, and drank that. Then he took his napkin, wiped his beak, and pushed the table out of the way. He felt much better.

To be all alone in a hotel room gives a person a cozy feeling and a feeling of importance. Louis felt great. But soon he began feeling rather lonely, too. He thought of Sam Beaver. He thought of Camp Kookooskoos. He thought of his father and mother and sisters and brothers, back home in Montana. He thought of Serena, the swan he loved, and wondered how she was. The words of the song he had played in the lobby came back to him:

> *There's a small hotel*
> *With a wishing well;*
> *I wish that we were there, together.*

How wonderful it would be, he thought, if Serena could be here at the Ritz to enjoy the hotel with him!

The waiter had left an evening paper on a table. Louis glanced at the front page. To his amazement, he saw a picture of himself on the lake in the Public Garden with the Swan Boat. A big headline said:

BOSTON GOES WILD OVER THE TRUMPET OF THE SWAN

The news story began:

> There's a new bird in town. His name is Louis. He is a Trumpeter Swan that really plays the trumpet. Incredible though it may seem, this rare and beautiful water bird has accepted employment with the Swan Boat management in the Public Garden and is entertaining boat riders with his smooth trumpet. Crowds gathered at the lake this afternoon after his arrival, and the sweet notes of his horn were heard in many parts of Boston. . . .

Louis read the article to the end and then tore it out of the paper. "Sam Beaver ought to know about this," he thought. From the writing desk in his room, Louis took a pen and a sheet of letter paper. This is what he wrote:

Dear Sam:

I am spending the night at the Ritz in fashionable surroundings. You were right about Boston—it is very pleasant. I was able to find work as soon as I arrived. I am associated with the Swan Boat at a salary of $100 a week. You may be interested in the enclosed clipping from today's paper. If all goes well, I'll soon have enough money to pay my father's debt to the music store, and then I will own the trumpet free and clear and will hope that by blowing it passionately I will be able to make a favourable impression on the young female I am in love with. Then everybody will be happy: my father's honour will be restored, the music shop in Billings will be repaid, and I can take a wife. I hope you are well. I miss you. A hotel room, even though it has every convenience, can be a lonely place.

Your friend,
Louis

Louis addressed an envelope to Sam, folded the letter, fitted the newspaper clipping in, and found a six-cent stamp in his moneybag. He sealed the envelope, pasted the stamp on, and dropped the letter in a mail chute outside the door of his room. "Now I'll go to sleep," he thought.

He went into the bathroom, used the toilet, then drew a full tub of cold water in the bathtub. He couldn't get Serena out of his mind. How wonderful it would be if only she were here! Before settling down for the night, he picked up his trumpet and played the song he had composed for her when he was in Ontario:

> *Oh, ever in the greening spring,*
> *By bank and bough retiring,*
> *For love shall I be sorrowing*
> *And swans of my desiring.*

He tried to play softly, but in a minute the phone rang in his room. Louis lifted the receiver and put it to his ear.

"I'm sorry, sir," a voice said, "but I'll have to ask you not to make so much noise. The Ritz does not allow its guests to play brass instruments in the bedrooms."

Louis hung up the phone and put his trumpet away. Then he turned out the lights, climbed into the tub, curved his long neck around to the right, rested his head on his back, tucked his bill under his wing, and lay there, floating on the water, his head cradled softly in his feathers. Soon he was asleep, dreaming of little lakes in the north in the springtime, dreaming of Serena, his true love.

Chapter 16

Philadelphia

LOUIS WORKED all the last week of September for the Swan Boat man in the Boston Public Garden. He was a great success and was becoming famous. On Saturday, the Boatman paid him a hundred dollars in cash, which Louis placed carefully in his moneybag. The Boatman, after paying the first night's bill at the Ritz Carlton Hotel, decided to let Louis sleep on the lake instead of in the hotel, and this suited Louis better. He slept with the ducks and geese on the lake, floating gracefully on the surface of the water, his head tucked under his wing.

Louis took good care of his trumpet. He kept it polished, and once a week he cleaned the spit out of it. He learned new songs whenever he could, by listening to people's radios and by attending concerts. He was very good at remembering music he had heard. He was really a natural-born musician—or, in his case, a natural-*hatched* musician.

One song he liked was "Beautiful Dreamer, Wake

Unto Me." Whenever he played it, he thought of Serena, and always, when he finished it, the passengers on the Swan Boat clapped loudly and cheered. Louis liked applause. It made him feel lighthearted and gay.

Sometimes, at the end of the afternoon, Louis played "Now the Day Is Over." He made it sound sweet and sad. One afternoon, when he was leading the last trip of the day, he played the "Cradle Song" by Brahms. The passengers sang the words:

Lul-la-by and good-night, With ros-es be-dight ___

A boy in the front seat of the boat pulled an air rifle from under his jacket and began shooting BB shots at Louis's trumpet. Whenever a shot hit the horn, it made a *pinging* sound. So the "Cradle Song" sounded something like this:

> *Lul-la - by* (ping)
> *and good - night* (ping)
> *With ros-es be - dight* (ping)

The children on the boat roared with laughter when they heard this, but the grown-up passengers were angry. One of them seized the boy's rifle. Another went home that night and wrote a letter to the *Boston Globe* urging a stronger gun-control law.

On some afternoons, at the end of the day, people gathered on the shores of the lake to listen while Louis played taps. It was a peaceful scene, a memorable hour. The Swan Boat had never enjoyed such popularity or made such a lot of money for the owner. But Louis knew that the boats would not run all winter. In a few days, the boats would be hauled out for the season, to wait quietly for the arrival of spring.

One day, when Louis was waiting for the boat to take its passengers aboard, a Western Union messenger boy appeared on a bicycle.

"I have a telegram for the swan," he said.

The Boatman seemed surprised, but he took the telegram and handed it to Louis, who opened it promptly. It was from a man in Philadelphia. The message said:

```
CAN OFFER YOU FIVE HUNDRED DOLLARS
A WEEK FOR NIGHTCLUB SPOT. TEN WEEK
ENGAGEMENT. PLEASE REPLY.
        (Signed) ABE ("LUCKY") LUCAS
                        HOTEL NEMO
```

Louis did some quick figuring. Five hundred dollars a week for ten weeks—that was five thousand dollars.

Five thousand dollars would easily pay his father's debt to the music store.

He took his slate and wrote:

> OFFER ACCEPTED. ARRIVE TOMORROW. MEET ME
> AT BIRD LAKE IN THE ZOO. SPLASHDOWN WILL BE
> AT FOUR FIFTY-TWO P.M. HOPE THIS WILL BE A
> CONVENIENT TIME FOR YOU.

Louis showed the message to the Western Union boy, who copied it on a telegraph blank.

"Send it collect!" wrote Louis.

The messenger nodded and rode away. Louis stepped back into the water, the boat's lines were cast off, and Louis led the way. He knew it was his last appearance with the Swan Boat, and he felt a little sad. It was a warm, quiet Sunday afternoon, the last Sunday in September. Louis played all his favorite tunes: "Lazy River," "Beautiful Dreamer," "Oh, Ever in the Greening Spring," "Now the Day Is Over," and then, as the boat neared the dock, he raised his trumpet and blew taps.

The last note echoed from the walls of the Ritz and lingered over the Public Garden. It was a sad farewell. For the people of Boston, it meant the end of summer. For the Boatman, it meant the end of the best week of business he had ever had. For Louis, it meant the end of another chapter in his adventurous life, out in the big world, trying to earn enough money to get his father and himself out of trouble. Louis slept peacefully that night, being very careful that his moneybag was safe. Next day he flew to Philadelphia to keep his appointment with Mr. Lucas, the man who had sent the telegram.

Louis had no trouble finding Philadelphia. Almost anybody can find Philadelphia who tries. Louis simply rose into the air with all his things around his neck, and when he was about a thousand feet high, he followed the railroad tracks to Providence, New London, New Haven, Bridgeport, Stamford, Cos Cob, Greenwich, Port Chester, Rye, Mamaroneck, New Rochelle, Pelham, Mount Vernon, and the Bronx. When he saw the Empire State Building, he veered off to the right, crossed the Hudson River, and followed the railroad tracks to Newark and Trenton and points south. At half past four, he reached the Schuylkill River. Just beyond, he spied the Philadelphia Zoo. Bird Lake looked very attractive from the air. It was crowded with waterfowl of all kinds—ducks and geese mostly. Louis thought he also saw two or three swans.

He circled, picked an open spot, and exactly at four fifty-two he splashed down. His trumpet banged against his slate, his slate knocked against his medal, his medal rapped against his chalk pencil, and his chalk pencil on its string wound itself around his moneybag. All in all, the splashdown caused quite a commotion. The ducks and geese were not expecting anything like this to happen—a big white Trumpeter Swan dropping down out of the sky, loaded with personal possessions.

Louis paid no attention to the other birds. He had a date to keep. He saw a man leaning on the wide railing in front of the Bird House. The man was dressed in a purple suit and wore a Tyrolean hat. His face looked shrewd and wise, as though he knew a great many things, many of them not worth knowing.

"That must be Abe 'Lucky' Lucas," thought Louis.

He swam quickly over.

"Ko-hoh!" he said, through his trumpet.

"My pleasure," replied Mr. Lucas. "You are right on time. The splashdown was sensational. Welcome to the Philadelphia Zoo, which crawls with rare mammals, birds, reptiles, amphibians, and fishes, including sharks, rays, and other fishlike vertebrates. Watch out for wild animals—this place is replete with them: snakes, zebras, monkeys, elephants, lions, tigers, wolves, foxes, bears, hippos, rhinos, woodchucks, skunks, hawks, and owls. I seldom come here; my work confines me to the throbbing heart of the city, among the money changers. I am under great pressure from my work. How was your trip from Boston?"

"Smooth," wrote Louis on his slate. "I made good time. What about my job?"

"A happy question," replied Mr. Lucas. "The job will start on October fifteenth. The contract has been finalized. Your place of employment is a nightclub of great renown, across the river—a place of high fashion and low prices, a jumpy joint. You will be called upon to make appearances each evening except Sunday, and play your trumpet for the happy customers. Once in a while you can join a jazz group: 'Louis the Swan on trumpet.' The pay is very good. My spirits are lifted by thinking about the pay. Wealth and happiness are around the corner for Louis the Swan and Lucky Lucas, the great of heart. My agent's fee is ten percent, a mere bagatelle."

"How do I get to the nightclub?" asked Louis, who only understood about half of what Mr. Lucas was saying.

"In a taxicab," replied Mr. Lucas. "Be at the North Entrance of the Zoo, Girard Avenue and Thirty-fourth Street, at nine o'clock on the evening of October fifteenth, a night that will live in memory. A cab will await your pleasure and will transport you to the club. The driver is a friend of mine. He, too, is under pressure from his work."

"Who's going to pay for the cab?" asked Louis on his slate.

"I am," replied Mr. Lucas. "Lucky Lucas, the generous of heart, pays for the cab for Louis the Swan. And by the way, I see that you are wearing a moneybag and that it is plump with moola. I suggest, from the kindness of my great heart, that you turn this moneybag over to me for safekeeping during your stay in Philadelphia, a place of many thieves and pickpockets."

"No, thank you," wrote Louis. "Will keep moneybag myself."

"Very well," said Mr. Lucas. "And now there is one other small matter I must bring to your attention. Most of the birds that swim on this luxury lagoon have undergone surgery. Candour compels me to tell you that the tip of one wing is usually removed by the management —a painless operation, popular with zoos the world over. 'Pinioned' is the word for it, I believe. It detains the water bird and prevents him from leaving the narrow confines of this public park and rising into the air, because when one wing is shorter than the other, the balance of the bird is upset. His attempt to take off would be crowned with failure. In short, he can't fly. Sensing in advance the revulsion *you* would feel toward having the tip of one of your powerful wings removed, I approached the Man in Charge of Birds and laid before him a proposition. He has agreed not to clip your wing. It is arranged. He is a man of honour. Your freedom of movement is assured. You will not be pinioned. But in return for this so great favour on the part of the management of the Philadelphia Zoo, you are to give a free concert here at the lake every Sunday afternoon for the people of Philadelphia, the peasantry, who come here to refresh themselves. Is it a deal?"

"Yes," wrote Louis. "Will give Sunday concert."

"Good!" said Mr. Lucas. "Farewell for the nonce! Be at the North Entrance at nine! October fifteen. A cab will await you. Play well, Sweet Swan! You will be the finest thing that has happened to Philadelphia since the Constitutional Convention of 1787."

Louis didn't understand this, but he nodded good-bye to Mr. Lucas and swam off toward the island in the centre of the lake. There he stepped ashore, straightened his things, preened his feathers, and rested. He was not sure he was going to like his new job. He was not sure he liked Mr. Lucas. But he needed money badly, and when you need money, you are willing to put up with difficulties and uncertainties. One *good thing* about the whole business was the Zoo itself. It seemed like an extremely nice place in spite of what he had heard about having your wing clipped. Louis had no intention of having a wing clipped.

"I'll sock anybody who tries *that* on me!" he said to himself.

He was pleased to see so many other water birds. There were many kinds of ducks and geese. In the distance, he saw three Trumpeter Swans. They were old residents of the Lake. Their names were Curiosity, Felicity, and Apathy. Louis decided he would wait a day or two before making their acquaintance.

Bird Lake has a fence around it. When the night came for him to start work, Louis polished his trumpet, put on all his things, flew over the fence, and landed at the North Entrance. He was there promptly at nine. The taxicab was there, waiting, just as Mr. Lucas had promised. Louis got in and was driven away to his new job.

Chapter 17

Serena

DURING THE next ten weeks, Louis got rich. He went every evening except Sundays to the nightclub and played his trumpet for the customers. He did not like the job at all. The place was big and crowded and noisy. Everyone seemed to be talking too loudly, eating too much, and drinking too much. Most birds like to go to sleep at sundown. They do not want to stay up half the night entertaining people. But Louis was a musician, and musicians can't choose their working hours—they must work when their employer wants them to.

Every Saturday night Louis collected his pay—five hundred dollars. Mr. Lucas was always on hand to receive his agent's fee of ten percent from Louis. After Louis had paid Mr. Lucas, he still had four hundred and fifty dollars left, and he would put this in his moneybag, hop into the waiting taxicab, and return to Bird Lake, arriving at around 3 A.M. His moneybag grew so stuffed with money, Louis was beginning to worry.

On Sunday afternoons, if the weather was good, crowds of people would gather on the shores of Bird Lake, and Louis would stand on the island in the middle of the lake and give a concert. This became a popular event in Philadelphia, where there isn't much going on on Sunday. Louis took the concert very seriously. By playing for the people, he was earning the right to remain free and not have a wing clipped.

He was always at his best on Sundays. Instead of playing jazz and rock and folk and country-and-western, he would play selections from the works of the great composers—Ludwig van Beethoven, Wolfgang Amadeus Mozart, and Johann Sebastian Bach—music he had learned by listening to records at Camp Kookooskoos. Louis also liked the music of George Gershwin and Stephen Foster. When he played "Summertime" from *Porgy and Bess*, the people of Philadelphia felt that it was the most thrilling music they had ever heard. Louis was considered so good on the trumpet he was invited to make a guest appearance with the Philadelphia Symphony Orchestra.

One day, about a week before Christmas, a great storm came up. The sky grew dark. The wind blew a howling gale. It made a whining noise. Windows rattled. Shutters came off their hinges. Old newspapers and candy wrappers were picked up by the wind and scattered like confetti. Many of the creatures in the Zoo became restless and uneasy. Over in the Elephant House, the elephants trumpeted in alarm. Lions roared and paced back and forth. The Great Black Cockatoo screamed. Keepers rushed here and there, shutting doors and windows and making everything secure against the awful force of the gale. The waters of Bird Lake were ruffled by the strong, mighty wind, and for a while the lake looked like a small ocean. Many of the water birds sought protection on the island.

Louis rode out the gale on the lake, in the lee of the island. He faced the wind and kept paddling with his feet, his eyes bright with wonder at the strength of the blast. Suddenly he saw an object in the sky. It was coming down out of the clouds. At first, he couldn't make out what it was.

"Maybe it's a flying saucer," he thought.

Then he realized that it was a large white bird, struggling desperately to come in against the wind. Its wings were beating rapidly. In a moment it splashed down and flopped ashore, where it lay sprawled out, almost as if it were dead. Louis stared and stared and stared. Then he looked again.

"It looks like a swan," he thought.

It *was* a swan.

"It looks like a *Trumpeter* Swan," he thought.

It *was* a Trumpeter Swan.

"My goodness," said Louis to himself, "it looks like Serena. It *is* Serena. She's here at last. My prayers have been answered!"

Louis was right. Serena, the swan of his desiring, had been caught by the fierce storm and blown all the way across America. When she looked down and saw Bird Lake, she ended her flight, almost dead from exhaustion.

Louis was tempted to rush right over. But then he thought, "No, that would be a mistake. She is in no

condition at the moment to perceive the depth of my affection and the extent of my love. She is too pooped. I will wait. I will bide my time. I will give her a chance to recover. Then I will renew our acquaintance and make myself known."

Louis did not go to his job that night; the weather was too bad. All night, he stayed awake, keeping watch, at a slight distance from his beloved. When morning came, the wind subsided. The skies cleared. The lake grew calm. The storm was over. Serena stirred and woke. She was still exhausted, and very mussy. Louis stayed away from her.

"I'll just wait," he thought. "When in love, one must take risks. But I'm not going to risk everything with a bird who is too tired to see straight. I won't hurry, and I won't worry. Back home on Upper Red Rock Lake, I was without a voice; she ignored me because I could not tell her of my love. Now, thanks to my brave father, I have my trumpet. Through the power of music, I will impress her with the intensity of my desire and the strength of my devotion. She will hear me say ko-hoh. I'll tell her I love her in a language anybody can understand, the language of music. She will hear the trumpet of the swan, and she will be mine. At least, I *hope* she will."

Usually, if a strange bird appeared on Bird Lake, one of the keepers would report its arrival to the Head

Man in Charge of Birds, whose office was in the Bird House. The Head Man would then give the order to have the new bird pinioned—have one of its wings clipped. But today, the keeper who usually tended the waterfowl was sick with the flu and had not come to work. Nobody noticed that a new Trumpeter Swan had arrived. Serena was being very quiet, anyway—she was not attracting any attention. There were now five Trumpeters on the lake. There were the original three captive swans, Curiosity, Felicity, and Apathy. There was, of course, Louis. And now there was the new arrival, Serena, still exhausted but beginning to revive.

Toward the end of the afternoon, Serena roused herself, looked at her surroundings, had a bite to eat, took a bath, then walked out of the water and stood for a long while preening her feathers. She felt distinctly better. And when her feathers were all smoothed out, she looked extremely beautiful—stately, serene, graceful, and very feminine.

Louis trembled when he saw how truly lovely she was. He was again tempted to swim over and say ko-hoh and see if she remembered him. But he had a better idea.

"There is no hurry," he thought. "She's not going to leave Philadelphia tonight. I will go to my job, and when I get back from work, I shall abide near her all through the night. Just at daylight, I'll awaken her with a song of love and desire. She will be drowsy; the sound of my trumpet will enter her sleepy brain and overcome her with emotion. My trumpet will be the first sound she hears. I will be irresistible. I will be the first thing she sees when she opens her eyes, and she will love me from that moment on."

Louis was well satisfied with his plan and began to make preparations. He swam ashore, removed his things, hid them under a bush, then returned to the water, where he fed and bathed. Then he fixed his feathers carefully. He wanted to look his best next morning, when the meeting was to take place. He drifted around for a while, thinking of all the songs he liked and trying to decide which one to play to wake Serena in the morning. He finally decided to play "Beautiful Dreamer, Wake Unto Me." He had always loved that song. It was sad and sweet.

"She will be a beautiful dreamer," thought Louis, "and she will wake unto me. The song fits the situation perfectly."

He was determined to play the song better than he had ever played it before. It was one of his best numbers. He really knew how to play it awfully well. Once, when he played it at one of his Sunday concerts, a music critic from a Philadelphia newspaper heard him, and next morning the paper said: "Some of his notes are like jewels held up to the light. The emotion he transmits is clean and pure and sustained." Louis had memorized that statement. He was proud of it.

Now he was anxious for morning to come, but he still had his job at the nightclub to go to. He knew the night would be long and that he wouldn't be able to sleep.

Louis swam ashore to pick up his things. When he looked under the bush, he received a terrible jolt: his medal was there, his slate and chalk pencil were there, his moneybag was there, but where was the trumpet? His trumpet was gone. Poor Louis! His heart almost stopped. "Oh, no!" he said to himself. "Oh, no!" Without his trumpet, his whole life would be ruined, all his plans for the future would collapse.

He was frantic with anger and fear and dismay. He dashed back into the water and looked up and down the lake. Far off, he saw a small Wood Duck that seemed to have something shiny in its mouth. It was the trumpet, all right! The duck was trying to play it. Louis was furious. He skimmed down the lake, going even faster than he had on the day he had saved Applegate from drowning. He swam straight for the duck, knocked him on the head with a swift blow from his wing, and grabbed the precious trumpet. The duck fainted. Louis wiped the horn, blew the spit out of it, and hung it around his neck, where it belonged.

Now he was ready. "Let the night come! Let the

hours pass! Let morning come, when my beautiful dreamer wakes unto me!"

Night came at last. Nine o'clock came. Louis went off to work, riding in the cab. The Zoo quieted down. The visitors had all gone home. Many of the animals slept or snoozed. A few of them—the great cats, the raccoon, the armadillo, the ones that enjoy the night-time—prowled and became restless. Bird Lake was clothed in darkness. Most of the waterfowl tucked their heads under their wings and slept. At one end of the lake, the three captive swans—Curiosity, Felicity, and Apathy—were already asleep. Near the island, Serena, the beautiful Serena, was fast asleep and dreaming. Her long white neck was folded neatly back; her head rested on soft feathers.

Louis got home from work at two in the morning. He flew in over the low fence and splashed down near Serena, making as little noise as possible. He did not try to sleep. The night was fair and crisp, as nights often are just before Christmas. Clouds drifted across the sky in endless procession, partially hiding the stars. Louis watched the clouds, watched Serena as she slept, and waited for day to come—hour after hour after hour.

At last, a faint light showed in the east. Soon, crea-tures would be stirring, morning would be here.

"This is my moment," thought Louis. "The time has come for me to waken my true love."

He placed himself directly in front of Serena. Then he raised the trumpet to his mouth. He tilted his head: the horn pointed slightly upward toward the sky, where the first light was showing.

He began his song.

"Beautiful dreamer," he played, "wake unto me . . ."

The first three or four notes were played softly. Then as the song progressed, the sound increased; the light in the sky grew brighter.

Beau - ti - ful dream-er wake un-to me

Star-light and dew-drops are wait-ing for thee..

Each note was like a jewel held to the light. The sound of Louis's trumpet had never before been heard at this early dawn-hour in the Zoo, and the sound seemed to fill the whole world of buildings and animals and trees and shrubs and paths and dens and cages. Sleepy bears, dozing in their grotto, pricked up their ears. Foxes, hiding in their dens, listened to the sweet and dreamy sound of the horn blown at the coming of light. In the Lion House, the great cats heard. In the Monkey House, the old baboon listened in wonder to the song.

Beau—ti—ful dream—er, wake un—to me . . .

The hippo heard, and the seal in his tank. The grey wolf heard, and the yak in his cage. The badger, the coon, the Ring-tailed Coati, the skunk, the weasel, the otter, the llama, the dromedary, the White-tailed Deer —all heard, listened, pricked up their ears at the song. The kudu heard, and the rabbit. The beaver heard, and the snake, who *has* no ears. The wallaby, the possum, the anteater, the armadillo, the peafowl, the pigeon, the bowerbird, the cockatoo, the flamingo—all heard, all were aware that something out of the ordinary was happening.

Philadelphians, waking from sleep in bedrooms where the windows were open, heard the trumpet. Not one person who heard the song realized that this was the moment of triumph for a young swan who had a speech defect and had conquered it.

Louis was not thinking about his large, unseen audience of animals and people. His mind was not on bears and buffaloes and cassowaries and lizards and hawks and owls and people in bedrooms. His mind was on Serena, the swan of his choice, the beautiful dreamer. He played for her and for her alone.

At the first note from his trumpet, she woke. She raised her head and her neck straightened until her head was held high. What she saw filled her with astonishment. She gazed straight at Louis. At first, she could hardly remember where she was. Directly in front of her, she saw a handsome young male swan, a cob of noble proportions. Held against his mouth was a strange instrument—something she had never seen before. And from this strange instrument came sounds that made her tremble with joy and with love. As the song went on, as the light grew stronger, she fell hopelessly in love with this bold trumpeter who had awakened her from her dreams. The dreams of night were gone. New dreams of day were upon her. She knew that she was full of sensations she had never had before—feelings of delight and ecstasy and wonder.

She had never seen a finer-looking young cob. She had certainly never seen *any* swan with so many personal possessions around his neck. And she had never been so thrilled by a sound before in her whole life.

"Oh!" she thought. "Oh, oh, oh, oh!"

The song ended. Louis lowered his trumpet and bowed solemnly to Serena. Then he raised his horn again.

"Ko-hoh!" he said.

"Ko-hoh!" replied Serena.

"Ko-hoh, ko-hoh!" said Louis through his trumpet.

"Ko-hoh, ko-hoh!" replied Serena.

Each felt drawn to the other by a mysterious bond of affection.

Louis swam once rapidly around Serena.

Then Serena swam once rapidly around Louis. This seemed to amuse them.

Louis dipped his neck and pumped it back and forth.

Serena dipped her neck and pumped it back and forth.

Louis splashed a little water into the air. Serena splashed a little water into the air. It was like a game. It was love at long last for Louis; it was love at first sight for Serena.

Then Louis decided to show off. "I'll play her my own composition," he thought. "The one I made up for her last summer at camp." Again he raised his trumpet.

> *Oh, ever in the greening spring*
> *By bank and bough retiring,*
> *For love shall I be sorrowing*
> *And swans of my desiring.*

The notes were clear and pure. They filled the Zoo with beauty. If Serena had been in any doubt before, she no longer was. She succumbed completely to this charmer, this handsome musician, this rich and talented cob.

Louis knew that his plan had succeeded. His beautiful dreamer had waked, and she had waked unto him. Never again would they be parted. All the rest of their lives they would be together. Thoughts of small quiet lakes in the woods, where canebrakes grew and blackbirds sang, filled Louis's mind. Thoughts of springtime and nesting and little cygnets. Oh, ever in the greening spring!

Louis had been told once by his father what happened to deep-sea divers when they go far, far down into the ocean. At great depths, where the pressure is great and the watery world is strange and mysterious, divers sometimes experience what they call the "rapture of the deep." They feel so completely peaceful and enchanted, they never want to return to the surface. Louis's father had warned him about this. "Always remember, when you dive deep," he had said, "that this feeling of rapture can lead you to your death. No matter how wonderful you feel down there, *don't ever forget to return to the surface*, where you can breathe again!"

Looking at Serena, Louis thought to himself, "I think love is like the rapture of the deep. I feel so good I just want to stay right where I am. I'm experiencing rapture of the deep even though I'm right on top of the water. I have never felt so good, so peaceful, so excited, so happy, so ambitious, so desirous.

If love is like this on a cold day in December in the Philadelphia Zoo, imagine what it's going to be like in spring on a remote lake in Canada!"

These were Louis's secret thoughts. He was the happiest bird alive. He was a real Trumpeter Swan at last. His defect of being without a voice had at last been overcome. He felt very grateful to his father.

Cautiously, he placed his head across Serena's long beautiful white neck. It seemed a very daring thing to do, but she seemed to like it. Then he backed away. Serena swam toward him. Cautiously, she placed *her* head across *his* neck. It rested there for a moment; then she swam away.

"What a daring thing!" she thought. "But he seems to like it. How pleasing to know that I have found an acceptable mate—a cob I can love and respect, a cob that appears to be not only musical but also quite wealthy. Look at all those *things*!" said Serena to herself. Her eyes feasted on the trumpet, the slate, the chalk pencil, the moneybag, the lifesaving medal.

"What a gay cob!" she thought. "What a dressy fellow!"

They swam off together toward the other end of the lake, where they could be alone. Then Louis, who was short on sleep, dozed off, while Serena ate her breakfast and fixed herself up.

Chapter 18

Freedom

THE NEWS of Serena's arrival on Bird Lake had finally reached the Head Man in Charge of Birds. He went out to look at her and was delighted. Then he gave an order to one of his keepers.

"See to it that she is pinioned this morning—right away, before she flies off and leaves us. That swan is a valuable bird. Make sure she doesn't get away!"

Louis was just waking from his nap when he saw two keepers approaching Serena, who was standing on the shore near the ornamental fence. One keeper carried a large net with a long handle. The other carried surgical instruments. They were sneaking up on Serena from behind, very slowly and quietly.

Louis knew right away what they were up to. He grew hot with rage. If those men succeeded in catching Serena and cutting a wing tip, all his plans would go wrong—she could never fly away to a lonely lake with him; she would have to remain in Philadelphia the rest of her life, a horrible fate.

"This is my moment," thought Louis. "Nobody is going to clip my Love's wing while *I'm* around."

He hustled over to the island and stripped for action. He chucked his trumpet and all his other stuff under a willow tree. Then he returned to the water and waited for the right time to attack.

The keeper holding the net was crawling quietly up on Serena from the rear. She did not notice him—she was just standing there, dreaming of Louis. Slowly, slowly the keeper raised his net. As he did so, Louis went into action. Lowering his long, powerful neck until it pointed straight out in front of him like a lance, he streaked across the water, straight at the keeper, his wings beating the air, his feet beating the water. In a flash, he reached the scene and drove his strong bill straight into the seat of the man's pants. It was a well-aimed jab. The keeper doubled up in pain and dropped the net. The other keeper tried to grab Serena by her throat. Louis beat him over the head with his wings, striking terrific blows and knocking the poor fellow off his feet. Surgical instruments bounced into the air. The net fell into the water. One keeper groaned and held his hand on his behind, where he had been stabbed. The other keeper lay on the ground, almost knocked out.

Serena slipped quickly into the water and glided gracefully away. Louis followed. He motioned for her

to stay on the lake. Then he raced back to the island, grabbed his trumpet, his slate, his chalk pencil, his medal, and his moneybag, flew over the balustrade, and walked boldly into the Bird House. He was still mad. He went straight to the office of the Head Man in Charge of Birds. He rapped on the door.

"Come in!" said a voice.

Louis entered. The Head Man was seated at his desk. "Hello, Louis!" he said.

"Ko-hoh!" replied Louis through his trumpet.

"What's on your mind?" asked the man.

Louis placed his trumpet on the floor and took his slate and chalk pencil from his neck. "I'm in love," he wrote.

The Head Man leaned back in his chair and put his hands behind his head. His face had a faraway look. He gazed out of the window for a moment in silence.

"Well," he said, "it's natural that you're in love. You're young. You're talented. In a couple of months, spring will be here. All birds fall in love in springtime. I suppose you're in love with one of my young swans."

"Serena," wrote Louis. "She arrived the day before yesterday. I used to know her slightly, back in Montana. She loves me, too."

"That doesn't surprise me," said the Head Man. "You're a very unusual young cob. Any young female swan would fall for you. You're a great trumpeter—

one of the best. I'm delighted to hear about this love affair, Louis. You and your bride can stay right here on Bird Lake and raise your family in comfort and safety, in the oldest zoo in the United States."

Louis shook his head.

"I have other plans," he wrote. Then he set his slate down and raised his trumpet. "They say that falling in love is wonderful . . ." It was an old song by Irving Berlin. The room was filled with the sound of love. The Head Man had a dreamy look in his eyes.

Louis set his horn down and took up his slate again. "I am taking Serena away with me in a day or two," he wrote.

"Oh, no you're not!" said the Head Man firmly. "Serena now belongs to the Zoo. She is the property of the people of Philadelphia. She came here because of an act of God."

"It wasn't an act of God," wrote Louis. "It was a high wind."

"Well, anyway," said the Head Man, "she's *my* swan."

"No, she's mine," wrote Louis. "She's mine by reason of the power of love—the greatest force on earth."

The Head Man became thoughtful. "You can't take Serena from the Zoo. She will never fly again. My keepers clipped one of her wings a few minutes ago."

"They tried to," wrote Louis, "but I beat them up."

The Head Man looked surprised. "Was it a good fight?"

"It was a fair fight," replied Louis. "They were sneaking up on her from behind, so I sneaked up on *them* from behind. They hardly knew what hit them."

The Head Man chuckled. "I wish I'd seen it," he said. "But look here, Louis, you've got to realize the position I'm in. I have a duty to the people of Philadelphia. Within the last couple of months, I've acquired *two* rare birds by accident—you and Serena. Two Trumpeter Swans! One arrived here blown by a gale, the other to keep a nightclub engagement. The whole business is most unusual for a zoo. I have my responsibility to the public. It is my duty as Head Man in Charge of Birds to see that Serena stays. You yourself, of course, are free to leave when you want to, because Mr. Lucas insisted that you remain free when we arranged for your Sunday concerts. But in Serena's case . . . well, Louis, she's got to have her left wing tip amputated. The Zoo can't afford to lose a young, beautiful, valuable Trumpeter Swan just because *you* happen to be in love. Besides, I think you're making a great mistake. If you and Serena stay here, you'll be safe. You'll have no enemies. You'll have no worries about your children. No fox, no otter, no coyote will ever attack you with intent to kill. You'll never go hungry. You'll never get shot. You'll never die of lead poisoning from eating the shotgun pellets that are on the bottom of all natural lakes and ponds. Your cygnets will be hatched each spring and will live a long life in perfect ease and comfort. What more can a young cob ask?"

"Freedom," replied Louis on his slate. "Safety is all well and good; I prefer freedom." With that, he picked up his trumpet and played "Button up your overcoat, when the wind blows free . . ."

The Head Man smiled. He knew just what Louis meant. For a while the two remained silent. Louis put his trumpet aside. Then he wrote: "I ask two favours. First, put off the operation on Serena until after Christmas—I'll guarantee she won't try to escape. Second, let me send a telegram."

"O.K., Louis," replied the Head Man. And he handed Louis a sheet of paper and a pencil. Louis wrote out a telegram to Sam Beaver. It said:

AM IN THE PHILADELPHIA ZOO. THIS IS
AN EMERGENCY. COME AT ONCE. I WILL
PAY YOUR PLANE FARE. AM NOW WEALTHY.
(Signed) LOUIS

He handed the telegram to the Head Man along with four dollars from his money bag. The Head Man was astounded. In all his days at the Zoo, this was the first time one of his birds had asked him to send a telegram. And of course he didn't know who Sam Beaver was. But he sent the wire and ordered his keepers to let Serena alone for a few days—which they were glad to do.

Louis thanked him and left. He returned to Serena, and they spent the day happily together, bathing, swimming, eating, drinking, and showing each other in a thousand small ways how much they loved each other.

Sam arrived at the Zoo on the day after Christmas. He was equipped as though he were going into the woods. Under one arm was a sleeping bag, neatly rolled. On his back was a rucksack containing his toothbrush, his comb, a clean shirt, a hand axe, a pocket compass, his notebook, a pencil, and some food. In his belt was a hunting knife. Sam was fourteen now and big for his age. He had never seen a large zoo. He and Louis were overjoyed to see each other again.

Louis introduced Sam to Serena. Then he opened his moneybag and showed Sam his earnings: hundred-dollar bills, fifty-dollar bills, twenty-dollar bills, tens, fives, ones, and some silver coins—a great pile.

"Goodness!" thought Sam. "I hope she's not marrying him for his money."

Louis took his slate and told Sam about the fight with the keepers and about how the Head Man wanted to keep Serena captive by clipping the tip of one wing. He told Sam it would ruin his life if Serena were to lose the power to fly. He explained that as soon as his father's debts were paid and the trumpet honestly belonged to him, he and Serena intended to leave civilization and return to a wild life. "The sky," he wrote on his slate, "is my living room. The woods are my parlour. The lonely lake is my bath. I can't remain behind a fence all my life. Neither can Serena—she's not built that way. Somehow or other we must persuade the Head Man to let Serena go."

Sam stretched out on the shore of Bird Lake and clasped his hands behind his head. He looked up at the great wide sky. It was a clear blue, with small white clouds floating slowly across. Sam knew how Louis felt about freedom. For a long time he lay there, thinking. Ducks and geese swam slowly by, back and forth, an endless procession of captive birds. They seemed happy and well. Curiosity, Felicity, and Apathy —the three Trumpeters—swam by and peered at the strange boy lying on the ground. Finally Sam sat up.

"Listen, Louis," he said. "How's this for an idea? You and Serena intend to raise a family every year, don't you?"

"Certainly," replied Louis on his slate.

"O.K.," said Sam. "In every family of cygnets, there is always one that needs special care and protection. Bird Lake would be a perfect place for this one little swan that needs extra security. This is a beautiful lake, Louis. This is a great zoo. If I can persuade the Head Man to let Serena remain free, would you be willing to donate one of your cygnets, now and then, if the Zoo needs another swan for the lake? If you agree, I'll go right in and see the Head Man about the matter."

It was now Louis's turn to think and think. After five minutes, he picked up his slate.

"Very well," he wrote. "It's a deal."

Then he picked up his trumpet. "Oh, ever in the greening spring," he played. "By bank and bough retiring . . ."

The waterfowl stopped swimming and listened. The keepers stopped what they were doing and listened. Sam listened. The Head Man in his office in the Bird House laid down his pencil, leaned back in his chair, and listened. The sound of Louis's horn was in the air, and the whole world seemed better and brighter and wilder and freer and happier and dreamier.

"That's a good tune," said Sam. "What is it?"

"Oh, just something I made up myself," wrote Louis on his slate.

Chapter 19

A Talk About Money

IN ALMOST everyone's life there is one event that changes the whole course of his existence. The day Sam Beaver visited the Philadelphia Zoo was the turning point in his life. Up until that day, he had not been able to decide what he wanted to be when he grew up. The minute he saw the Zoo, all his doubts vanished. He knew he wanted to work in a zoo. Sam loved every living thing, and a zoo is a great storehouse of living things—it has just about every creature that creeps or crawls or jumps or runs or flies or hides.

Sam was eager to see them all. But he had Louis's problem to solve first. He must save Serena from captivity. So he picked up his rucksack and his sleeping bag and walked into the Bird House and entered the office. He walked tall and straight, as though he were on a forest trail. The Head Man liked Sam's appearance and noticed that he looked a little like an Indian.

"So you're Sam Beaver," said the Head Man, as Sam advanced on him.

"Why did you come here?" asked the Head Man.

"To defend freedom," replied Sam. "I heard you intended to clip the wing of a swan. I'm here to ask you not to do it."

Sam sat down, and they talked for a whole hour. Sam assured the Head Man that Louis was an old friend. He told about discovering the swan's nest almost three years ago in Canada, about how Louis came into the world lacking a voice, about Louis's attending school in Montana and learning to read and write, about the theft of the trumpet by Louis's father, the old cob, and about Camp Kookooskoos and the Swan Boat in Boston.

The Head Man listened with great attention, but he wasn't sure he believed a word of this strange tale.

Then Sam explained his proposal for allowing Serena to go free instead of making a captive bird out of her. He said he thought it would be a good arrangement for the Zoo, because any time they wanted a young Trumpeter Swan, Louis would give them one of his cygnets. The Head Man was fascinated.

"You mean to say you came all the way to Philadelphia to help a bird?"

"Yes, sir," replied Sam. "I would go anywhere to help a bird. Besides, Louis is special. He's an old friend. We went to the same school. You've got to admit he's quite a bird."

"He sure is," said the Head Man. "His Sunday afternoon concerts have been the biggest attraction the Zoo has ever had. We had a gorilla once named Bamboo—he's dead now. Bamboo was great, but Louis draws even more of a crowd than Bamboo did. We have sea lions that draw big crowds, but nothing to compare with Louis when he plays that horn on Sunday afternoons. People go crazy. And music is good for the animals, too—it soothes them, and they forget the cares of the day. I'm going to miss Louis when he's gone. The whole Zoo will miss him terribly. I wish he'd stay and keep his bride right here—it would be just great."

"Louis would pine away in captivity. He would die," replied Sam. "He needs wild places—little ponds, swamps, cattails, Red-winged Blackbirds in the spring, the chorus of the frogs, the cry of the loon at night. Louis is following a dream. We must all follow a dream. Please let Serena go, sir! Please don't clip her wing!"

The Head Man closed his eyes. He was thinking of little lakes deep in the woods, of the colour of bulrushes, of the sounds of night and the chorus of frogs. He was thinking of swans' nests, and eggs, and the hatching of eggs, and the cygnets following their father in single file. He was thinking of dreams he had had as a young man.

"All right," he said, suddenly. "Serena can go. We will not clip her wing. But how can I be sure that

Louis will bring me a young Trumpeter Swan when I need one? How do I know he's honest?"

"He's an honourable bird," said Sam. "If he weren't honest and true to his word, he wouldn't have bothered to go out and earn a lot of money to pay the store-keeper back for the trumpet his father swiped."

"How much money has Louis got, anyway?" asked the Head Man.

"He's got four thousand six hundred and ninety-one dollars and sixty-five cents," said Sam. "We just counted it a few minutes ago. He received one hundred dollars from Camp Kookooskoos for playing bugle calls, and all he spent was sixty cents for postage stamps. So he arrived in Boston with ninety-nine dollars and forty cents. Then the Swan Boat man paid him a hundred dollars for one week's work, but he spent three dollars in tips at the hotel where he spent a night. So he had a hundred and ninety-six dollars and forty cents when he got to Philadelphia. The nightclub paid him five hundred dollars a week for ten weeks, which came to five thousand dollars, but he had to pay his agent ten percent of the five thousand dollars, and he also spent seventy-five cents for some new chalk pencils and four dollars to send the telegram to me. So that makes a total of four thousand six hundred and ninety-one dollars and sixty-five cents. It's a lot of money for a bird."

"It sure is," said the Head Man. "It sure is."

"But he is going to pay my aeroplane fare from Montana to Philadelphia and back again. That will bring the total down to four thousand four hundred and twenty dollars and seventy-eight cents."

The Head Man looked staggered by these figures.

"It's *still* a lot of money for a bird," he said. "What's he going to do with it all?"

"He will give it to his father, the old cob."

"And what's *he* going to do with it?"

"He will fly back to the music store in Billings and give it to the owner, to pay for the stolen trumpet."

"Give *all* of it?"

"Yes."

"But a trumpet isn't worth four thousand four hundred and twenty dollars and seventy-eight cents."

"I know," said Sam. "But there was some damage to the store itself. The old cob was going like the dickens when he crashed through the plate-glass window. He shook things up pretty badly."

"Yes," said the Head Man. "But it *still* wouldn't take all that money to make things right."

"I guess not," said Sam. "But Louis has no use for money anymore, so he's going to turn it all over to the owner of the music store."

The subject of money seemed to interest the Head Man greatly. He thought how pleasant it would be not to have any more use for money. He leaned back in his chair. He found it hard to believe that one of his swans had been able to save more than four thousand dollars and that the money was right out there, hanging around his neck in a moneybag.

"When it comes to money," he said, "birds have it easier than men do. When a bird earns some money, it's almost all clear profit. A bird doesn't have to go to a supermarket and buy a dozen eggs and a pound of butter and two rolls of paper towels and a TV dinner and a can of Ajax and a can of tomato juice and a pound and a half of ground round steak and a can of sliced peaches and two quarts of fat-free milk and a bottle of stuffed olives. A bird doesn't have to pay rent on a house, or interest on a mortgage. A bird doesn't insure its life with an insurance company and then have to pay premiums on the policy. A bird doesn't own a car and buy petrol and oil and pay for repairs on the car and take the car to a car wash and pay to get it washed. Animals and birds are lucky. They don't keep acquiring things, the way men do. You can teach a monkey to drive a motorcycle, but I have never known a monkey to go out and *buy* a motorcycle."

"That's right," replied Sam. "But some animals do like to acquire things, even though they don't pay anything for them."

"Such as?" asked the Head Man.

"A rat," said Sam. "A rat will fix up a home for himself, but then he'll bring home all sorts of little objects—trinkets and stuff. Anything he can find that catches his eye."

"You're right," said the Head Man. "You're absolutely right, Sam. You seem to know quite a lot about animals."

"I like animals," said Sam. "I love to watch them."

"Then come with me and we'll explore the Zoo," said the Head Man, getting up from his chair. "I don't feel like working anymore today. I'll show you the Zoo." And away they went, the two of them.

That night Sam slept in the Head Man's office, by special permission. He unrolled his sleeping bag on the floor and crawled in. The plane taking him back home would leave in the morning. Sam's head was full of everything he had seen in the Zoo. And before he turned out the light he took his notebook out of his rucksack and wrote a poem. This is what he wrote:

SAM BEAVER'S POEM

Of all the places on land and sea,
Philadelphia's zoo is the place for me.
There's plenty to eat and a lot to do,
There's a Frigate Bird and a tiny Shrew;
There's a Vesper Rat and a Two-toed Sloth,
And it's fair to say that I like them both.

373

There's a Canada Goose and a Polar Bear
And things that come from Everywhere.
There are lots of things that you've never seen
Like the Kinkajou and the Wolverine.
You really have to go to the zoo
To see a newborn Wallaroo
Or a Fallow Deer or a White-tailed Gnu.
There are wondrous birds on a beautiful lake,
There's a Timber Wolf and a Hognose Snake.
There are animals with great appeal,
Like the Hummingbird and the Harbour Seal.
There are pony rides, there are birds of prey,
And something happening every day.
There are Wolves and Foxes, Hawks and Owls,
And a great big pit where the Lion prowls.
There are quiet pools and pleasant cages,
Where Reptiles lie and the Tiger rages.
The houses are clean, the keepers are kind,
And one Baboon has a pink behind.
The entire aim of a well-kept zoo
Is to bring the animal world to You.

(signed) **Sam** Beaver

Sam left the poem on the Head Man's desk.

Early the next morning, long before the Zoo people
came to work, Sam left Philadelphia by plane. Louis
and Serena went along with him to the airport. They
wanted to wave good-bye. They also planned to leave

Philadelphia, right then and there, and fly back to Montana. When the airport officials saw two big white birds out on the airstrip, they raised a terrible fuss. The men in the control tower sent warning messages to the pilots of incoming planes. Members of the ground crew came piling out of buildings and rushed toward Louis and Serena to chase them away. Sam was sitting by a window inside his plane, ready for takeoff, and he saw the whole thing.

Louis grabbed his trumpet.

"Off we go," he played, "into the wild blue yonder!" The notes carried across the airport and startled everyone. "Ko-hoh! Ko-hoh!" called Louis. He put his trumpet away and started racing down the airstrip, with Serena racing after him. Just then, Sam's plane started into the wind for the takeoff. The two swans flew alongside. They were in the air before the plane was, and flying fast. Sam waved from the window. Louis's lifesaving medal gleamed in the morning sun. The plane rose and started to climb. Louis and Serena climbed fast, too.

"Good-bye, Philadelphia!" thought Louis. "Good-bye, Bird Lake! Good-bye, nightclub!"

The plane, with its greater speed, gained on the swans. They began to drop behind. For a little while they headed west, following the plane. Then Louis motioned to Serena that he was going to change course.

He banked to the left and swung toward the south.

"We'll go home by the southern route and take our time about it," he said to himself.

And that's what they did. They flew south across Maryland and Virginia. They flew south across the Carolinas. They spent a night in Yemassee and saw huge oak trees with moss hanging from their branches. They visited the great swamps of Georgia and saw the alligator and listened to the mockingbird. They flew across Florida and spent a few days in a bayou where doves moaned in the cedars and little lizards crawled in the sun. They turned west into Louisiana. Then they turned north toward their home in Upper Red Rock Lake.

What a triumphant return it would be! When he left Montana, Louis had been penniless. Now he was rich. When he left, he had been unknown. Now he was famous. When he left, he had been alone in the world. Now he had his bride by his side—the swan that he loved. His medal was around his neck, his precious trumpet dangled in the breeze, his hard-earned money was in the bag. He had accomplished what he had set out to do. All in a few short months!

Freedom felt so wonderful! Love felt so good!

Chapter 20
Billings

ON A BRIGHT clear day in January, Louis and Serena came home to the Red Rock Lakes. From among the thousands of waterfowl, they quickly found the members of their own families—their fathers and mothers and sisters and brothers. It was a noisy homecoming. Everybody wanted to say hello at once. Ko-hoh, ko-hoh, ko-hoh! The wanderers were home at last.

Louis's father, the old cob, made a graceful speech—rather long, but sincere.

Louis raised his trumpet and played "There's no place like home. Home, home sweet home!" There was a great deal of gossip among the waterfowl about Louis's having persuaded Serena to be his wife. Everybody congratulated the happy couple. And all the brothers and sisters of Louis and Serena gathered around and looked at Louis's possessions. They were much impressed by his worldly goods. They liked the lifesaving medal, they loved the sound of the trumpet, and they were eager to see the money in the moneybag. But Louis did not open the bag. Instead, he took his father and mother to one side. They all three stepped out on shore, where Louis slipped the moneybag off his neck and, with a bow, handed it to the old cob. Four thousand four hundred and twenty dollars and seventy-eight cents.

Then Louis took his slate and wrote a note to the owner of the music store in Billings so his father would have something to show him when he got there. The note said:

To the Storekeeper of Billings:
Enclosed please find $4,420.78. It will pay you
for the trumpet and the damage to the store.
Sorry about the inconvenience this has caused you.

The old cob was not able to count money, and he was not able to read, but he took the moneybag and the slate and hung them around his neck. He felt sure he could now pay his debt for the stolen trumpet.

"I shall go," he said to his wife. "I shall redeem my honour. I shall return to Billings, the scene of my crime —a great city, teeming with life—"

"We've heard that before," remarked his wife. "Just take the money and the note and beat it for Billings as fast as you can go. And when you get there, for heavens' sakes be careful! The owner of that music store has a gun. He will remember that the last time he saw a swan coming at him he got robbed. So watch yourself! You're on a dangerous mission."

"Danger!" said the old cob. "Danger! I *welcome* danger and adventure. Danger is my middle name. I would risk my life to redeem my honour and recapture my sense of decency. I shall pay my debt and blot out the foul mark that sullies my good name. I shall rid myself forever of the shame that comes from thievery and wrongdoing. I shall—"

"If you don't stop talking," said his wife, "you won't get to Billings before the stores close."

"You are right, as usual," replied the cob. He adjusted the moneybag and the slate for flight. Then he took off into the air and headed toward the northeast, flying fast and high. His wife and son watched him until he faded from view.

"What a swan!" said his wife. "You have a good father, Louis. I hope nothing happens to him. To tell you the truth, I'm worried."

The old cob flew fast and far. When he spied the churches and factories and shops and homes of Billings, he circled once, then began his downward glide—straight for the music store.

"My hour has come," he said to himself. "My mo-

379

ment of truth is at hand. I shall soon be out of debt, out from under the cloud of shame and dishonour that has cast a shadow over my life for lo these many months."

The cob had been seen already by people down below. One of the salesmen in the music store was standing by the front window, looking out. When he saw the big white bird approaching, he yelled to the storekeeper: "Large bird approaching. Get your gun!"

The storekeeper grabbed his shotgun and raced to the sidewalk. The cob was low in the sky, gliding straight for the store.

The storekeeper raised his gun. He fired both barrels in quick succession. The old cob felt a twinge of pain in his left shoulder. Thoughts of death filled his mind. Looking back, he saw a bright red drop of blood staining his breast. But he kept going, straight for the storekeeper.

"The end is near," he said to himself. "I shall die in the performance of duty. I have only a few moments remaining to live. Man, in his folly, has given me a mortal wound. The red blood flows in a steady trickle from my veins. My strength fails. But even in death's final hour, I shall deliver the money for the trumpet. Good-bye, life! Good-bye, beautiful world! Good-bye, little lakes in the north! Farewell, springtimes I have known, with their passion and ardour! Farewell, loyal wife and loving sons and daughters! I, who am about to die, salute you. I must die gracefully, as only a swan can."

With that, he sank to the sidewalk, held out the moneybag and the slate to the astonished storekeeper, and fainted away at the sight of his own blood. He lay limp on the sidewalk, to all appearances a dying swan.

A crowd quickly gathered.

"What's this?" exclaimed the storekeeper, bending over the bird. "What's going on here?"

He quickly read the note on the slate. Then he tore open the moneybag and began pulling out hundred-dollar bills and fifty-dollar bills.

A policeman hurried to the scene and started to hold the crowd back.

"Stand back!" he shouted. "The swan is wounded. Give him air!"

"He's dead," said a little boy. "The bird is dead."

"He *is not* dead," said the salesman. "He's scared."

"Call an ambulance!" screamed a lady in the crowd.

A small pool of blood formed under the neck of the old cob. He seemed lifeless. Just then a game warden appeared.

"Who shot this bird?" he demanded.

"I did," said the storekeeper.

"Then you're under arrest," said the warden.

"What for?" asked the storekeeper.

"For shooting a Trumpeter Swan. These birds are protected by law. You can't pull a gun on a wild swan."

"Well," replied the storekeeper, "you can't arrest *me*, either. I happen to know this bird. He's a thief. *He's* the one you should arrest. He's been here before, and he stole a trumpet from my store."

"Call an ambulance!" cried the lady.

"What's that you've got in your hand?" asked the policeman. The storekeeper quickly stuffed the money

back into the moneybag and held the bag and the slate behind his back.

"Come on, show it to me!" said the cop.

"I want to see it, too," said the warden.

"We *all* want to see it!" cried a fellow in the crowd. "What's in that bag?"

The storekeeper sheepishly handed the moneybag and the slate to the game warden. The warden stood straight, put on his glasses, and read the note in a loud

voice: "To the Storekeeper of Billings: Enclosed please find four thousand four hundred and twenty dollars and seventy-eight cents. It will pay you for the trumpet and the damage to the store. Sorry about the inconvenience this has caused you."

At the mention of the sum of money, the crowd gasped. Everyone started talking at once.

"Call an ambulance!" screamed the lady.

"I'll have to take that money to the station house," said the policeman. "This is a complicated case. Anything that involves money is complex. I'll take the money and keep it safe until the matter is decided."

"No, you won't!" said the game warden. "The money is mine."

"Why?" asked the policeman.

"Because," replied the warden.

"Because *what*?" asked the policeman.

"Because the law says the bird is in my custody. The money was on the bird. Therefore, the money goes to me until this is settled."

"Oh, no, you don't!" said the storekeeper, angrily. "The money is mine. It says so right here on this slate. The four thousand four hundred and twenty dollars and seventy-eight cents is mine. Nobody's going to take it away from me."

"Yes, they are!" said the policeman. " *I* am."

"No, *I* am," said the game warden.

"Is there a lawyer in the crowd?" asked the store-keeper. "We'll settle this matter right here and now."

A tall man stepped forward.

"I'm Judge Ricketts," he said. "I'll decide this case. Now then, who saw the bird arrive?"

"I did," said the salesman.

"Call an ambulance!" screamed the lady.

"I saw the bird, too," said a small boy named Alfred Gore.

"O.K.," said the judge. "Describe what happened, exactly as you saw it."

The salesman spoke first. "Well," he said, "I was looking out the window and saw a swan approaching. So I hollered. The boss got his gun and fired, and the bird fell to the sidewalk. There was a drop or two of blood."

"Did you notice anything special about the bird?" asked Judge Ricketts.

"He carried money," replied the salesman. "You don't often see any money on a bird, so I noticed it."

"All right," said the judge. "Now we'll let Alfred Gore tell it as *he* saw it. Describe what you saw, Alfred!"

"Well," said the little boy, "I was very thirsty, and so I wanted to go to a candy store and get something to drink."

"Just tell what you saw, please, Alfred," said the

judge. "Never mind how thirsty you were."

"I was coming along the street," continued Alfred, "because I was very thirsty. So I was coming along the street on my way to the candy store to get something to drink, and there, up in the sky, all of a sudden there was a big white bird right over me in the sky and he was sliding down out of the sky like *this*." Alfred held out his arms and imitated a bird. "And so when I saw the big bird I stopped thinking about how thirsty I was and pretty soon this enormous bird, he was enormous, was on the sidewalk and he was dead and there was blood all over everything and that's what I saw."

"Did you notice anything special about the bird?" asked Judge Ricketts.

"Blood," said Alfred.

"Anything else?"

"No, just blood."

"Did you hear a gun?"

"No, just blood," said Alfred.

"Thank you!" said the judge. "That will be all."

Just then a siren started wailing—woooaw, woooaw, woooaw. An ambulance came screaming down the street. It stopped in front of the crowd. Two men jumped out. They carried a stretcher and set it down next to where the swan lay. The old cob lifted his head and looked around. "I have been at death's door," he thought, "and now I think I am returning to life. I am reviving. I shall live! I shall return on strong wings to the great sky. I shall glide gracefully again on the ponds of the world and hear the frogs and take pleasure in the sounds of night and the coming of day."

As he was thinking these pleasant thoughts, he felt himself being lifted. The ambulance attendants put his slate around his neck, picked him up, laid him gently on the stretcher, and carried him into the ambulance, which had a red light whirling round and around on top of it. One of the men placed an oxygen mask over the old cob's head and gave him some oxygen. And away they drove, making a great deal of noise, to the hospital. There, he was put to bed and given a shot of penicillin. A young doctor came in and examined the wound where the shotgun pellet had hit him. The doctor said the wound was superficial. The old cob didn't know what "superficial" meant, but it sounded serious.

Nurses gathered around. One of them took the swan's blood pressure and wrote something on a chart. The old cob was beginning to feel very well again. It felt good to be in bed, being cared for by nurses— one of whom was quite pretty. The doctor washed the wound and put a Band-Aid on it.

Meantime, back on the sidewalk in front of the

music store, the judge was announcing his decision.

"On the basis of the testimony," he said solemnly, "I award the money to the storekeeper, to make up for the loss of the trumpet and damage to the store. I am placing the swan in the custody of the game warden."

"Your Honour," said the warden, "don't forget that the storekeeper is under arrest for shooting a wild swan."

"It was a case of false arrest," said the judge wisely. "The storekeeper fired his gun at the bird because he was afraid his store would be robbed again. He did not know that the swan was bringing money to pay for the trumpet. The gun was fired in self-defense. Everyone is innocent, the swan is honest, the debt is paid, the storekeeper is rich, and the case is dismissed."

A cheer went up from the crowd. The warden looked sulky. The policeman looked glum. But the storekeeper was beaming. He was a happy man. He felt that justice had been done.

"I have an announcement," he said. "I am only going to keep just enough of this money to pay for the stolen trumpet and the repair bills for my store. All the rest of the money will be given to a good cause if I can think of just the right one. Can anyone think of a worthy cause that needs money?"

"The Salvation Army," suggested a woman.

"No," said the storekeeper.

"The Boy Scouts?" suggested a boy.

"No," said the storekeeper.

"The American Civil Liberties Union?" suggested a man.

"Nope," said the storekeeper. "Nobody has thought of just the right place for me to send this money."

"How about the Audubon Society?" asked a little fellow whose nose looked like the beak of a bird.

"Great! You've got it!" cried the storekeeper. "A bird has been very good to me, and now I want to do something for birds. The Audubon Society is kind to birds. I want this money to be used to help birds. Some birds are in real trouble. They face extinction."

"What's extinction?" asked Alfred Gore. "Does it mean they stink?"

"Certainly not," said the storekeeper. "Extinction is what happens when you're extinct—when you don't exist anymore because there are no others like you. Like the passenger pigeon and the eastern Heath Hen and the Dodo and the Dinosaur."

"The Trumpeter Swan was *almost* extinct," said the game warden. "People kept shooting them, like this crazy storekeeper. But now they are making a comeback."

The storekeeper glared at the warden.

"*I'll* say they're making a comeback," he said. "The swan that was just here *came back* to Billings with four thousand four hundred and twenty dollars and seventy-eight cents and gave it all to me. I call that making a very good comeback. I can't imagine where he *got* all that money. It's a mighty funny thing."

The storekeeper went back into his music store, the policeman went back to the station house, the judge went back to the courthouse, the game warden walked off down the street toward the hospital, and Alfred Gore, who was still thirsty, continued his journey to the candy store. All the rest of the people wandered away.

At the hospital, the old cob lay peacefully in bed thinking beautiful thoughts. He felt thankful to be alive and relieved to be out of debt.

It was getting dark. Many of the patients in the hospital were asleep already. A nurse came into the cob's room to open his window.

When she came back a few minutes later to take the cob's temperature and give him a back rub, the bed was empty—the room was deserted. The cob had jumped out of the window, spread his broad wings, and headed for home through the cold night sky. He flew all night, crossed the mountains, and arrived home soon after daylight, where his wife was waiting for him.

"How did it go?" she asked.

"Very well," he said. "An extraordinary adventure. I was shot at, just as you predicted. The storekeeper pointed a gun at me and fired. I felt an agonizing pain in my left shoulder—which I've always considered the more beautiful of my two shoulders. Blood gushed from my wound in torrents, and I sank gracefully to the sidewalk, where I handed over the money and thus regained my honour and my decency. I was at death's door. A great multitude of people gathered. Blood was everywhere. I became faint and passed out with dignity in front of all. The police arrived—dozens of them. Game wardens flocked to the scene in great numbers, and there was a tremendous argument about the money."

"How did you know all this if you were unconscious?" asked his wife.

"My dear," said the cob, "I wish you wouldn't interrupt me when I am telling the story of my trip. Seeing my grave condition, someone in the crowd summoned an ambulance, and I was taken to the hospital, where I was put to bed. I looked very beautiful lying there, my black bill contrasting with the snowy white sheets. Doctors and nurses attended me and comforted me in

391

my hour of suffering and pain. You can judge how serious my wound was when I tell you that one of the doctors examined it and said it was superficial."

"It doesn't look bad to me," said his wife. "I think you just got nicked. If it had been bad, you couldn't have flown back so soon. Anyway, superficial or not, I'm glad to see you home safe. I always miss you when you're gone. I don't know why, but I do."

And with that, she placed her head across his neck and gave him a slight nudge. Then they had breakfast and went for a swim in an open place in the frozen lake. The cob pulled his Band-Aid off and threw it away.

Chapter 21

The Greening Spring

LOUIS AND Serena were more in love than ever. When spring came, they flew north, Louis wearing his trumpet and his slate and his chalk pencil and his medal, Serena wearing nothing at all. Now that he no longer had to work and earn, Louis felt a great sense of relief. No more would he have to carry a moneybag around his neck.

The two swans flew high and fast, ten thousand feet above the earth. They arrived at last at the little pond in the wilderness where Louis had been hatched. This was his dream—to return with his love to the place in Canada where he had first seen the light of day. He escorted Serena from one end of the pond to the other and back again. He showed her the tiny island where his mother's nest had been. He showed her the log Sam Beaver had been sitting on when Louis had pulled his shoelace because he couldn't say ko-hoh. Serena was enchanted. They were in love. It was spring. The frog was waking from his long sleep. The turtle was coming to life again after his nap. The chipmunk felt the warm air, soft and kind, blow through the trees, just as it did in that springtime when Louis's father and mother had visited the pond to nest and raise their young.

The sun shone down, strong and steady. Ice was melting; patches of open water appeared on the pond. Louis and Serena felt the changing world, and they stirred with new life and rapture and hope. There was a smell in the air, a smell of earth waking after its long winter. The trees were putting out tiny green buds, the buds were swelling. A better, easier time was at hand. A pair of Mallard Ducks flew in. A sparrow with a white throat arrived and sang, "Oh, sweet Canada, Canada, Canada!"

Serena chose a muskrat lodge on which to build her nest. It was the right height above the water. The muskrats had built it of mud and sticks. Louis had hoped his wife might decide to make her nest in the same spot where his mother had built hers, but females are full of notions; they want their own way, pretty much, and Serena knew what she was doing. Louis was so delighted when he saw her begin to construct the nest, he didn't really care where it was. He raised his horn to his mouth and played the beginning of an old song called "It's delightful to be married, to be-be-

be-be, be-be-be-be married . . ." Then he helped by bringing a few pieces of coarse grass.

Rain or shine, cold or warm, every day was a happy day for the two swans. In time, the eggs were laid and the cygnets were hatched—four of them. The first sound the baby swans heard was the pure, strong sound of their father's trumpet.

"Oh, ever in the greening spring," he played, "By bank and bough retiring . . ."

Life was gay and busy and sweet in the little lonely pond in the north woods. Once in a while Sam Beaver would show up for a visit, and they would have great times together.

Louis never forgot his old jobs, his old friends, or his promise to the Head Man in Charge of Birds in Philadelphia. As the years went by, he and Serena returned each spring to the pond, nested, and had their young. And each year, at the end of summer, when the moult was over and the flight feathers grew back in and the cygnets were ready to try their wings, Louis took his family for a long pleasure trip across America. He led them first to Camp Kookooskoos, where he had saved the life of Applegate Skinner and won his medal. The camp would be closed for the season, but Louis liked to revisit it and wander around, remembering the boys and how he had earned his first hundred dollars as camp bugler.

Then the swans would fly to Boston, where the Swan Boat man always gave them a big welcome. Louis would polish up his horn, blow the spit out of it, and swim in front of the boats again, playing "Row, row, row your boat," and the people of Boston would hear the familiar sound of the trumpet of the swan and would flock to the Public Garden. Then the Boat-man would treat Louis and Serena to a night at the Ritz Hotel, while the cygnets spent the night by them-selves on the lake, watched over by the Boatman. Serena dearly loved the Ritz. She ate dozens of water-cress sandwiches and gazed at herself in the mirror and swam in the bathtub. And while Louis stood and looked out of the window at the Public Garden down below, Serena would walk round and around, turning lights on and off for the fun of it. Then they would both get into the bathtub and go to sleep.

From Boston, Louis would lead his family to the Philadelphia Zoo and show them Bird Lake. Here, he would be greeted warmly by the Head Man in Charge of Birds. If the Zoo needed a young Trumpeter Swan to add to its collection of waterfowl, Louis would donate one of his cygnets, just as he had promised. In later years, Philadelphia was also the place where they would see Sam Beaver. Sam took a job with the Zoo just as soon as he was old enough to go to work. He and Louis always had a great time when they got together. Louis would get out his slate, and they would have a long talk about old times.

After visiting Philadelphia, Louis would fly south with his wife and children so they could see the great savannas where alligators dozed in the swamp water and Turkey Buzzards soared in the sky. And then they would return home to spend the winter in the Red Rock Lakes of Montana, in the lovely, serene Centennial Valley, where all Trumpeter Swans feel safe and unafraid.

The life of a swan must be a very pleasant and interesting life. And of course Louis's life was particularly pleasant because he was a musician. Louis took good care of his trumpet. He kept it clean and spent hours polishing it with the tips of his wing feathers. As long as he lived, he felt grateful to his father, the brave cob who had risked his life in order to give him the trumpet he needed so badly. Every time Louis looked at Serena, he remembered that the sound of the trumpet was what had made her willing to become his mate.

Swans often live to be very old. Year after year, Louis and Serena returned in spring to the same small pond in Canada to raise their family. The days were peaceful. Always, just at the edge of dark, when the young cygnets were getting sleepy, Louis would raise

his horn and play taps, just as he used to do at camp long ago. The notes were sad and beautiful as they floated across the still water and up into the night sky.

One summer, when Sam Beaver was about twenty, he and his father were sitting in their camp in Canada. It was after supper. Mr. Beaver was rocking in a chair, resting after a day of fishing. Sam was reading a book.

"Pop," said Sam, "what does 'crepuscular' mean?"

"How should I know?" replied Mr. Beaver. "I never heard the word before."

"It has something to do with rabbits," said Sam. "It says here that a rabbit is a crepuscular animal."

"Probably means timid," said Mr. Beaver. "Or maybe it means that it can run like the dickens. Or maybe it means stupid. A rabbit will sit right in the middle of the road at night and stare into your headlights and never get out of the way, and that's how a lot of rabbits get run over. They're stupid."

"Well," said Sam, "I guess the only way to find out what 'crepuscular' means is to look it up in the dictionary."

"We haven't got a dictionary here," said Mr. Beaver. "You'll have to wait till we get back to the ranch."

Just then, over at the pond where the swans were, Louis raised his horn and played taps, to let his children know that the day had come to an end. The wind was right, and the sound carried across the swamp.

Mr. Beaver stopped rocking.

"That's funny!" he said. "I thought I heard the sound of a trumpet just then."

"I don't see how you could," replied Sam. "We're alone in these woods."

"I know we are," said Mr. Beaver. "Just the same, I thought I heard a trumpet. Or a bugle."

Sam chuckled. He had never told his father about the swans in the pond nearby. He kept their secret to himself. When he went to the pond, he always went alone. That's the way he liked it. And that's the way the swans liked it.

"What ever happened to your friend Louis?" asked Mr. Beaver. "Louis was a trumpeter. You don't suppose *he's* somewhere around here, do you?"

"He might be," said Sam.

"Have you heard from him recently?" asked Mr. Beaver.

"No," replied Sam. "He doesn't write anymore. He ran out of postage stamps, and he has no money to buy stamps with."

"Oh," said Mr. Beaver. "Well, the whole business about that bird was very queer—I never did fully understand it."

Sam looked across at his father and saw that his eyes had closed. Mr. Beaver was falling asleep. There was hardly a sound to disturb the stillness of the woods.

Sam was tired and sleepy too. He got out his note-book and sat down at the table by the light of the kerosene lamp. This is what he wrote:

Tonight I heard Louis's horn. My father heard it, too. The wind was right, and I could hear the notes of taps, just as darkness fell. There is nothing in all the world I like better than the trumpet of the swan. What does "crepuscular" mean?

Sam put his notebook away. He undressed and slid into bed. He lay there, wondering what "crepuscular" meant. In less than three minutes he was fast asleep.

On the pond where the swans were, Louis put his trumpet away. The cygnets crept under their mother's wings. Darkness settled on woods and fields and marsh. A loon called its wild night cry. As Louis relaxed and prepared for sleep, all his thoughts were of how lucky he was to inhabit such a beautiful earth, how lucky he had been to solve his problems with music, and how pleasant it was to look forward to another night of sleep and another day tomorrow, and the fresh morn-ing, and the light that returns with the day.

图书在版编目(CIP)数据

吹小号的天鹅: 汉英对照 / (美)怀特
(White, E.B.)著;任溶溶译. —上海: 上海译文出版
社,2016.1(2025.5重印)
ISBN 978-7-5327-7047-2

Ⅰ.①吹… Ⅱ.①怀… ②任… Ⅲ.①英语-汉语-
对照读物 ②童话-美国-现代 Ⅳ.①H319.4: I

中国版本图书馆 CIP 数据核字(2015)第 190813 号

The Trumpet of the Swan by E.B.White. Illustrated by Fred Marcellino.
Text copyright © 1970 by E.B.White
Illustrations copyright © 2000 by Fred Marcellino
Chinese translation copyright © 2016
by Shanghai Translation Publishing House
Text published by arrangement with ICM Partners
Illustrations published by arrangement with HarperCollins Children's Books
ALL RIGHTS RESERVED

图字: 09-1998-127号

吹小号的天鹅

〔美〕E·B·怀特/著 任溶溶/译 〔美〕弗雷德·马尔切利诺/绘
责任编辑/黄昱宁 装帧设计/张志全工作室

上海译文出版社有限公司出版、发行
网址:www.yiwen.com.cn
201101 上海市闵行区号景路 159 弄 B 座
常熟市文化印刷有限公司印刷

开本 787×1092 1/32 印张 13 插页 2 字数 175,000
2016 年 1 月第 1 版 2025 年 5 月第 9 次印刷
印数: 28,001—30,000 册

ISBN 978-7-5327-7047-2
定价:49.00 元